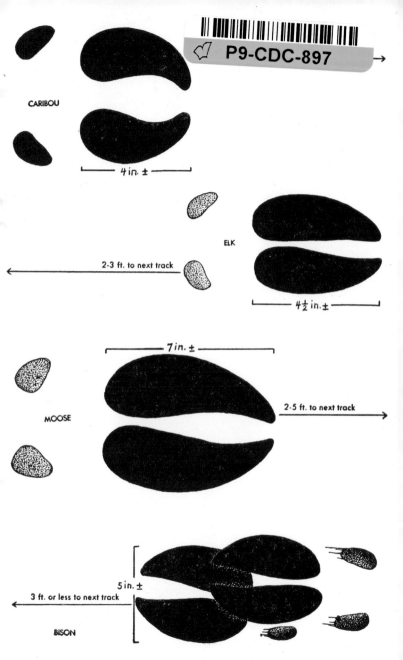

CARIBOU

4 in. ±

ELK

2-3 ft. to next track

4½ in. ±

7 in. ±

MOOSE

2-5 ft. to next track

5 in. ±

3 ft. or less to next track

BISON

# A Field Guide to the Mammals

BOOKS BY WILLIAM HENRY BURT
AND RICHARD PHILIP GROSSENHEIDER

THE MAMMALS OF MICHIGAN

A FIELD GUIDE TO THE MAMMALS

THE PETERSON FIELD GUIDE SERIES

# A Field Guide to the Mammals

Giving Field Marks of all Species
Found North of the Mexican Boundary

*Text and Maps by*
WILLIAM HENRY BURT

*Illustrations by*
RICHARD PHILIP GROSSENHEIDER

*Sponsored by*
*National Wildlife Federation*
*and*
*National Audubon Society*

HOUGHTON MIFFLIN COMPANY BOSTON
The Riverside Press Cambridge

SIXTH PRINTING, SEPTEMBER 1961

LIBRARY OF CONGRESS CARD NUMBER 52-8269

The Riverside Press
CAMBRIDGE · MASSACHUSETTS
PRINTED IN THE U.S.A.

# Editor's Note

BECAUSE so many mammals are nocturnal we do not know as much about them as we do about birds. We find their tracks in the mud by the riverbank, and in the snow, but except for the squirrels and a few others, we get scarcely more than an occasional glimpse of these shy creatures. Because our views of mammals are often so brief it is even more important than it is with birds to know exactly what to look for — to know their "field marks."

Dr. William H. Burt and Richard P. Grossenheider have combined their talents to produce this Field Guide, one which Ernest Thompson Seton would have enthusiastically endorsed, because it was he who pointed out that each animal has its particular "badge" or "identification tag" by which it may be known at a glance. This idea was first developed fully in my *Field Guide to the Birds*, in which I reduced all eastern birds to simple patterns. An added innovation was the use of arrows pointing to distinctive field marks. The success of the book and its companion volume, *A Field Guide to Western Birds*, was immediate, far exceeding the expectations of the author and the publisher. It was inevitable that students would urge us to extend the system to other fields of natural history, thus the Field Guide Series was launched.

*A Field Guide to the Mammals* is not the first book on which Dr. Burt and Mr. Grossenheider have collaborated. Many readers already know their work through that splendid volume *The Mammals of Michigan*. Dr. Burt, through years of teaching at the University of Michigan, his custodianship of the mammal collection at the museum in Ann Arbor, and through his recent editorship of the *Journal of Mammalogy*, is ideally equipped to inform us in the clearest, most direct terms about North American mammals. He is familiar with mammals both in the wild and in the hand, hence he knows where to draw the line between field marks and taxonomic characters. A few small mammals, it will be seen, simply cannot be identified with certainty except in the hand, using dentition and skull characters. Dr. Burt has avoided the problem of subspecies, as that too is properly within the realm of the specialist and the specimen tray. Moreover, had he treated them at this stage in our taxonomic knowledge the book would probably become obsolete in a short time.

Richard Grossenheider's drawings are so sensitive in handling that one must study them carefully to fully appreciate their artistry. He loves the small mammals in particular and no one has ever portrayed them with greater understanding. The exquisite textural quality of his drawings reminds one of an earlier master, Albrecht Dürer.

George Sutton, the distinguished wildlife artist, in eulogizing Grossenheider's work writes, "Those who study these drawings will, I am confident, concur that they possess that rarest of qualities — the life-spark. This subtle quality in a picture invariably puzzles me. I have studied living birds and mammals for years, and believe I know *why* they look alive. But the aliveness of a picture is amazing and wondrous nonetheless. There must be something of the small mammal in Dick Grossenheider himself — something very sensitive to sounds, something keenly aware of passing shadows, something ever on the alert for signs and warnings — else how could his drawings have the *autobiographical* authenticity they possess?"

When you start out on a camping trip take this book with you. Do not leave it on your library shelf; it is a Field Guide intended to be used.

ROGER TORY PETERSON

### CONSERVATION NOTE

Mammals and all wildlife are part of our American heritage. They contribute to our happiness and standard of living.

Help support the cause of wildlife conservation by taking an active part in the work of the National Wildlife Federation, National Audubon Society, Izaak Walton League, and other conservation organizations. They deserve your support.

Should your interest in mammals be scientific, even in an amateur way, you shall want to subscribe to the *Journal of Mammalogy* or the *Journal of Wildlife Management*.

R. T. P.

# Preface

Most mammals, unlike birds, are nocturnal and secretive in their habits. They are, therefore, much more difficult to see and identify in the field. An exception is the squirrel family. Tree Squirrels, Ground Squirrels, Chipmunks, Woodchucks, and Prairie Dogs are active by day and present themselves in favorable situations for the field naturalist. Also in this category are many of the big game mammals, Deer, Elk, Moose, Caribou, Sheep, Goats, Bison, Prong-horns, and Muskox, as well as the marine mammals, Whales, Dolphins, Seals, and Sea Lions. Cats, Foxes, Coyotes, Rabbits, and Hares, too, although most active at night, are often seen by day. Most of the small mammals, Bats, Moles, Shrews, Mice, and Rats, sleep during the day and come out only as darkness falls. Although one occasionally sees these small mammals in daytime, particularly in early morning or just before darkness, they are difficult to iden-tify unless he has them in his hand. Even then, some are puzzling and cannot be determined by external characters alone. We have attempted, therefore, throughout the Field Guide to the Mammals, to indicate which kinds might be confused. If characterizations sometimes seem vague it is because those species being discussed do not possess outstanding field marks. We feel that it is better to treat obscure species this way than to give characters which nobody can see. It is often as important to know where the animal is seen as it is to know all its body characters. Each kind of mam-mal has its own habitat preference. Some kinds are confined to a very limited set of conditions, others are more generally adapted and are not restricted in habitat. One would not expect to see a Tree Squirrel on the open prairie far from trees, nor would one ex-pect to see a Prairie Dog in a forest. But, foxes might be seen in both situations. Throughout the text, some indication is usually given to advise the reader where to expect to find each species. With the exception of some of the bats and marine species, migra-tions of mammals are slight or non-existent. They stay put. This is an aid in identification by elimination. One need not be concerned about any species that does not occur in his area. For those who wish to keep a record of the kinds of mammals they have seen and identified, there is a Life List (p. xvii) of all the species mentioned.

We have purposely avoided any treatment of subspecies. We feel that the ordinary person will be satisfied to know which species he is seeing. If he is concerned about the subspecies he should turn to the more technical literature and to the specialists in mammal-ogy. Further, with our present lack of knowledge of many kinds of mammals it would be impossible to treat them at the subspecific level. For some groups this could be done, but for others it could not without a revision of the group.

The shaded parts of the maps represent the approximate areas within which the different species might be expected. They do not mean that the species will be found over the entire shaded area, but wherever suitable conditions, within the area, prevail the species might be expected. For example, the actual area where the Beaver (p. 111) is found would include only narrow strips along streams and lakes, and there would be more blank space than shaded if it were truly indicated. The outer boundaries of the dis-tributions as outlined on the maps should be interpreted as being approximate. Some species will undoubtedly be found beyond the boundaries indicated, others probably will fall short of them. On some maps you will see question marks. These indicate that we do not know even the approximate position of the boundary of the range of the species. Present, not past distributions are indi-cated. There are no maps showing distributions of the strictly marine mammals, Whales, Dolphins, Porpoises, Seals, Sea Lions, etc. Instead, there is a short statement of the part of the coast where they might occur.

There are accounts of 373 species in the text. This is probably a minimum. A few extras have been included in the section on "Remarks." Many so-called species have been grouped under single headings because it is difficult or impossible to find dis-tinctive characters. We believe it is better to do it this way and indicate relationships than to list them under separate headings, implying differences that do not exist.

We wish to thank our many colleagues, especially the Graduate Students, for help and constructive advice. To single out any one would be unfair to the others — they all contributed in a substan-tial way.

# Contents

# Illustrations

# Distribution Maps

# How to Use This Book

To USE the Field Guide effectively, we suggest the following pro-
cedure. First, by thumbing through the plates of illustrations,
determine the kind or large group to which the mammal in question
belongs. Arrows point to the outstanding recognition marks mentioned on the page opposite the drawing. Second, turn to the
maps showing the ranges of the species in this group. A rapid
perusal of the maps will show you which kinds are to be found in
your area. You need be concerned *only* with these. Usually there
will be no more than two or three kinds to select from for any given
locality. Third, turn to the text where one of the species is treated.
Read the characters given and also those given for "Similar
species." Here, *be concerned only with those found in your area.*
This should give you the answer in most instances. If it is one of
the "Similar species," turn to the account of that one and see if
the characters fit. In many instances, you should arrive at the
answer from the illustration alone, in others from the illustration
plus the map. Here is an example. Follow this through and you
will know how to use the Guide. You are in Northern Wisconsin.
You see a small mammal in the woods, it is brightly colored,
brownish, and has stripes on its sides and face. In a perusal of the
illustrations you come to a plate (p. 88) showing squirrel-like mammals, and all have stripes on them. The animal you saw fits those
labeled "Chipmunk." You now turn to the maps (p. 76) where
the ranges of chipmunks are shown. You discover that in Northern
Wisconsin there are two species, the Eastern Chipmunk and the
Least Chipmunk. You need not be concerned about the other
thirteen species. Both chipmunks being illustrated, you should
determine the kind from the drawings alone. If not, turn to Eastern Chipmunk (p. 71) and read the account under "Recognition."
If this does not fit, under "Similar species" look for Least Chipmunk. Here you will find that the body stripes reach to the base of
the tail, and the rump is not reddish. If the animal you saw has
these marks it is a Least Chipmunk. To double-check, turn to the
account under Least Chipmunk. This should not be necessary,
but it is always good to have an extra check on any identification.

Mammal skulls are often picked up in the field or taken from owl
pellets. Many of these can be identified, at least to the large group
to which they belong, by comparing them with the pictures (pp. 152,
153, 156, 157, 164, 165, 168, 169). They may be, in many instances,
identified to the species by just counting the teeth and referring to
the list of dental formulæ (pp. 179–182).

The measurement "head and body" is of the outstretched animal from tip of nose to base of tail. The tail measurement does not include the hairs at the tip — it is of the tail vertebræ. There are 25 millimeters to an inch if it is desirable to convert from one to the other system.

Page references for each species refer to the plate of illustrations, **boldface type,** and the distribution map, regular type. Page references on the pages opposite the plates refer to the text, *italics,* and the distribution maps, regular type.

# My Life List

....VIRGINIA OPOSSUM
....MEXICAN OPOSSUM
....STARNOSE MOLE
....EASTERN MOLE
....HAIRYTAIL MOLE
....TOWNSEND MOLE
....PACIFIC MOLE
....CALIFORNIA MOLE
....SHREW-MOLE
....MASKED SHREW
....MT. LYELL SHREW
....MALHEUR SHREW
....SMOKY SHREW
....ARCTIC SHREW
....TUNDRA SHREW
....UNALASKA SHREW
....PRIBILOF SHREW
....MERRIAM SHREW
....SOUTHEASTERN SHREW
....LONGTAIL SHREW
....GASPÉ SHREW
....TROWBRIDGE SHREW
....VAGRANT SHREW
....DUSKY SHREW
....PACIFIC SHREW
....ORNATE SHREW
....ASHLAND SHREW
....SANTA CATALINA SHREW
....SUISUN SHREW
....INYO SHREW
....DWARF SHREW
....NORTHERN WATER SHREW
....ALASKA WATER SHREW
....PACIFIC WATER SHREW
....PIGMY SHREW
....DESERT SHREW
....LEAST SHREW

....SHORTTAIL SHREW
....LEAFCHIN BAT
....LEAFNOSE BAT
....HOGNOSE BAT
....LONGNOSE BAT
....LITTLE BROWN MYOTIS
....YUMA MYOTIS
....MISSISSIPPI MYOTIS
....GRAY MYOTIS
....CAVE MYOTIS
....ARIZONA MYOTIS
....KEEN MYOTIS
....LONG-EARED MYOTIS
....FRINGED MYOTIS
....INDIANA MYOTIS
....LONG-LEGGED MYOTIS
....CALIFORNIA MYOTIS
....SMALL-FOOTED MYOTIS
....WESTERN PIPISTREL
....EASTERN PIPISTREL
....BIG BROWN BAT
....EVENING BAT
....SILVER-HAIRED BAT
....HOARY BAT
....RED BAT
....SEMINOLE BAT
....WESTERN YELLOW BAT
....EASTERN YELLOW BAT
....SPOTTED BAT
....WESTERN BIG-EARED BAT
....EASTERN BIG-EARED BAT
....PALLID BAT
....BUNKER BAT
....FLORIDA FREETAIL BAT
....MEXICAN FREETAIL BAT
....POCKETED FREETAIL BAT
....BIG FREETAIL BAT

....WESTERN MASTIFF BAT

....EASTERN MASTIFF BAT

....BLACK BEAR

....GRIZZLY BEAR

....BIG BROWN BEAR

....POLAR BEAR

....RACCOON

....COATI

....RINGTAIL CAT

....MARTEN

....FISHER

....SHORTTAIL WEASEL

....LONGTAIL WEASEL

....LEAST WEASEL

....MINK

....BLACK-FOOTED FERRET

....WOLVERINE

....RIVER OTTER

....SEA OTTER

....SPOTTED SKUNK

....STRIPED SKUNK

....HOODED SKUNK

....HOGNOSE SKUNK

....BADGER

....RED FOX

... KIT FOX

....GRAY FOX

....ARCTIC FOX

....COYOTE

....GRAY WOLF

....RED WOLF

....JAGUAR

....OCELOT

....MARGAY CAT

....MOUNTAIN LION

....JAGUARUNDI CAT

....LYNX

....BOBCAT

....CALIFORNIA SEA LION

....NORTHERN SEA LION

....ALASKA FUR SEAL

....GUADALUPE FUR SEAL

....HARBOR SEAL

....RIBBON SEAL

....RINGED SEAL

....SADDLEBACK SEAL

....BEARDED SEAL

....GRAY SEAL

....HOODED SEAL

....ELEPHANT SEAL

....WALRUS

....WOODCHUCK

....YELLOWBELLY MARMOT

....HOARY MARMOT

....OLYMPIC MARMOT

....VANCOUVER MARMOT

....TOWNSEND GROUND SQUIRREL

....WASHINGTON GROUND
                                        SQUIRREL

....IDAHO GROUND SQUIRREL

....RICHARDSON GROUND SQUIRREL

....UINTA GROUND SQUIRREL

....BELDING GROUND SQUIRREL

....COLUMBIAN GROUND SQUIRREL

....ARCTIC GROUND SQUIRREL

....THIRTEEN-LINED GROUND
                                        SQUIRREL

....MEXICAN GROUND SQUIRREL

....SPOTTED GROUND SQUIRREL

....FRANKLIN GROUND SQUIRREL

....ROCK SQUIRREL

....CALIFORNIA GROUND SQUIRREL

....YUMA ANTELOPE SQUIRREL

....WHITETAIL ANTELOPE
                                        SQUIRREL

....SAN JOAQUIN ANTELOPE
                                        SQUIRREL

....MOHAVE GROUND SQUIRREL

....ROUNDTAIL GROUND SQUIRREL

....GOLDEN-MANTLED SQUIRREL

....BLACKTAIL PRAIRIE DOG

....WHITETAIL PRAIRIE DOG

....EASTERN CHIPMUNK

....ALPINE CHIPMUNK

....LEAST CHIPMUNK

....YELLOW PINE CHIPMUNK

....PANAMINT CHIPMUNK

....COLORADO CHIPMUNK

....UINTA CHIPMUNK
....CHARLESTON MOUNTAIN
            CHIPMUNK
....REDTAIL CHIPMUNK
....GRAYNECK CHIPMUNK
....TOWNSEND CHIPMUNK
....SONOMA CHIPMUNK
....LONG-EARED CHIPMUNK
....MERRIAM CHIPMUNK
....CLIFF CHIPMUNK
....RED SQUIRREL
....CHICKAREE
....SPRUCE SQUIRREL
....WESTERN GRAY SQUIRREL
....EASTERN GRAY SQUIRREL
....ARIZONA GRAY SQUIRREL
....TASSEL-EARED SQUIRREL
....APACHE FOX SQUIRREL
....EASTERN FOX SQUIRREL
....SOUTHERN FLYING SQUIRREL
....NORTHERN FLYING SQUIRREL
....NORTHERN POCKET GOPHER
....PIGMY POCKET GOPHER
....SIERRA POCKET GOPHER
....TOWNSEND POCKET GOPHER
....VALLEY POCKET GOPHER
....BAILEY POCKET GOPHER
....GIANT POCKET GOPHER
....PLAINS POCKET GOPHER
....SOUTHEASTERN POCKET
            GOPHER
....MEXICAN POCKET GOPHER
....MEXICAN POCKET MOUSE
....WYOMING POCKET MOUSE
....PLAINS POCKET MOUSE
....MERRIAM POCKET MOUSE
....SILKY POCKET MOUSE
....APACHE POCKET MOUSE
....ARIZONA POCKET MOUSE
....LITTLE POCKET MOUSE
....SAN JOAQUIN POCKET MOUSE
....GREAT BASIN POCKET MOUSE
....WHITE-EARED POCKET MOUSE
....LONGTAIL POCKET MOUSE

....BAILEY POCKET MOUSE
....DESERT POCKET MOUSE
....ROCK POCKET MOUSE
....NELSON POCKET MOUSE
....SAN DIEGO POCKET MOUSE
....CALIFORNIA POCKET MOUSE
....SPINY POCKET MOUSE
....HISPID POCKET MOUSE
....HEERMANN KANGAROO RAT
....MORRO BAY KANGAROO RAT
....MOHAVE KANGAROO RAT
....PANAMINT KANGAROO RAT
....STEPHENS KANGAROO RAT
....GIANT KANGAROO RAT
....BANNERTAIL KANGAROO RAT
....TEXAS KANGAROO RAT
....MERRIAM KANGAROO RAT
....FRESNO KANGAROO RAT
....ORD KANGAROO RAT
....PACIFIC KANGAROO RAT
....SANTA CRUZ KANGAROO RAT
....BIG-EARED KANGAROO RAT
....GREAT BASIN KANGAROO RAT
....DESERT KANGAROO RAT
....DARK KANGAROO MOUSE
....PALE KANGAROO MOUSE
....BEAVER
....NORTHERN GRASSHOPPER
            MOUSE
....SOUTHERN GRASSHOPPER
            MOUSE
....EASTERN HARVEST MOUSE
....PLAINS HARVEST MOUSE
....WESTERN HARVEST MOUSE
....SALT MARSH HARVEST MOUSE
....FULVOUS HARVEST MOUSE
....PIGMY MOUSE
....CACTUS MOUSE
....CALIFORNIA MOUSE
....CANYON MOUSE
....DEER MOUSE
....SITKA MOUSE
....OLDFIELD MOUSE
....WHITE-FOOTED MOUSE

.... COTTON MOUSE

.... BRUSH MOUSE

.... WHITE-ANKLED MOUSE

.... PIÑON MOUSE

.... ROCK MOUSE

.... GOLDEN MOUSE

.... FLORIDA MOUSE

.... RICE RAT

.... HISPID COTTON RAT

.... LEAST COTTON RAT

.... YELLOWNOSE COTTON RAT

.... EASTERN WOODRAT

.... SOUTHERN PLAINS WOODRAT

.... WHITETHROAT WOODRAT

.... DESERT WOODRAT

.... MEXICAN WOODRAT

.... DUSKY-FOOTED WOODRAT

.... BUSHYTAIL WOODRAT

.... SOUTHERN BOG LEMMING

.... NORTHERN BOG LEMMING

.... BROWN LEMMING

.... HUDSON BAY COLLARED
                        LEMMING

.... GREENLAND COLLARED
                        LEMMING

.... UNALASKA COLLARED LEMMING

.... MOUNTAIN PHENACOMYS

.... UNGAVA PHENACOMYS

.... MACKENZIE PHENACOMYS

.... PACIFIC PHENACOMYS

.... TREE PHENACOMYS

.... BRITISH COLUMBIA REDBACK
                        VOLE

.... WRANGELL ISLAND REDBACK
                        VOLE

.... TUNDRA REDBACK VOLE

.... ST. LAWRENCE ISLAND
                  REDBACK VOLE

.... BOREAL REDBACK VOLE

.... CALIFORNIA REDBACK VOLE

.... MEADOW VOLE

.... MOUNTAIN VOLE

.... CALIFORNIA VOLE

.... TUNDRA VOLE

.... ALASKA VOLE

.... TOWNSEND VOLE

.... LONGTAIL VOLE

.... MEXICAN VOLE

.... YELLOW-CHEEKED VOLE

.... YELLOWNOSE VOLE

.... RICHARDSON VOLE

.... PRAIRIE VOLE

.... OREGON VOLE

.... SAGEBRUSH VOLE

.... PINE VOLE

.... FLORIDA WATER RAT

.... MUSKRAT

.... NORWAY RAT

.... BLACK RAT

.... HOUSE MOUSE

.... APLODONTIA

.... MEADOW JUMPING MOUSE

.... WESTERN JUMPING MOUSE

.... WOODLAND JUMPING MOUSE

.... NUTRIA

.... PORCUPINE

.... PIKA

.... ARCTIC HARE

.... TUNDRA HARE

.... WHITETAIL JACKRABBIT

.... SNOWSHOE HARE

.... EUROPEAN HARE

.... ANTELOPE JACKRABBIT

.... BLACKTAIL JACKRABBIT

.... EASTERN COTTONTAIL

.... MOUNTAIN COTTONTAIL

.... NEW ENGLAND COTTONTAIL

.... DESERT COTTONTAIL

.... BRUSH RABBIT

.... MARSH RABBIT

.... SWAMP RABBIT

.... PIGMY RABBIT

.... PECCARY

.... EUROPEAN WILD BOAR

.... ELK

.... MULE DEER

.... WHITETAIL DEER

.... MOOSE

....WOODLAND CARIBOU
....BARREN GROUND CARIBOU
....GREENLAND CARIBOU
....PRONGHORN
....BISON
....MUSKOX
....BIGHORN SHEEP
....WHITE SHEEP
....MOUNTAIN GOAT
....ARMADILLO
....MANATEE
....ATLANTIC RIGHT WHALE
....PACIFIC RIGHT WHALE
....BOWHEAD WHALE
....GRAY WHALE
....FINBACK WHALE
....RORQUAL
....PIKED WHALE
....BLUE WHALE
....HUMPBACK WHALE
....SPERM WHALE
....PIGMY SPERM WHALE
....SPOTTED DOLPHIN
....LONGBEAK DOLPHIN
....COMMON DOLPHIN

....ATLANTIC BOTTLENOSE
                      DOLPHIN
....PACIFIC BOTTLENOSE DOLPHIN
....RIGHT WHALE DOLPHIN
....ATLANTIC WHITE-SIDED
                      DOLPHIN
....PACIFIC WHITE-SIDED DOLPHIN
....WHITEBEAK DOLPHIN
....ATLANTIC KILLER WHALE
....PACIFIC KILLER WHALE
....GRAMPUS
....FALSE KILLER
....COMMON BLACKFISH
....PACIFIC BLACKFISH
....SHORT-FINNED BLACKFISH
....ATLANTIC HARBOR PORPOISE
....DALL PORPOISE
....WHITE WHALE
....NARWHAL
....BAIRD BEAKED WHALE
....SOWERBY WHALE
....TRUE BEAKED WHALE
....PACIFIC BEAKED WHALE
....GOOSEBEAK WHALE
....BOTTLENOSE WHALE

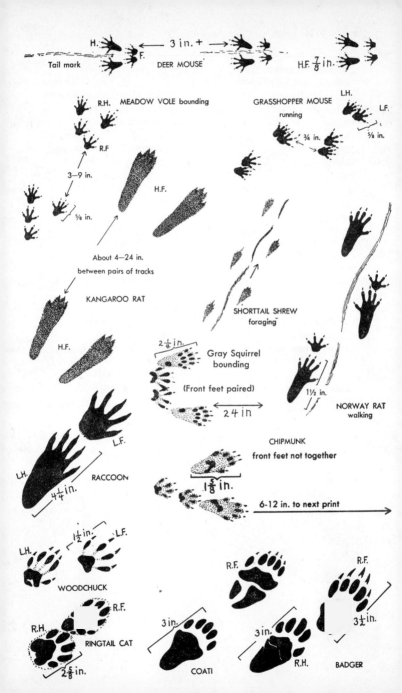

Tail mark     H.     ← 3 in. + →     DEER MOUSE     H.F. 7/8 in.

F.

R.H.    MEADOW VOLE bounding     GRASSHOPPER MOUSE    L.H.

running    L.F.

R.F     ¾ in.     ⅝ in.

3—9 in.

⅝ in.     H.F.

About 4—24 in.
between pairs of tracks

KANGAROO RAT     SHORTTAIL SHREW
foraging

H.F.

2¼ in.    Gray Squirrel
bounding

(Front feet paired)

← 24 in →     1½ in.    NORWAY RAT
walking

L.F.

L.H.    RACCOON    CHIPMUNK
front feet not together

4¼ in.     1⅝ in.     6-12 in. to next print →

L.H.    1½ in.    L.F.

WOODCHUCK

R.H.    R.F.    RINGTAIL CAT    R.F.     R.F.

2⅝ in.     3 in.    COATI    3 in.     3½ in.

R.H.    BADGER

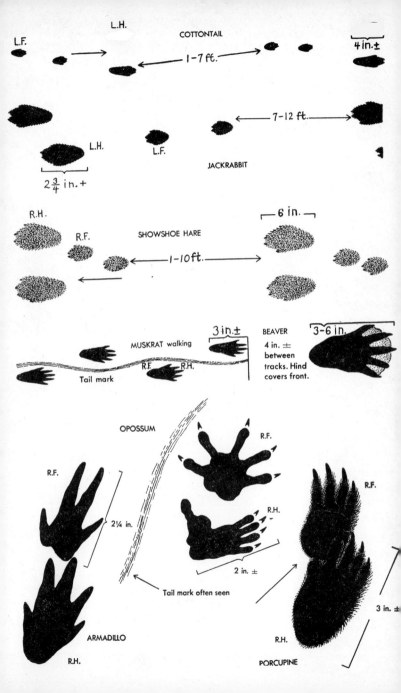

L.H.

COTTONTAIL

L.F.

1-7 ft.

4 in. ±

7-12 ft.

L.H.

L.F.

JACKRABBIT

2¾ in. +

R.H.

R.F.

SNOWSHOE HARE

6 in.

1-10 ft.

3 in. ±

MUSKRAT walking

BEAVER

4 in. ± between tracks. Hind covers front.

3-6 in.

Tail mark

R.F.

R.H.

OPOSSUM

R.F.

R.H.

2 in. ±

Tail mark often seen

R.F.

2¼ in.

R.F.

3 in. ±

ARMADILLO

R.H.

R.H.

PORCUPINE

# Opossums: Didelphiidæ

THESE are the only marsupials (pouched mammals) in North America. The female has a *fur-lined pouch* on her belly in which the young are carried. 'Possums have five toes on each foot. The *inside toe on the hind foot is opposable and without a claw.* The tail is scaly and rattail-like in appearance. 'Possums eat almost any kind of food, and live in any place that will afford shelter.

**VIRGINIA OPOSSUM.** *Didelphis virginiana.* pp. **132**, 2
  **Recognition:** — Head and body, 15–20 in.; tail, 9–13 in.; wt., 4–12 lb. About the size of a house cat, but with heavier body and shorter legs, spreading toes, long pointed nose, *white face*, paper-thin *black ears*, and a *rat-like tail.* Color usually grayish, but varies from white to nearly black. Tail black at base for *one-third or less* of length. Prefers farming areas, usually active only at night.
  **Similar species:** — Mexican Opossum; tail black for basal one-half of length.

**MEXICAN OPOSSUM.** *Didelphis marsupialis.* p. 2
  **Recognition:** — Head and body, 15–18 in.; tail, 10–16 in. There are two color phases. The gray phase is similar to the Virginia Opossum — in the black phase the tips of the body hairs are black. *Basal one-half of tail black.*
  **Similar species:** — Virginia Opossum; basal one-third or less of the tail black.

# Moles: Talpidæ

MOLES live most of their lives *beneath* the surface of the ground. Their presence may be detected by the *low ridges* they push up as they move just beneath the surface; also by the *earth mounds*, each consisting of from one-half to two gallons of earth, which they push up from beneath. There is no indication of an entrance to the burrow. The front feet are *broad* and the palms usually face outward. The eyes are of *pinhead size* or smaller; some are covered with a thin skin; *no external ears*; fur soft and thick. They do not occur in the Rocky Mountain or Great Basin area. Length, from tip of nose to tip of tail, 4–9 in.

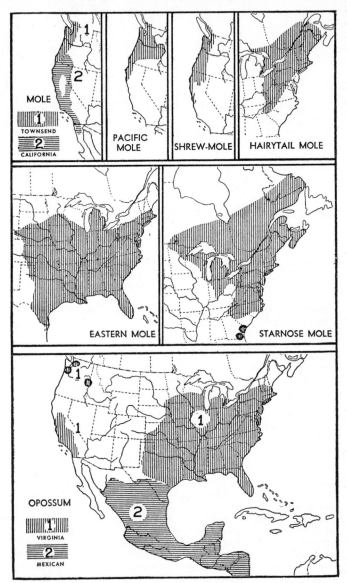

MOLE

1 TOWNSEND

2 CALIFORNIA

PACIFIC MOLE

SHREW-MOLE

HAIRYTAIL MOLE

EASTERN MOLE

STARNOSE MOLE

OPOSSUM

1 VIRGINIA

2 MEXICAN

**STARNOSE MOLE.** *Condylura cristata.*                          pp. **8**, 2
    **Recognition:** — Head and body, 4½–5 in.; tail, 3–3½ in.; wt., 35–80 gm. This is the only kind of mammal that has the end of the nose *surrounded by finger-like fleshy projections* (22 tentacles), giving the appearance of a star. Eyes small but apparent. Front feet as long as broad. Fur, dark brown or black. Tail *hairy*, constricted near body. Prefers wet ground near lakes or streams.
    **Similar species:** — Eastern Mole and Hairytail Mole; both have naked noses without finger-like projections.

**EASTERN MOLE.** *Scalopus aquaticus.*                          pp. **8**, 2
    **Recognition:** — Head and body, 4½–6½ in.; tail, 1–1½ in.; wt., 50–120 gm. Front feet *broader than long*, palms turn *outward;* end of nose naked with nostrils opening *upward;* tail *naked*. Eyes covered with thin skin. Fur with a silvery sheen. Prefers sandy loam. Common about lawns, golf courses, gardens, and low meadows.
    **Similar species:** — Hairytail Mole; tail haired, not naked. Starnose Mole; end of nose surrounded by 22 finger-like projections.

**HAIRYTAIL MOLE.** *Parascalops breweri.*                       pp. **8**, 2
    **Recognition:** — Head and body, 4½ in.; tail, 1–1½ in. The smallest of the eastern moles. Front feet as broad as long, nose pointed, eyes not apparent, tail distinctly *haired*.
    **Similar species:** — Starnose Mole; has 22 finger-like projections around nose. Eastern Mole; larger, naked tail.

**TOWNSEND MOLE.** *Scapanus townsendi.*                         pp. **8**, 2
    **Recognition:** — Head and body, 6–7 in.; tail, 2± in. Front feet *broader than long;* nose naked; nostrils open *upward;* tail slightly haired; blackish brown to black. Found principally in moist places where the soil is easily worked.
    **Similar species:** — Pacific Mole; smaller.

**PACIFIC MOLE.** *Scapanus orarius.*                            p. 2
    **Recognition:** — Head and body, 5–5¼ in.; tail, 1⅛ in. Front feet *broader than long*, nose naked; nostrils open above; tail slightly haired; color, blackish brown to black.
    **Similar species:** — Townsend Mole; larger. California Mole; difficult to distinguish in the flesh. Where the two occur together, specimens should be sent to a museum for identification.

**CALIFORNIA MOLE.** *Scapanus latimanus.*                       p. 2
    **Recognition:** — Head and body, 5–6 in.; tail, 1½ in. Front feet *broader than long*; nose naked; nostrils open upward; tail slightly haired; blackish brown to black.
    **Similar species:** — Pacific Mole; difficult to distinguish. Where

the two occur together specimens should be sent to a museum for identification.

**SHREW–MOLE.** *Neürotrichus gibbsi.*                          pp. **8**, 2
  **Recognition:** — Head and body, 3–3½ in.; tail, 1–1½ in. Front feet *longer than broad;* nose naked; nostrils open *to the sides;* eyes *small but apparent;* tail *haired.* Smallest of the North American moles, this miniature edition is found along the humid northwest coast.
  **Similar species:** — Water Shrew; front feet not conspicuously broad, nose not naked. Trowbridge Shrew; smaller.


# Shrews: Soricidæ

THESE bundles of energy are *mouse-size* with small *bead-like eyes, a long pointed nose,* and ears concealed, or nearly concealed by their soft fur. They always have *five toes* on each foot; most mice have four toes on the front foot. Many shrews are difficult to identify; if questionable, they should be sent to a museum. They are found over most of the North American continent. Usually they prefer moist situations, but some are found in the sagebrush regions of our arid West.


**MASKED SHREW.** *Sorex cinereus.*                          pp. **8**, 5
  **Recognition:** — Head and body, 2–2½ in.; tail, 1¼–2 in.; wt., 3½–5½ gm. In the North and down the Rocky and Appalachian Mountains, particularly in *moist habitat,* this small *grayish-brown* sprite is usually the commonest of the shrews.
  **Similar species:** — Least Shrew; shorter tail. Pigmy Shrew; slightly smaller, but can be distinguished for certain only by the unicuspids (single-cusped teeth in upper jaw), three instead of five on each side. Smoky Shrew; larger, brownish. Merriam Shrew; pale grayish, whitish underparts. Arctic, Longtail, Vagrant, Dusky, and Trowbridge shrews; all larger. Gaspé, Dwarf, and Southeastern shrews; about same size, but ranges overlap only slightly.


**MT. LYELL SHREW.** *Sorex lyelli.*                          p. 5
  **Recognition:** — Head and body, 2¼ in.; tail, 1½ in. Found only in a small section of the high Sierras, *6900 feet altitude and above.*


**MALHEUR SHREW.** *Sorex preblei.*                          p. 5
  **Recognition:** — Head and body, 2–2¼ in.; tail, 1½ in. Restricted to the *Malheur area* of eastern Oregon. One of the *smallest* of western shrews.
  **Similar species:** — Merriam Shrew; larger. Vagrant Shrew; larger.

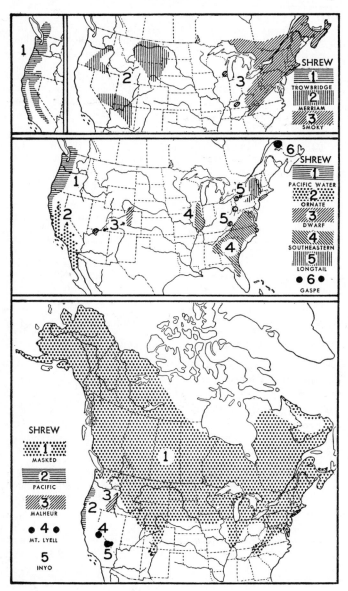

SHREW
1 TROWBRIDGE
2 MERRIAM
3 SMOKY

SHREW
1 PACIFIC WATER
2 ORNATE
3 DWARF
4 SOUTHEASTERN
5 LONGTAIL
● 6 ● GASPE

SHREW
1 MASKED
2 PACIFIC
3 MALHEUR
● 4 ● MT. LYELL
5 INYO

**SMOKY SHREW.**   *Sorex fumeus.*                              p. 5
   **Recognition:** — Head and body, 2½–3 in.; tail, 1¾–2 in.  A *dull brown* shrew, *uniformly-colored*, except for the *bicolor tail* (yellow-ish below, brown above) and *pale feet*.  This is a common shrew within its range.
   **Similar species:** — Masked Shrew; smaller, underparts paler than upper parts.  Longtail Shrew; longer tail.  Pigmy Shrew; smaller.  Arctic Shrew; shorter tail, body not uniform color.  Gaspé Shrew; smaller.  Least Shrew; shorter tail.

**ARCTIC SHREW.**   *Sorex arcticus.*                       pp. **8,** 12
   **Recognition:** — Head and body, 2¾–3 in.; tail, 1½–1⅝ in.; wt., 7–11 gm.  The most *brilliantly colored* and most attractive of the shrews — the back, sides, and belly all contrast.  In winter, *tricolor*, with back nearly black; in summer, *brown*, duller than winter.
   **Similar species:** — Masked Shrew; smaller.  Smoky Shrew; longer tail, uniform body color.  Dusky Shrew; not tricolor, light brown.  Pigmy Shrew; smaller, light brown.

**TUNDRA SHREW.**   *Sorex tundrensis.*                        p. 12
   **Recognition:** — Head and body, 2⅖–3 in.; tail, 1¼ in.  Similar to the Arctic Shrew, probably of the same species.  Not quite as distinctly tricolor.  On St. Lawrence Island, known as *S. jacksoni.*
   **Similar species:** — Masked Shrew; smaller.  Dusky Shrew; not tricolor.  Pigmy Shrew; smaller, grayish brown.

**UNALASKA SHREW.**   *Sorex hydrodromus.*
   Confined to *Unalaska Island,* Aleutian Islands, Alaska.

**PRIBILOF SHREW.**   *Sorex pribilofensis.*
   Confined to *St. Paul Island,* Pribilof Group.

**MERRIAM SHREW.**   *Sorex merriami.*                      pp. **8,** 5
   **Recognition:** — Head and body, 2¼–2½ in.; tail 1½ in.  This *pale, grayish-drab* shrew with *nearly white underparts and feet* is found in parts of our arid West where one normally would not expect shrews.  It is quite rare.
   **Similar species:** — Masked Shrew; brownish, slightly larger.  Dwarf Shrew; smaller.  Dusky Shrew; larger, brownish.  Vagrant Shrew; larger, dark feet.  Malheur Shrew; smaller.

**SOUTHEASTERN SHREW.**   *Sorex longirostris.*               p. 5
   **Recognition:** — Head and body, 2–2½ in.; tail, 1–1½ in.  This *dark brown* shrew with *paler underparts* is the only longtail shrew found over most of its range in the Atlantic Plain and Piedmont region.
   **Similar species:** — Masked Shrew; about same, ranges overlap only slightly.  Least Shrew; shorter tail.

**LONGTAIL SHREW.** *Sorex dispar.* p. 5

**Recognition:** — Head and body, 2¾ in.; tail, 2⅕–2½ in. This large, *dark grayish* shrew, with slightly paler underparts and with a nearly *uniform-colored tail*, has a restricted range. It is not a common shrew anywhere.

**Similar species:** — Masked Shrew; smaller. Smoky Shrew; shorter, bicolor tail. Least Shrew; shorter tail. Pigmy Shrew; smaller.

**GASPÉ SHREW.** *Sorex gaspensis.* p. 5

**Recognition:** — Head and body, 2–2⅕ in.; tail 2 in. Similar to the Longtail Shrew, but slightly smaller, and confined to *Gaspé Peninsula.*

**Similar species:** — Masked Shrew; smaller. Smoky Shrew; bicolor tail. Arctic Shrew; tricolor body. Pigmy Shrew; smaller.

**TROWBRIDGE SHREW.** *Sorex trowbridgei.* p. 5

**Recognition:** — Head and body, 2½–2⅘ in.; tail 2–2½ in. A fairly large shrew with nearly uniform dark *mouse-gray* to *brownish* body and a distinctly *bicolor tail, nearly white below.*

**Similar species:** — Pacific Shrew; larger, tail not bicolor. Vagrant Shrew; shorter tail. Ornate Shrew; smaller. Dusky Shrew; light brown, underparts whitish.

**VAGRANT SHREW.** *Sorex vagrans.* p. 10

**Recognition:** — Head and body, 2⅓–2⅘ in.; tail 1½–1⅘ in. This small *reddish-brown* to *nearly black* shrew is the common shrew in our western mountains.

**Similar species:** — Trowbridge Shrew; larger. Pacific Shrew; larger. Masked Shrew; smaller, grayish brown. Dwarf Shrew; smaller, pale brown. Merriam Shrew; smaller, pale gray. Pigmy Shrew; smaller, grayish brown. Dusky Shrew; grayish brown.

**DUSKY SHREW.** *Sorex obscurus.* p. 10

**Recognition:** — Head and body, 2½–3 in.; tail, 1⅗–2½ in. This shrew is difficult to distinguish from some of the other shrews that occur in the same areas. In case of doubt, specimens should be sent to some museum. Upper parts *dull brown*, underparts *whitish*; tail *bicolor.*

**Similar species:** — Vagrant Shrew; reddish brown or blackish. Pigmy Shrew; smaller. Arctic Shrew; tricolored. Tundra Shrew; tricolored. Masked Shrew; smaller, grayish. Dwarf Shrew; smaller. Merriam Shrew; pale gray, smaller, found on desert. Trowbridge Shrew; dark underparts.

**PACIFIC SHREW.** *Sorex pacificus.* p. 5

**Recognition:** — Head and body, 3⅓ in.; tail, 2–2¾ in. This *large brown* western shrew is exceeded in size only by the Western Water Shrew. It is generally medium brown, including tail, feet, and underparts.

## SHREWS AND MOLES

**MASKED SHREW**                                          pp. *4*, 5
    Grayish brown, long tail, pointed nose.

**LEAST SHREW**                                           pp. *13*, 12
    Brownish, short tail.

**MERRIAM SHREW**                                         pp. *6*, 5
    Small, pale grayish.

**ARCTIC SHREW**                                          pp. *6*, 12
    Tricolor pattern.

**SHORTTAIL SHREW**                                       pp. *13*, 12
    Lead color, short tail, no ears.

**NORTHERN WATER SHREW**                                  pp. *11*, 12
    Blackish, stiff hairs on hind feet.

**SHREW–MOLE**                                            pp. *4*, 2
    Broad feet, hairy tail, naked nose.

**STARNOSE MOLE**                                         pp. *3*, 2
    Projections around nose.

**HAIRYTAIL MOLE**                                        pp. *3*, 2
    Tail hairy, feet broad, nose naked.

**EASTERN MOLE**                                          pp. *3*, 2
    Tail naked, nose naked, feet broad.
    *Pale phase:* Silvery
    *Dark phase:* Slate color

**TOWNSEND MOLE**                                         pp. *3*, 2
    Broad feet.

Shrew-mole snout,
top view

H. F., Water Shrew,
fringe of stiff hairs

Surface mole tunnel from above

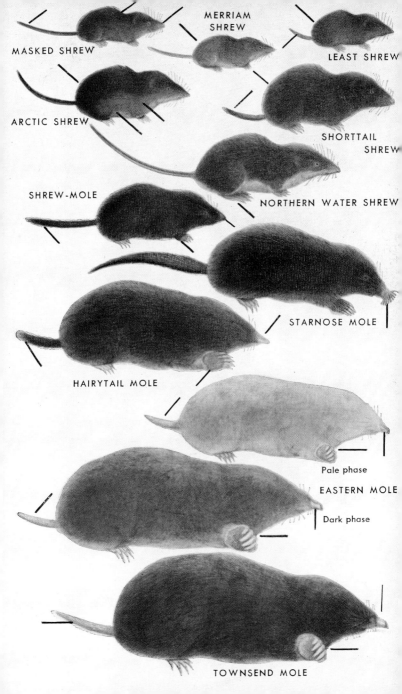

MERRIAM SHREW

MASKED SHREW

LEAST SHREW

ARCTIC SHREW

SHORTTAIL SHREW

SHREW-MOLE

NORTHERN WATER SHREW

STARNOSE MOLE

HAIRYTAIL MOLE

Pale phase

EASTERN MOLE

Dark phase

TOWNSEND MOLE

LITTLE BROWN
MYOTIS

LONG-EARED MYOTIS

EASTERN
BIG-EARED BAT

CALIFORNIA
MYOTIS

EASTERN PIPISTREL

SMALL-FOOTED
MYOTIS

WESTERN PIPISTREL

PALLID BAT

BIG BROWN BAT

Plate 2                                                    9

# BATS

**LITTLE BROWN MYOTIS**                          pp. *16*, **15**
  Brown, ears medium, size small.

**LONG–EARED MYOTIS**                            pp. *19*, **17**
  Pale brown, ears large.

**EASTERN BIG–EARED BAT**                        pp. *29*, **28**
  Lumps on nose, large ears joined in middle.

**CALIFORNIA MYOTIS**                            pp. *21*, **20**
  Small, bases of hairs dark.

**SMALL–FOOTED MYOTIS**                          pp. *21*, **17**
  Black mask, small.

**EASTERN PIPISTREL**                            pp. *22*, **23**
  Yellowish brown, blunt tragus.

**WESTERN PIPISTREL**                            pp. *22*, **23**
  Ashy, pale, small, blunt tragus.

**PALLID BAT**                                   pp. *29*, **20**
  Pale yellowish gray, large ears, simple nose.

**BIG BROWN BAT**                                pp. *22*, **28**
  Brown, large, blunt tragus.

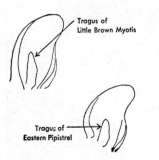

Tragus of Little Brown Myotis

Tragus of Eastern Pipistrel

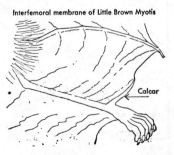

Interfemoral membrane of Little Brown Myotis

Calcar

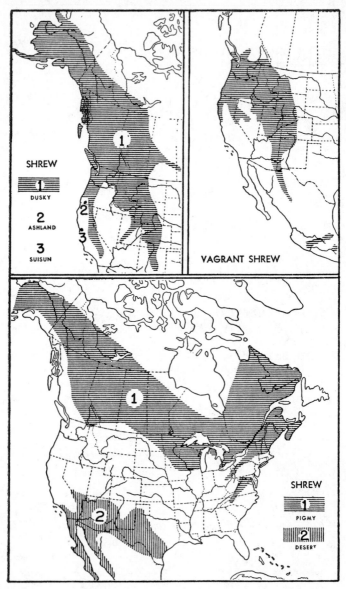

SHREW

1 DUSKY

2 ASHLAND

3 SUISUN

VAGRANT SHREW

SHREW

1 PIGMY

2 DESERT

**Similar species:** — Trowbridge Shrew; bicolor tail, smaller. Dusky Shrew; smaller, bicolor tail. Western Water Shrew; larger, blackish, stiff hairs on sides of hind feet.

**ORNATE SHREW.** *Sorex ornatus.* p. 5
**Recognition:** — Head and body, 2⅓–2½ in.; tail, 1½–1⅘ in. This small *grayish-brown* shrew, *pale beneath*, is the only shrew found over much of its range.
**Similar species:** — Trowbridge Shrew; larger, dark underparts. Desert Shrew; pale ash gray, found on desert.

**ASHLAND SHREW.** *Sorex trigonirostris.* p. 10
**Recognition:** — Head and body, 2½ in.; tail 1⅓ in. This small *grayish-brown* shrew is known only from *Ashland*, Oregon. It may be the same as the Ornate Shrew.

**SANTA CATALINA SHREW.** *Sorex willetti.*
**Recognition:** — Head and body, 2⅗ in.; tail, 1½ in. This shrew is known only from *Santa Catalina Island*, California. No other shrew is known from the island.

**SUISUN SHREW.** *Sorex sinuosus.* p. 10
**Recognition:** — Head and body, 2⅕–2½ in.; tail, 1½ in. This *nearly black* shrew is known only from *Grizzly Island*, near Suisun, Solano County, California.

**INYO SHREW.** *Sorex tenellus.* p. 5
**Recognition:** — Head and body, 2⅖ in.; tail, 1⅗ in. This small *grayish-brown* shrew is known only from a few *high mountain peaks* in California and Nevada.

**DWARF SHREW.** *Sorex nanus.* p. 5
**Recognition:** — Head and body, 2½ in.; tail, 1¾ in. This *small* rare shrew is known from a few scattered locations within its general range. Its color is a *pale grayish brown.*
**Similar species:** — Merriam Shrew; pale gray, larger. Masked Shrew; larger. Dusky Shrew; larger. Vagrant Shrew; larger.

**NORTHERN WATER SHREW.** *Sorex palustris.* pp. **8**, 12
**Recognition:** — Head and body, 3⅓ in.; tail, 2½–3 in.; wt., 10–16 gm. Along the *streams* of the north and of the mountain ranges this *large blackish-gray* shrew may be found. In some areas the underparts are silver, in others they are only slightly paler than the back. The *stiff hairs along the sides of the hind feet* will distinguish it from all but the Pacific Water Shrew.
**Similar species:** — Pacific Water Shrew; brownish, larger.

**ALASKA WATER SHREW.** *Sorex alaskanus.* p. 12
**Recognition:** — Head and body, 3⅕–3½ in.; tail, 2½–3 in. This water shrew is known only from *Point Gustavus*, Glacier Bay,

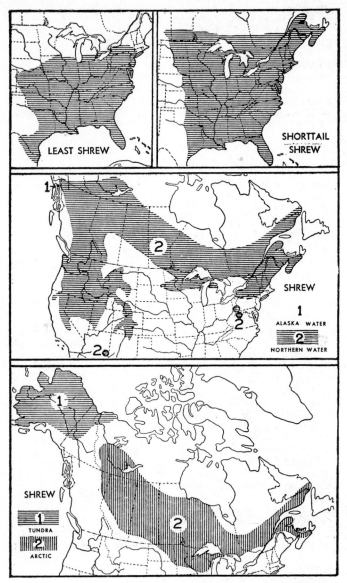

LEAST SHREW

SHORTTAIL
SHREW

SHREW

1
ALASKA WATER

2
NORTHERN WATER

SHREW

1
TUNDRA

2
ARCTIC

Alaska. It is probably of the same species as the Northern Water Shrew.

## PACIFIC WATER SHREW. *Sorex bendirei.* p. 5

**Recognition:** — Head and body, 3½–3⅜ in.; tail, 2½–3⅛ in. Along the humid Pacific Coast, near and in *streams*, lives this *large, dark-brown* shrew. The hind feet have *stiff, bristle-like hairs along their sides*, adaptations for swimming.

**Similar species:** — The only other shrew with stiff hairs on the hind feet is the Northern Water Shrew. It is blackish.

## PIGMY SHREW. *Microsorex hoyi.* p. 10

**Recognition:** — Head and body, 2–2½ in.; tail, 1–1⅔ in.; wt., 2⅛–4 gm. By weight, this is probably the *smallest living mammal*. It weighs about the same as a dime. Eyes, tiny black beads; nose, pointed, long.

**Similar species:** — Masked Shrew; longer tail, cannot be distinguished for certain without examining the teeth, has five upper unicuspids (single cusped teeth) on each side of upper jaw. Smoky Shrew; larger. Arctic Shrew; larger, more brightly colored. Dusky Shrew; larger. Longtail Shrew; larger. Gaspé Shrew; larger. Vagrant Shrew; larger.

## DESERT SHREW. *Notiosorex crawfordi.* p. 10

**Recognition:** — Head and body, 2± in.; tail, 1± in. Among the *sagebrush* and other low *desert shrubs* in the arid southwest, this *pale ashy* shrew has been found on few occasions. It is found only on the low desert.

**Similar species:** — Merriam Shrew; slightly larger, darker. Other shrews occurring in the same general area will be found in the mountains in moist situations.

## LEAST SHREW. *Cryptotis parva.* pp. 8, 12

**Recognition:** — Head and body, 2⅛–2½ in.; tail, ½–¾ in.; wt., 4–6½ gm. This small, *cinnamon, shorttail* shrew inhabits the open *grassy areas* of eastern United States. By its color and extremely short tail it may be distinguished from all other shrews.

**Similar species:** — Shorttail Shrew; larger, plumbeous. Other shrews; longer tails.

## SHORTTAIL SHREW. *Blarina brevicauda.* pp. 8, 12

**Recognition:** — Head and body, 3–4 in.; tail, ¾–1⅛ in.; wt., 12–23 gm. This *plumbeous-colored*, shorttail shrew, with *no external ears* and with eyes so small that they are *barely apparent*, is one of the commonest mammals of eastern United States. It is found in nearly every land habitat available to it.

**Similar species:** — Least Shrew; smaller, brown. Other shrews; longer tails.

# Bats: Chiroptera

THESE are the only *truly flying* mammals. The hand is formed into a wing with a membrane of skin extending between the hand bones to the forearm, side of body, and hind leg. Most of them also have a membrane connecting the legs (including the tail). This is the interfemoral membrane. The only measurement given in the following accounts is that of the forearm (from the elbow to the wrist). This indicates the relative size of the animal fairly accurately. The calcar is a cartilaginous support for the free edge of the interfemoral membrane. It is anchored to the inside of the foot and extends out along the edge of the membrane. If it is "keeled" there will be a definite extension of the free edge of the membrane beyond the calcar. If the calcar lies along the free edge, it is not keeled. The tragus is a leaf-like structure in the ear.

# Leafnose Bats: Phyllostomatidæ

MEMBERS of this family usually have a *leaf-like, triangular flap* of thick skin *projecting upward from the tip of the nose.* Members of this family are the only ones, considered here, that possess these leaf-like structures around the nose.

**LEAFCHIN BAT.** *Mormoops megalophylla.*                    p. 15
   **Recognition:** — Forearm, 2–2⅕ in. A brownish bat with prominent *leaf-like folds of skin across chin,* reaching from ear to ear, the central one, in front of lower lip, covered with small *wart-like prominences;* end of tail appears on *upper side of interfemoral membrane;* face short; forehead high. This tropical bat barely gets into southern United States. We have no other bat with the above characters.   ·

**LEAFNOSE BAT.** *Macrotus californicus.*                pp. **24,** 15
   **Recognition:** — Forearm, 2 in. This *large-eared, grayish* bat has a distinct *leaf-like flap* of thick skin *projecting upward from the tip of the nose.* It may be found in colonies in caves and mine tunnels of our southwestern desert.
   **Similar species:** — Hognose Bat; long, slender rostrum, small ears, dark brown. Longnose Bat; long rostrum, no tail.

**HOGNOSE BAT.** *Choeronycteris mexicana.*                pp. **24,** 15
   **Recognition:** — Forearm, 1¾ in. This bat has a *long, slender nose* with a triangular *flap* of skin projecting upward from the tip. The ears are small, barely projecting above the head; color, dark brown; tail extends *less than halfway to edge of interfemoral mem-*

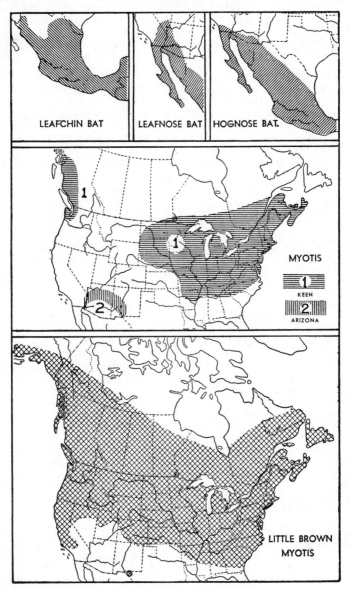

LEAFCHIN BAT  LEAFNOSE BAT  HOGNOSE BAT.

MYOTIS

1 KEEN

2 ARIZONA

LITTLE BROWN
MYOTIS

*brane.* It is a tropical bat that barely gets into southern United States.

**Similar species:** — Leafnose Bat; ears large, tail extends to edge of interfemoral membrane. Longnose Bat; no tail.

**LONGNOSE BAT.** *Leptonycteris nivalis.* p. 20
    **Recognition:** — Forearm, 2⅖ in. This rather large, brownish bat has an extremely *long slender nose* with a *leaf-like projection* of thick skin on its end. The ears are medium large and extend well above the top of the head. The interfemoral membrane is narrow; there is *no tail.* This bat barely reaches the southern border of the United States, being tropical.
    **Similar species:** — Hognose Bat; tail present. Leafnose Bat; tail present.

# Plainnose Bats: Vespertilionidæ

MEMBERS of this family have *simple, unmodified muzzles.* They all have *complete* interfemoral membranes, and in all the *tail reaches to* the *back edge of the membrane, but not noticeably beyond.*

# Myotis Group of Bats: Vespertilionidæ (in part)

THIS is the largest and most widely distributed group of bats. They are all relatively *small,* some shade of *brown,* have simple snouts, and a rather long *pointed tragus* (a leaf-like projection arising from the base of the inside of the external ear). The membranes are always complete, and the tail reaches to the edge of the interfemoral membrane. This membrane is sometimes scantily haired, especially at the base, but *never thickly covered with hair.*

    Many of the species are difficult to identify, even in a museum. In the following accounts, this should be borne in mind. In case of doubt, specimens should be sent to some authority for identification.

**Similar species:** — Big Brown Bat; larger. Evening Bat; tragus blunt. Pipistrel; tragus blunt.

**LITTLE BROWN MYOTIS.** *Myotis lucifugus.* pp. **9,** 15
    **Recognition:** — Forearm, 1½ in. This is the commonest and most widely distributed species of the myotis group. They may be found in caves, buildings, or hollow trees by day; in the evening, at deep dusk, they may be seen flying near water or edges of forests. The ear is moderate in size, when laid forward it reaches

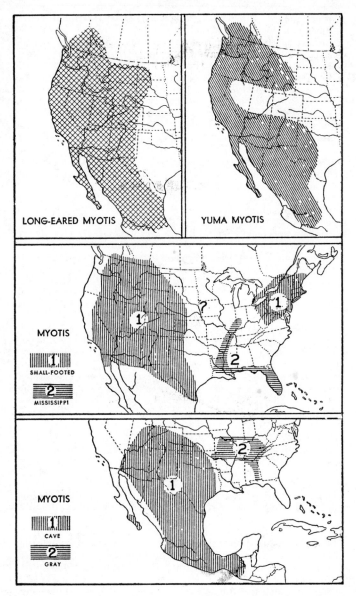

LONG-EARED MYOTIS

YUMA MYOTIS

MYOTIS

1 SMALL-FOOTED

2 MISSISSIPPI

MYOTIS

1 CAVE

2 GRAY

to the nostril. Hairs on back have *long glossy tips*. This glossy sheen is fairly characteristic.
**Similar species:** — Yuma Myotis; smaller. Mississippi Myotis; larger, duller color. Gray Myotis; larger. Cave Myotis; larger. Keen Myotis; ears large (when laid forward, reach beyond nose). Long-eared Myotis; ears large (when laid forward, reach beyond nose). Fringed Myotis; conspicuous fringe of hairs along edge of interfemoral membrane. Indiana Myotis; definite keel on calcar. Long-legged Myotis; larger, fur not glossy. California Myotis; smaller. Small-footed Myotis; smaller. Big Brown Bat; larger. Evening Bat; rounded tragus.

**YUMA MYOTIS.** *Myotis yumanensis.* p. 17
**Recognition:** — Forearm, 1⅓–1½ in. This is one of the commonest of the western myotis. It is usually found in colonies by day, flying near water or forest edges in the evening. Interfemoral membrane *haired nearly to knees.* Color, *dull brownish* with hairs dark at their bases.
**Similar species:** — Little Brown Myotis; larger, hair glossy. Cave Myotis; larger. Arizona Myotis; ochraceous, glossy fur. Keen Myotis; ears large (when laid forward extend beyond nose). Long-eared Myotis; ears large. Fringed Myotis; conspicuous fringe of hairs along edge of tail membrane. Long-legged Myotis; larger. California Myotis; smaller. Small-footed Myotis; smaller. Big Brown Bat; larger.

**MISSISSIPPI MYOTIS.** *Myotis austroriparius.* p. 17
**Recognition:** — Forearm, 1½–1⅗ in. Found in the lower Mississippi Valley and southeastern United States, this bat is not common. It is a *dull yellowish brown.*
**Similar species:** — Little Brown Myotis; smaller, glossy fur. Gray Myotis; larger, hairs not dark at bases. Keen Myotis; ears large. Indiana Myotis; smaller. Big Brown Bat; larger. Evening Bat; rounded tragus.

**GRAY MYOTIS.** *Myotis grisescens.* p. 17
**Recognition:** — Forearm, 1⅗–1⅘ in. This bat inhabits our southeastern *caves* in large colonies. It is a *dull grayish brown* with the hairs about the same color to the bases.
**Similar species:** — Little Brown Myotis; smaller, fur glossy and dark at bases. Mississippi Myotis; smaller. Indiana Myotis; smaller. Big Brown Bat; larger. Evening Bat; blunt tragus.

**CAVE MYOTIS.** *Myotis velifer.* p. 17
**Recognition:** — Forearm, 1⅗–1⅘ in. One of the common bats of the *caves* of the Southwest, where it is found in colonies by day. Color, *dull brown;* ears, moderate in size; wing membrane arises *from base of toes.*
**Similar species:** — Little Brown Myotis; smaller. Yuma My-

otis; smaller. Arizona Myotis; smaller. Long-eared Myotis; smaller, ears larger. Fringed Myotis; fringe of hairs along edge of tail membrane. Long-legged Myotis; smaller. California Myotis; smaller. Small-footed Myotis; smaller. Big Brown Bat; larger.

**ARIZONA MYOTIS.** *Myotis occultus.* p. 15

**Recognition:** — Forearm, $1\frac{2}{5}$–$1\frac{3}{5}$ in. This is a relatively rare bat with a limited distribution in the Southwest. Its color is strongly *ochraceous*, and the hairs of the back have burnished tips. It has a *glossy sheen.*

**Similar species:** — Yuma Myotis; brown. Cave Myotis; larger. Long-eared Myotis; ears large. Fringed Myotis; fringe of hairs at edge of tail membrane. Long-legged Myotis; underside of wing furred to elbow. California Myotis; smaller. Small-footed Myotis; smaller. Big Brown Bat; larger.

**KEEN MYOTIS.** *Myotis keeni.* p. 15

**Recognition:** — Forearm, $1\frac{2}{5}$–$1\frac{3}{5}$ in. This northern member of the myotis group may be distinguished from all other myotis within its range, except the Long-eared Myotis, by the size of its ears. When laid forward, the ears *extend about* $\frac{1}{16}$ *in. beyond the nose.* The Long-eared Myotis has even larger ears. The Keen Myotis is *dark brown.*

**Similar species:** — Little Brown Myotis; ears smaller. Yuma Myotis; ears smaller. Mississippi Myotis; ears smaller. Long-eared Myotis; ears larger (extend $\frac{1}{5}$ in. beyond nose when laid forward). Fringed Myotis; fringe of hairs on edge of tail membrane. Indiana Myotis; ears smaller. Long-legged Myotis; ears smaller. California Myotis; smaller. Big Brown Bat; larger. Evening Bat; blunt tragus.

**LONG-EARED MYOTIS.** *Myotis evotis.* pp. 9, 17

**Recognition:** — Forearm, $1\frac{2}{5}$–$1\frac{3}{5}$ in. This species is found in the western, *thinly forested* areas, usually around buildings or trees. It is not a cave bat. Nowhere is it common. It may be distinguished from all other species of myotis by its *large black ears* (when laid forward they extend about $\frac{1}{5}$ in. beyond the nose). Its general coloration is a *pale brown.*

**Similar species:** — Little Brown Myotis; smaller ears. Yuma Myotis; smaller ears. Cave Myotis; larger, with smaller ears. Arizona Myotis; smaller ears. Keen Myotis; slightly smaller ears, dark brown. Fringed Myotis; distinct fringe of hairs on edge of interfemoral membrane, smaller ears. Long-legged Myotis; smaller ears. California Myotis; smaller. Small-footed Myotis; smaller. Big Brown Bat; larger.

**FRINGED MYOTIS.** *Myotis thysanodes.* p. 20

**Recognition:** — Forearm $1\frac{3}{5}$–$1\frac{4}{5}$ in. Buffy brown in color, this bat may be distinguished from all other myotis by the presence

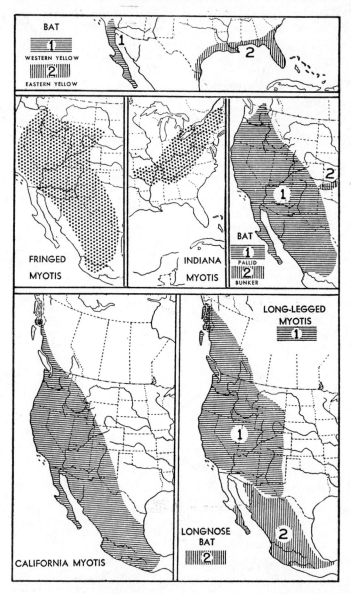

BAT
1 WESTERN YELLOW
2 EASTERN YELLOW

FRINGED MYOTIS

INDIANA MYOTIS

BAT
1 PALLID
2 BUNKER

LONG-LEGGED MYOTIS
1

CALIFORNIA MYOTIS

LONGNOSE BAT
2

of a *conspicuous fringe of stiff hairs along the free edge of the interfemoral (tail) membrane*. It also has relatively large ears. Found in buildings and caves.

**Similar species:** — The following species of myotis may be found within the range of the Fringed Myotis. All but the Cave Myotis are smaller, and none has the distinct fringe on the edge of the tail membrane. Little Brown Myotis, Yuma Myotis, Cave Myotis, Arizona Myotis, Keen Myotis, Long-eared Myotis, Long-legged Myotis, California Myotis. The Big Brown Bat is larger and does not possess the fringe.

**INDIANA MYOTIS** *Myotis sodalis.* p. 20

**Recognition:** — Forearm, $1\frac{2}{5}$–$1\frac{3}{5}$ in. This is a *cave* bat, rare over most of its range. Calcar with definite *keel.* It is very difficult to distinguish from the Little Brown Myotis, especially in the field.

**Similar species:** — Little Brown Myotis; no definite keel on calcar. Mississippi Myotis; larger. Gray Myotis; larger, hairs not dark at bases. Keen Myotis; larger ears. Small-footed Myotis; smaller. Big Brown Bat; larger. Evening Bat; rounded tragus.

**LONG–LEGGED MYOTIS.** *Myotis volans.* p. 20

**Recognition:** — Forearm, $1\frac{1}{2}$–$1\frac{3}{5}$ in. An inhabitant of the West, this species of myotis may be distinguished from other species of myotis by the *short rounded ears*, *small foot*, well-developed *keel on calcar*, and fur on the under side of the membranes as far out as the elbow and knee. It is found in open forests.

**Similar species:** — Little Brown Myotis; smaller. Yuma Myotis; smaller. Cave Myotis; larger. Arizona Myotis; under side of wing not furred to elbow. Keen Myotis; larger ears. Long-eared Myotis; larger ears. Fringed Myotis; larger, fringe on edge of tail membrane. California Myotis; smaller. Small-footed Myotis; smaller. Big Brown Bat; larger.

**CALIFORNIA MYOTIS.** *Myotis californicus.* pp. 9, 20

**Recognition:** — Forearm, $1\frac{1}{5}$–$1\frac{2}{5}$ in. One of the small species of myotis. Color varies from light buff (in desert) to rich brown (along northwest coast). Color of bases of hairs is *much darker than that of tips.*

**Similar species:** — Sometimes difficult to distinguish from the Yuma Myotis (usually larger, larger foot) or the Small-footed Myotis (*distinct black mask across face*). The Little Brown Myotis, Cave Myotis, Arizona Myotis, Keen Myotis, Long-eared Myotis, Fringed Myotis, Long-legged Myotis, and Big Brown Bat are all larger.

**SMALL–FOOTED MYOTIS.** *Myotis subulatus.* pp. 9, 17

**Recognition:** — Forearm, $1\frac{1}{5}$–$1\frac{2}{5}$ in. This is the *smallest* myotis in the eastern area and, except for the California Myotis, the western area also. Its *long silky fur* is almost *yellowish* and it has a distinct *black mask* across the face. The ears are black. In some parts of the range this is a rare bat, in other parts it is fairly common.

**Similar species:** — Yuma Myotis; larger, no black mask. Little Brown Myotis, Cave Myotis, Arizona Myotis, Keen Myotis, Long-eared Myotis, Fringed Myotis, Indiana Myotis, and Long-legged Myotis; all larger. California Myotis; brown mask, ears dark brown (sometimes difficult to distinguish). Big Brown Bat; larger. Evening Bat; rounded tragus.

# Other Plainnose Bats:
# Vespertilionidæ (in part)

**WESTERN PIPISTREL.** *Pipistrellus hesperus.* pp. **9**, 23
  **Recognition:** — Forearm, 1–1⅛ in. Tragus *blunt* with tip bent forward; color, *whitish gray* or *yellowish gray*. *Smallest* of the bats here considered. The Western Pipistrel may be found throughout the low *arid* country of the West. In daytime they seek refuge in crevices in cliffs or in buildings. They *fly early*, before sundown, in an erratic fashion. The small size and pale coloration distinguish them from other bats.
  **Similar species:** — California Myotis; larger, buffy to brown, pointed tragus. Yuma Myotis; larger, pointed tragus. Small-footed Myotis; black mask, pointed tragus. Other bats; larger.

**EASTERN PIPISTREL.** *Pipistrellus subflavus.* pp. **9**, 23
  **Recognition:** — Forearm 1⅜± in. Tragus *blunt* and straight; color *yellowish brown* to *drab brown*. One of the *smallest* of the eastern bats. Hang in crevices or buildings by day; *fly early, before sundown;* flight erratic. Small size and blunt tragus distinguish these from other bats.
  **Similar species:** — Small-footed Myotis; pointed tragus, brown. Indiana Myotis; pointed tragus, brown. Other bats; larger.

**BIG BROWN BAT.** *Eptesicus fuscus.* pp. **9**, 28
  **Recognition:** — Forearm, 1⅘–2 in. Pale brown (on desert) to dark brown; membranes black; tragus blunt. One of the commonest and most widely distributed of our bats. Inhabits buildings, also crevices and caves. Large size and color distinguish this from all other bats.
  **Similar species:** — Evening Bat; smaller. All myotis; smaller.

**EVENING BAT.** *Nycticeius humeralis.* p. 23
  **Recognition:** — Forearm, 1⅖–1½ in. Dark brown; black membranes; *blunt tragus.* Common in the South, rare in the North. Shelter in hollow trees and buildings; steady, straight flight.

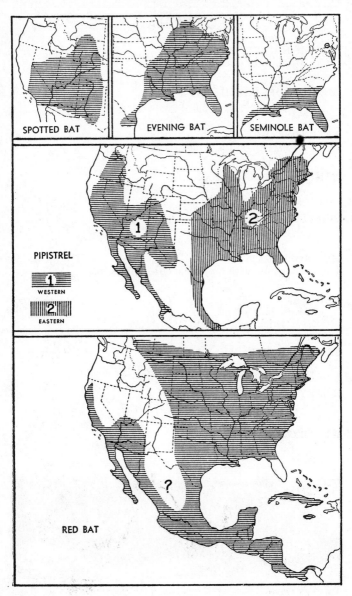

## OTHER BATS

**SILVER–HAIRED BAT**                                    pp. *27*, 26
    Blackish brown with white-tipped hairs.


**MEXICAN FREETAIL BAT**                            pp. *31*, 30
    Tail extends beyond membrane, chocolate brown.


**LEAFNOSE BAT**                                        pp. *14*, 15
    Projection on tip of nose, large ears.


**EASTERN YELLOW BAT**                              pp. *27*, 20
    Yellowish brown, tail membrane furred at base.


**SPOTTED BAT**                                          pp. *29*, 23
    White spots, large ears.


**HOGNOSE BAT**                                          pp. *14*, 15
    Long nose with projection on end, ears small.


**RED BAT**                                              pp. *27*, 23
    *Female:* Pale reddish, frosted.
    *Male:* Brick red, frosted.


**SEMINOLE BAT**                                         pp. *27*, 23
    Mahogany-brown, frosted.


**HOARY BAT**                                            pp. *27*, 26
    Frosted, yellow throat.


**WESTERN MASTIFF BAT**                             pp. *31*, 30
    Large, chocolate brown, tail beyond membrane.

Little Brown
Myotis sleeping
in cave

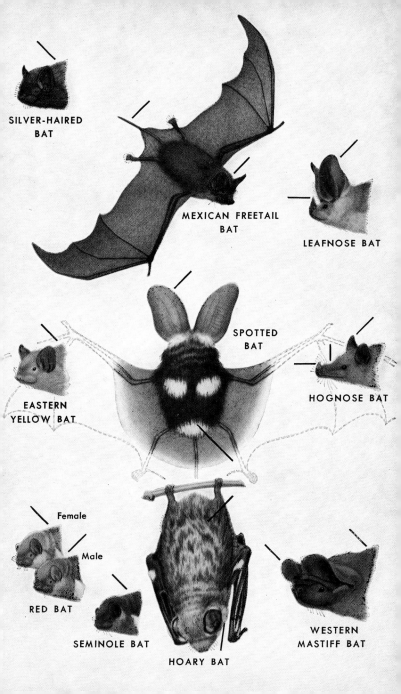

SILVER-HAIRED
BAT

MEXICAN FREETAIL
BAT

LEAFNOSE BAT

SPOTTED
BAT

EASTERN
YELLOW BAT

HOGNOSE BAT

Female

Male

RED BAT

SEMINOLE BAT

HOARY BAT

WESTERN
MASTIFF BAT

BIG BROWN BEAR

GRIZZLY BEAR

POLAR BEAR

Blue phase       Cinnamon phase       Black phase

BLACK BEAR

Plate 4                                                    25

# BEARS

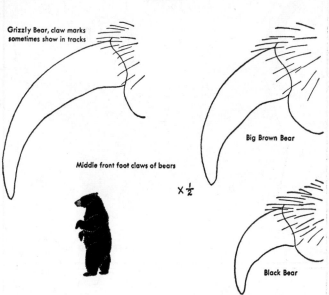

**Grizzly Bear, claw marks sometimes show in tracks**

**Big Brown Bear**

**Middle front foot claws of bears**

$\times \frac{1}{2}$

**Black Bear**

**GRIZZLY BEAR**                                    pp. *32*, 35
   Hump on shoulders, large fore claws.

**BIG BROWN BEAR**                                  pp. *34*, 33
   Hump on shoulders, large, moderate fore claws.

**POLAR BEAR**                                      pp. *34*, 33
   White.

**BLACK BEAR**                                      pp. *32*, 33
   *Blue phase, cinnamon phase, black phase:* No hump on shoulders, claws small, face brown.

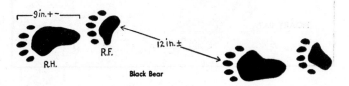

Black Bear

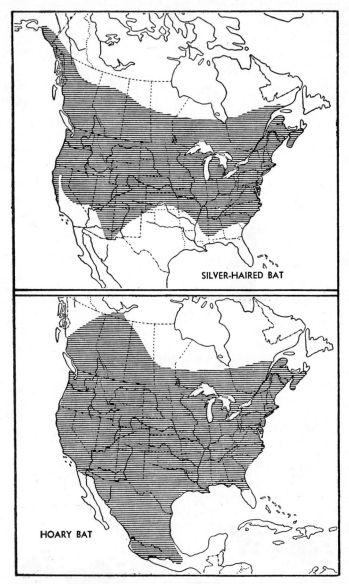

SILVER-HAIRED BAT

HOARY BAT

The combination of size, color, and blunt tragus distinguishes this from all other species in its range.

**Similar species:** — Big Brown Bat; larger. All myotis; pointed tragus.

**SILVER-HAIRED BAT.** *Lasionycteris noctivagans.* pp. **24,** 2⁶

**Recognition:** — Forearm, 1⅔ in. A *blackish-brown* bat with hairs on middle of back *tipped with white,* and tail membrane furred above on basal half. Inhabits *forested* regions. Distinguished from all other bats by color.

**Similar species:** — Hoary Bat; larger, throat buffy. Red Bat; brick or rusty red. Seminole Bat; mahogany.

**HOARY BAT.** *Lasiurus cinereus.* pp. **24,** 2⁶

**Recognition:** — Forearm, 2+ in. Yellowish brown to mahogany-brown, with hairs tipped with white over most of body, and with a buffy throat, this bat has the tail membrane heavily furred on top to edges; ears rounded. This magnificent bat inhabits the *forested* regions. It is solitary, and hangs in *trees* by day. Size and color distinguish it.

**Similar species:** — Silver-haired Bat; smaller. Red Bat; smaller. Seminole Bat; smaller.

**RED BAT.** *Lasiurus borealis.* pp. **24,** 23

**Recognition:** — Forearm, 1½–1⅔ in. This *brick-red* to *rusty-red* bat, with the hairs *tipped with white,* and the tail membrane fully furred above, inhabits the *forested* areas. It is solitary. Females are distinctly paler than males. Common throughout its range.

**Similar species:** — Hoary Bat; larger. Silver-haired Bat; blackish brown. Seminole Bat; mahogany-brown.

**SEMINOLE BAT.** *Lasiurus seminolus.* pp. **24,** 23

**Recognition:** — Forearm, 1½–2⅔ in. This bat inhabits the *forests,* chiefly, of southeastern United States. It is a rich *mahogany-brown* with the hairs *tipped with white.* Similar, in other respects, to the Red Bat.

**Similar species:** — Red Bat; brick-red or rusty red. Hoary Bat; larger. Silver-haired Bat; blackish brown. Eastern Yellow Bat; tail membrane heavily furred for only basal third, yellowish.

**WESTERN YELLOW BAT.** *Dasypterus ega.* p. **20**

**Recognition:** — Forearm, 1⅘–2⅛ in. This large, pale, *yellowish-brown* bat barely enters southern California. The tail membrane is heavily *furred only on its basal one-third.*

**Similar species:** — Hoary Bat; tail membrane completely furred.

**EASTERN YELLOW BAT.** *Dasypterus intermedius.* pp. **24,** 20

**Recognition:** — Forearm, 1⅘–2⅛ in. A large, pale, *yellowish-brown* bat with tail membrane heavily *furred only on its basal*

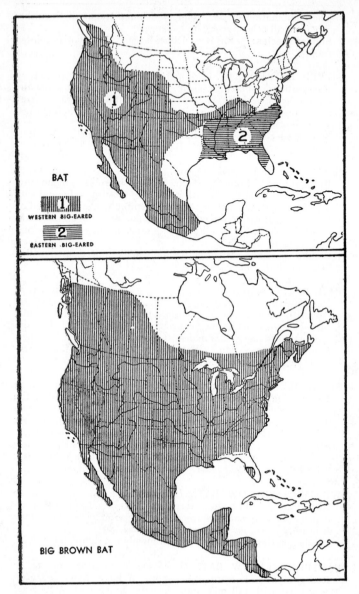

BAT

1   WESTERN BIG-EARED

2   EASTERN BIG-EARED

BIG BROWN BAT

*one-third.* Nowhere common. This and the Western Yellow Bat may belong to the same species. At present they are considered distinct. Also considered distinct is *Dasypterus floridanus*, which is included on the range map with the species *intermedius*.
**Similar species:** — Hoary Bat, Red Bat, and Seminole Bat; all have tail membrane heavily furred to edge.

**SPOTTED BAT.** *Euderma maculata.*                    pp. **24**, 23
   **Recognition:** — Forearm, 2 in. This rare and spectacular bat has *huge ears*, is *dark sepia* with a *white spot* at the *base of the tail* and another on *each shoulder*. It is the only bat with such contrasting colors.

**WESTERN BIG–EARED BAT.** *Corynorhinus rafinesquei.* p. 28
   **Recognition:** — Forearm, 1⅜–1⅘ in. This species may be recognized by the extremely *large ears* (over an inch in height) which are *joined across the forehead*. On its nose, in front of the eyes, are two prominent lumps. The general color is clove brown. Tail membrane is naked. This is a *cave* bat.
   **Similar species:** — Pallid Bat and Bunker Bat; ears separate, no prominent lumps on nose.

**EASTERN BIG–EARED BAT.** *Corynorhinus macrotis.* pp. **9**, 28
   **Recognition:** — Forearm, 1⅜–1⅘ in. Within its range, this bat may be distinguished from all others by the *tremendous ears* (over an inch high) which are *joined in the middle.* Two prominent lumps on top of its nose are further characters. Color *pale brown.* This and the Western Big-eared Bat are at present considered to be separate species. Inhabits *caves.*

**PALLID BAT.** *Antrozous pallidus.*                    pp. **9**, 20
   **Recognition:** — Forearm, 2–2⅜ in. This *large-eared* (over an inch in height) *pallid* bat is one of the common bats of the West. It has a simple muzzle, and the ears are *not joined.* Color, yellowish drab (palest in desert and darkest along North Pacific Coast).
   **Similar species:** — Western Big-eared Bat; ears joined.

**BUNKER BAT.** *Antrozous bunkeri.*                    p. 20
   **Recognition:** — Forearm, 2⅛ in. This bat has a limited range. It may prove to be the same as the Pallid Bat, but at present is considered distinct. Characters as given for the Pallid Bat.

# Freetail Bats: Molossidæ

MEMBERS of this family have the tail extending *well beyond the back edge of the tail membrane.* They all have *short*, dense, *dark brown* fur, and give off a *musty odor.* They are primarily cave bats, but

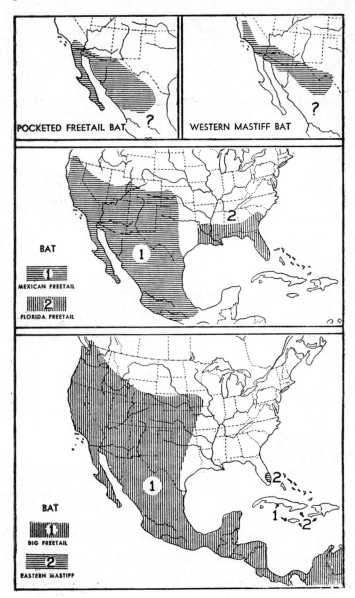

POCKETED FREETAIL BAT ?

WESTERN MASTIFF BAT ?

BAT

1
MEXICAN FREETAIL

2
FLORIDA FREETAIL

BAT

1
BIG FREETAIL

2
EASTERN MASTIFF

are also found in buildings. They are colonial in habits. The Carlsbad Caverns house one of the largest colonies (of the Mexican Freetail Bat) in this country.

**FLORIDA FREETAIL BAT.** *Tadarida cynocephala.* p. 30
**Recognition:** — Forearm, 1⅗–1⅘ in. This is the only freetail bat in its size range within the geographic range of the species. The short *velvety fur* is warm brown. Tail *extends well beyond membrane.*
**Similar species:** — Eastern Mastiff Bat; larger.

**MEXICAN FREETAIL BAT.** *Tadarida mexicana.* pp. **24**, 30
**Recognition:** — Forearm 1⅔–1⅘ in. This is the common freetail bat of the West, where it may be found in caves or buildings, usually in *large colonies.* The short *velvety fur* is usually *mummy brown.* Smallest of the freetails within its range. Probably the same species as the Florida Freetail, but considered distinct at present.
**Similar species:** — Pocketed Freetail, Big Freetail, and Western Mastiff Bats; all larger.

**POCKETED FREETAIL BAT.** *Tadarida femorosacca.* p. 30
**Recognition:** — Forearm, 1⅘–2 in. This rare bat barely ranges into the United States in the Southwest. Size alone should distinguish it from the other freetails in its range.
**Similar species:** — Mexican Freetail; smaller. Big Freetail; larger. Western Mastiff Bat; larger.

**BIG FREETAIL BAT.** *Tadarida macrotis.* p. 30
**Recognition:** — Forearm, 2⅓–2½ in. This rare freetail ranges over much of the West. It is the largest of the freetail bats, but is exceeded in size by the Western Mastiff Bat.
**Similar species:** — Mexican Freetail and Pocketed Freetail; smaller. Western Mastiff Bat; larger.

**WESTERN MASTIFF BAT.** *Eumops perotis.* pp. **24**, 30
**Recognition:** — Forearm, 2⅞–3⅛ in. This is the *largest* of the bats here considered. It has a limited range in our Southwest where, during the day, it hangs on tall buildings or on cliffs. The *free tail,* extending well beyond the membrane, and *large size* serve to distinguish it.
**Similar species:** — Freetail Bats; all smaller.

**EASTERN MASTIFF BAT.** *Eumops glaucinus.* p. 30
**Recognition:** — Forearm, 2⅓–2⅖ in. This *large* tropical bat with a *free tail* is rare. It is known only from Florida in the United States.
**Similar species:** — Florida Freetail Bat; smaller.

# Flesh-eaters: Carnivora

THIS order includes those mammals that are primarily *meat eaters*. Many of them eat berries, nuts, and fruits also, but usually their main diet is flesh. They vary in size from the small Least Weasel, wt. about ⅒ lb., to the Big Brown Bear which will weigh over 1500 lb. All have *five toes on the front foot*, some have the inner toe high on the foot, and only four toes touch the ground. They may have four or five toes on the hind foot. Large *canine teeth* are present in all.

# Bears: Ursidæ

IN THIS family we have the *largest* living carnivores. They walk on the entire foot, as does man, have five toes on both front and back feet, and have *short tails* which are practically concealed in the long fur. The ears are relatively small and rounded.

**BLACK BEAR.** *Ursus americanus.* pp. **25**, 33
  **Recognition:** — Head and body, 5–6 ft.; height at shoulders, 2–3 ft.; wt., 200–400 lb. This is the commonest and most widely distributed of the bears; it is also the smallest. In the East it is primarily a forest and swamp inhabitant; in the West it is found chiefly in the mountains. Color varies from *black*, in the East, to *cinnamon* or black, in the West, to *nearly white* on Gribble Island, British Columbia. The "Blue" or "Glacier" Bear from near Yakutat Bay, Alaska, is probably a color phase of the Black Bear. The face is always *brown* and there is usually a small patch of *white* on the breast.
  **Similar species:** — Grizzly Bear; larger, hump on shoulders. Big Brown Bear; larger.

**GRIZZLY BEAR.** *Ursus horribilis.* pp. **25**, 35
  **Recognition:** — Head and body 6–7 ft.; height at shoulders, 3–3½ ft.; wt., 325–850 lb. The Grizzly Bear ranges from *yellowish to* dark brown, *nearly black*, and usually has *white tips* on the hairs, especially on the back — giving it the *frosted* or grizzly effect. Claws on front feet long (about 4 in.) and curved. A *noticeable hump* is present above the shoulders. Found chiefly in mountainous areas.
  **Similar species:** — Black Bear; smaller, claws on front foot not noticeably large, no distinct hump in shoulder region. Big Brown Bear; larger.
  **Remarks:** — There are some seventy-four "species" of Grizzly Bears recognized in the literature. Obviously, this is too many,

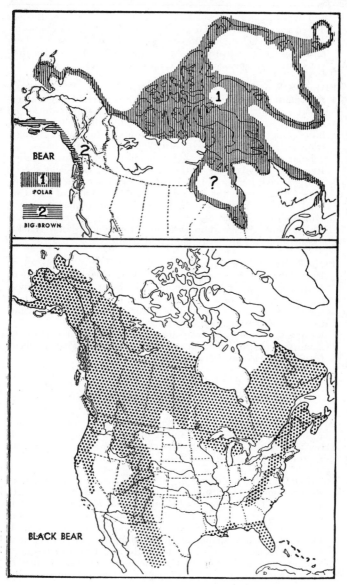

BEAR

1
POLAR

2
BIG-BROWN

?

BLACK BEAR

and to try to treat them separately would lead only to confusion. These are all treated as Grizzly Bears here, but this does not imply that all belong to the species *horribilis*. Most of them probably do. *Ursus inopinatus*, the Yellow Bear, from Rendezvous Lake, Mackenzie, Canada, may be distinct.

**BIG BROWN BEAR.** *Ursus middendorffi.* pp. **25, 33**
**Recognition:** — Head and body about 8 ft.; height at shoulders about 4–4½ ft.; weight up to 1500 lb. or more. This is the *largest* of the bears. The claws are relatively smaller than in the Grizzly, but size is the best character separating the two. Color ranges from *yellowish to dark brown*, often with white-tipped hairs.
**Similar species:** — Grizzly Bear; smaller. Black Bear; smaller.
**Remarks:** — According to the literature there are eight species of Big Brown Bears. All are included under one general heading here. Those from the islands are: *sitkensis*, Baranof and Chicagof Islands, Alaska; *shirisi*, Admiralty Island, Alaska; *nuchek*, Hinchinbrook Island and mainland, Alaska; *middendorffi*, Kodiak Island, Alaska; and *sheldoni*, Montague Island, Alaska. Mainland forms are: *gyas*, *dalli*, and *kenaiensis*.

**POLAR BEAR.** *Thalarctos maritimus.* pp. **25, 33**
**Recognition:** — Head and body, 6½–7½ ft.; height at shoulders, 3–4 ft.; wt., 600–1100 lb. or more. The Polar Bear spends most of its time on *ice floes*. When on land, it usually remains near shore. By its large size and *white* fur it may be distinguished from all other bears within its range.
**Remarks:** — The Polar Bears on the east coast of Greenland and along the coast of Labrador are usually listed as distinct species (*eogrœnlandicus* and *labradorensis*).

# Raccoons, Coatis: Procyonidæ

MEMBERS of this family are medium-sized, about that of a small dog; have five toes on front and hind feet; walk on entire foot; claws not retractile; tail with distinct *yellowish-white rings* or with very indistinct rings.

**RACCOON.** *Procyon lotor.* pp. **72, 35**
**Recognition:** — Head and body, 18–28 in.; tail, 8–12 in.; wt., 12–35 lb. This *grizzled gray* animal with a *black mask* over its eyes and alternating *rings* of yellowish white and black on its tail is found wherever there are streams or lakes within its range. It lives in trees, if available, and feeds along the water's edge. A shrill cry, almost a whistle, in the night might be a raccoon.
**Similar species:** — Ringtail Cat; slender body, tail as long or longer than head and body. Coati; tail as long as head and body, indistinctly ringed

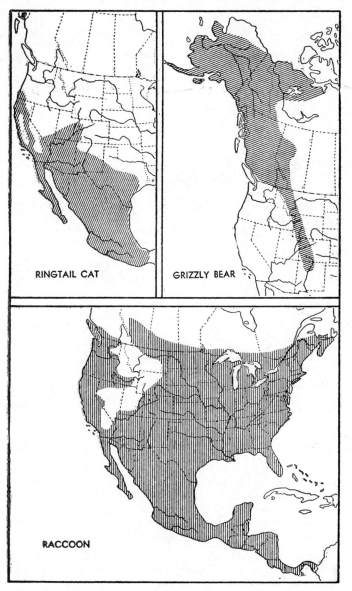

RINGTAIL CAT

GRIZZLY BEAR

RACCOON

**COATI.** *Nasua narica.*                              pp. **72**, 37

> **Recognition:** — Head and body, 20–25 in.; tail, 20–25 in.; wt.,
> 15–25 lb.  This *long-snouted*, grizzled-brownish invader from the
> tropics barely enters southern United States.  Its *long tail* which
> is often carried erect is indistinctly ringed, and it has *white spots
> above and below each eye.*  It has five toes on each foot, and walks
> on the entire foot.  A tough nose pad aids in its rooting activities
> for grubs and tubers.  The *nose is whitish.*
> **Similar species:** — Raccoon; tail distinctly ringed, shorter.  Red
> Fox; white tip on tail.

# Ringtail Cats: Bassariscidæ

**RINGTAIL CAT.** *Bassariscus astutus.*               pp. **72**, 35

> **Recognition:** — Head and body, 14–16 in.; tail, 15 in.  The Ring-
> tail Cat is found in the arid west and southwest, chiefly in rough
> country.  The *long tail is ringed* with whitish and blackish-brown
> rings, and the claws are semi-retractile.  There is thick fur be-
> tween the pads of the feet.  The ears and eyes are large, and the
> animal is most graceful.  This is the only species of this family
> which occurs north of the Mexican border.
> **Similar species:** — Raccoon; shorter tail, black mask.

# Weasels, Skunks, etc.: Mustelidæ

MEMBERS of this family are varied in size and color.  Usually they
have long slender bodies and short legs; short, rounded ears; and
anal scent glands.

**MARTEN.** *Martes americana.*                         pp. **40**, 37

> **Recognition:** — Head and body, males, 16–17 in., females, 14–15
> in.; tail, males, 8–9 in., females, 7–8 in.; weight, males, 2–4 lb.
> This graceful fur-bearer of the *northern forests* has soft, dense,
> *yellowish-brown* fur shading to *dark brown* on the bushy tail and
> on the legs.  It has a *pale buff patch* on the throat and breast, and
> the belly is paler than the back.
> **Similar species:** — Mink; white patch on chin.  Fisher; dark
> brown, grizzled on head and back, larger.

**FISHER.** *Martes pennanti.*                          pp. **40**, 37

> **Recognition:** — Head and body, 20–25 in.; tail, 13–15 in.; wt.,
> 4½–10 lb.  This magnificent fur-bearer of the northern forests is
> *dark brown to nearly black* with *white-tipped hairs* over most of its

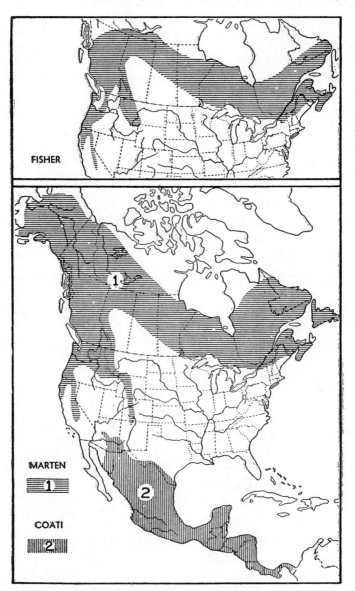

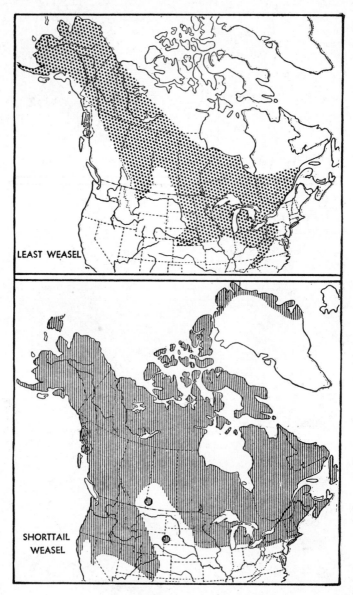

LEAST WEASEL

SHORTTAIL
WEASEL

body, giving it a *frosted* appearance. It has a long, slim body and
a bushy tail. The Fisher is more at home in the trees than it is
on the ground.
**Similar species:** — Marten; smaller, buffy patch on throat and
breast. Wolverine; yellowish stripes on sides and rump.

**SHORTTAIL WEASEL.** *Mustela erminea.*                    pp. **41**, 38
    **Recognition:** — Head and body, male, 6–9 in., female, 5–7½ in.;
tail, male, 2¼–4 in.; female, 2–3 in.; wt., male, 2½–3⅔ oz.,
female, 1½–2½ oz. Largest in East and North, smallest in
West. Males are one-fifth to one-fourth larger than females.
This small, lithe carnivore is nowhere common. It is *dark brown*
with *white underparts and feet* in summer, *white in winter*, but always with a *black tip on tail.* In summer, it has a *white line down
its hind leg*, connecting the white of the underparts with that of
the toes. It may be found in nearly every land habitat within
its range.
    **Similar species:** — Longtail Weasel; respective sexes larger,
tail longer, no white line on hind leg. Least Weasel; no black
tip on tail. Mink; uniform color.

**LONGTAIL WEASEL.** *Mustela frenata.*                    pp. **41**, 43
    **Recognition:** — Head and body, males, 9–10½ in., females, 8–9
in.; tail, males, 4–6 in., females, 3–5 in.; wt., males, 6–8¾ oz.,
females, 3–3½ oz. This, the most widely distributed, and most
common of the weasels, is found in all possible land habitats. It
is distinguished by its long slender body, long neck, head slightly
larger than neck, *yellowish-white underparts*, black tip on tail, and
*no whitish line down inside of hind leg.* In winter, in the northern
part of its range, it is white except for the black tip on the tail.
In some parts of its range it has a white bridle across its face and
the head is usually of a darker brown than the body.
    **Similar species:** — Shorttail Weasel; respective sexes smaller,
white line down inside of hind leg. Least Weasel; smaller, no
black tip on tail. Mink; nearly uniform dark brown.

**LEAST WEASEL.** *Mustela rixosa.*                    pp. **41**, 38
    **Recognition:** — Head and body, males, 6–6½ in., females,
5½–6 in.; tail, males, 1⅛–1½ in., females, 1–1⅛ in.; wt., females, 45–50 gm. This is the *smallest* living carnivore. It is rare
throughout most of its range. It is brown above, whitish below
in summer, white all over in winter. Sometimes there are a few
black hairs, but no black tip, at the end of its short tail.
    **Similar species:** — Shorttail and Longtail weasels; both have
black tips on tails.

**MINK.** *Mustela vison.*                    pp. **41**, 43
    **Recognition:** — Head and body, males, 13–17 in., females, 12–14
in.; tail, males, 7–9 in., females, 5–8 in.; wt., 1¼–2¼ lb. The

## FUR–BEARING MAMMALS

**MARTEN**                                                    pp. *36*, 37
    Brown, bushy tail, yellowish breast.

**FISHER**                                                    pp. *36*, 37
    Blackish brown, frosted on head and shoulders.

**WOLVERINE**                                                 pp. *42*, 44
    Dark brown, yellowish stripes across hips.

**SEA OTTER**                                                 p. *42*
    Sea coast, head and neck yellowish.  Floats on back.

**RIVER OTTER**                                               pp. *42*, 47
    Rich brown, tail thick at base.

L.H. 2 in.

Marten   L.F.

L.H. $2\frac{3}{4}$ in.

River Otter

L.F.

L.H.

River Otter slide on snow or mud bank, about 8 in. wide

Wolverine (Thumb print occasionally registers)

5 in. ±

L.F.

L.H.

3 in.

Fisher

L.F.

MARTEN

FISHER

WOLVERINE

SEA OTTER

RIVER OTTER

LEAST WEASEL

Winter

SHORTTAIL
WEASEL

Summer
Male

Northeast
Female

LONGTAIL WEASEL

Southwest

BLACK-FOOTED FERRET

MINK

Plate 6                                                                41

# WEASELS AND MINK

**LEAST WEASEL**                                               pp. *39*, 3⁸
  Short tail, no black tip.

**SHORTTAIL WEASEL**                                           pp. *39*, 3⁸
  *Winter:* White, medium tail with black tip.
  *Summer:* Brown, white down hind leg to foot.

**LONGTAIL WEASEL**                                            pp. *39*, 43
  Hind leg brownish, black tip on long tail.
  *Northeast:* No white on face.
  *Southwest:* White on face.

**BLACK–FOOTED FERRET**                                        pp. *42*, 44
  Black forehead and feet.

**MINK**                                                       pp. *39*, 43
  Rich brown, white on chin.

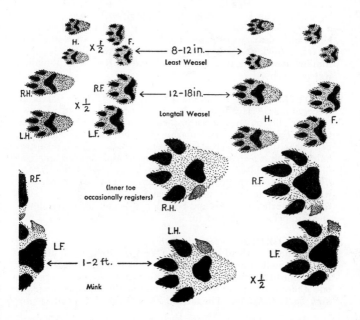

Mink is confined to streams and lakes within its range. It is usually *rich dark brown* with a *white chin patch* and sometimes scattered small white spots on its belly. The tail is slightly bushy.
**Similar species:** — Weasels; white or yellowish underparts.
Marten; yellow patch on throat and breast. River Otter; larger.

**BLACK–FOOTED FERRET.** *Mustela nigripes.*           pp. **41**, 44
   **Recognition:** — Head and body, 15–18 in.; tail, 5–6 in. This
large weasel-like inhabitant of the *prairies* may be recognized by
its *yellowish brown to buffy* body, *black forehead*, black-tipped tail,
and *black feet*.
   **Similar species:** — Kit Fox; bushy tail, feet not black.

**WOLVERINE.** *Gulo luscus.*                              pp. **40**, 44
   **Recognition:** — Head and body, 29–32 in.; tail, 7–9 in., wt.,
20–35 lb. In general appearance, except for the bushy tail, the
Wolverine looks like a small bear. It is *dark brown, paler on the
head*, and has *two broad yellowish stripes* which start at the shoulders and join on the rump. Its feet are large for its size. It lives
in the forests of high mountains and the north country.
   **Similar species:** — Fisher; without yellowish stripes.

**RIVER OTTER.** *Lutra canadensis.*                       pp. **40**, 47
   **Recognition:** — Head and body, 26–30 in.; tail, 12–17 in.; wt.,
10–20 lb. This large weasel-like mammal, *rich brown above* with
a *silvery sheen below*, and with small ears and a *broad snout*, is
found only near or in *streams and lakes*. Its feet are *webbed* and
its tail is thick at the base, tapering toward the tip.
   **Similar species:** — Beaver; tail flat and scaly. Mink; smaller,
feet not webbed.

**SEA OTTER.** *Enhydra lutris.*                               p. **40**
   **Recognition:** — Head and body, 30–36 in.; tail 11–13 in. Known
to occur only on the *sea coast* of southern California and among
the Aleutian Islands. This marine mustelid, usually seen in kelp
beds near shore, is deep *glossy brownish black* with white-tipped
hairs, giving it a frosted effect. The head and neck are grayish-
or yellowish-white. Its feet are completely *webbed and flipper-
like*. Sea Otters are protected at all times. For many years they
were thought to be extinct along the California Coast.
   **Similar species:** — Seals and Sea Lions; shorter tails, well-developed flippers, and shorter fur.

**SPOTTED SKUNK.** *Spilogale putorius.*                   p. **45**, 46
   **Recognition:** — Head and body, 9–13½ in.; tail, 4½–9 in.; wt.,
1–2 lb. Smallest in the West, largest in Midwest and East. This
handsome little carnivore is *black* with a *white spot on the forehead*,
one *under each ear*, and with *four broken white stripes along the
neck, back, and sides*. The tail has a white tip. The relative pro-

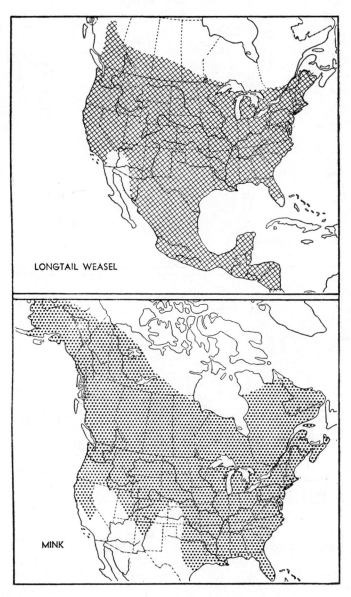

LONGTAIL WEASEL

MINK

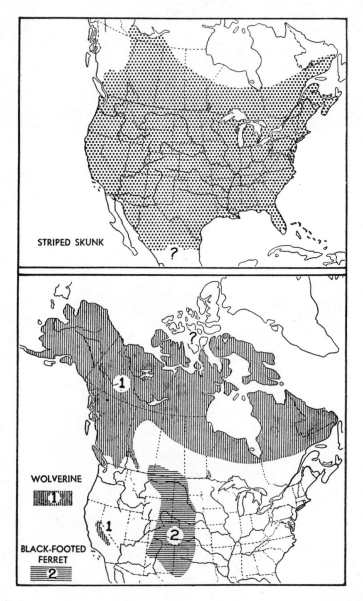

STRIPED SKUNK

?

WOLVERINE

1

BLACK-FOOTED
FERRET

2

portions of white and black vary considerably. There is no other mammal with a similar color pattern.

**Remarks:** — There are about eight species of Spotted Skunks, north of the Mexican boundary, listed in the literature. These may eventually be reduced to two or three — or even to one.

**STRIPED SKUNK.** *Mephitis mephitis.*                        p. 44
  **Recognition:** — Head and body, 13–18 in.; tail, 7–10 in.; wt., 6–10 lb. The Striped Skunk is probably the best known, and most widely known, mammal here considered. About the size of a House Cat, it may be recognized by its *black body, narrow white stripe* up middle of forehead, and *broad white area* on nape which usually divides into a V at about the shoulders. The resulting two white lines may continue back to the base of the bushy tail, which may or may not have a white tip. There is much variation in the length and width of the side stripes. Scent glands are well developed. Often the presence of a skunk is detected by *odor* rather than by sight. Found in practically all land habitats. Lives in ground dens and beneath abandoned buildings.
  **Similar species:** — Spotted Skunk; smaller, white lines broken. Hooded Skunk; tail longer, white V on back rarely present. Hognose Skunk; white back stripe not divided.

**HOODED SKUNK.** *Mephitis macroura.*                        p. 46
  **Recognition:** — Head and body, 12–16 in.; tail, 14–15 in. This is a southern skunk that barely enters southern United States. There are two general color patterns with intermediate variants in this species. In one, the entire back is chiefly *white*, including tail; in the other, the back is nearly all *black* and there are two white side stripes — the belly is *black*. The hair on the neck

Striped Skunk

Spotted Skunk

Hognose Skunk

Hooded Skunk

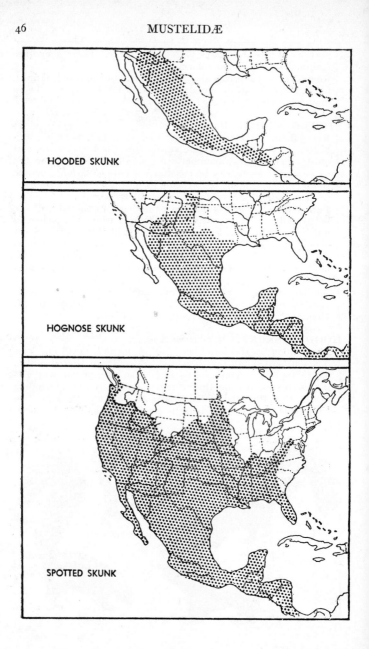

HOODED SKUNK

HOGNOSE SKUNK

SPOTTED SKUNK

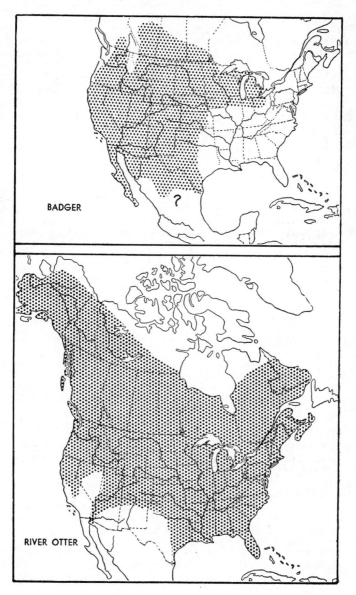

BADGER

RIVER OTTER

usually spreads out into a *ruff*. The tail is *as long as head and body*.

**Similar species:** — Striped Skunk; white V on back, tail shorter. Hognose Skunk; long, bare snout, entire back and tail white with no black hairs, tail shorter.

**HOGNOSE SKUNK.** *Conepatus leuconotus.* p. 45, 46

**Recognition:** — Head and body, 14–19 in.; tail, 7–12 in.; wt., 5–10 lb. The Hognose Skunk is well named. It has a long, *pig-like snout* which is *naked* for about an inch *on top*. It roots for grubs. A two-tone affair, its *entire back and tail are white* and the lower sides and belly are black. The fur is short and coarse.

**Similar species:** — Striped Skunk; white blaze on forehead. Hooded Skunk; if white on back, usually mixed with black, tail longer.

**BADGER.** *Taxidea taxus.* pp. **72**, 47

**Recognition:** — Head and body, 18–22 in.; tail, 4–6 in.; wt., 13–25 lb. This heavy-bodied, short-legged, *yellowish-gray* animal has a *median white stripe* from its nose over the top of its head, *white cheeks*, and a *black spot* in front of each ear. The feet are *black* and the front claws are extremely long. The belly and short tail are yellowish. No other North American mammal has the above characters. It is found chiefly in treeless country.

# Dogs, Foxes, Wolves: Canidæ

MEMBERS of this family are all *dog-like* in general appearance. They have five toes on each front foot (the inside toe is high) and four on the back foot (some domestic dogs have a fifth toe). All have a scent gland at the base of the tail, on top. Its position is revealed by the black-tipped hairs without underfur.

**RED FOX.** *Vulpes fulva.* pp. **56**, 49

**Recognition:** — Head and body, 22–25 in.; tail, 14–16 in.; wt., 10–15 lb. This fox has many color variations (Cross and Silver Foxes), but the normal color is *reddish yellow*, slightly darkened on the back, with a mixture of black in the *long bushy tail*, which has a *white tip*, and with *black legs and feet*. In the far north, the black may be reduced on the feet. The conspicuous white tip on the tail will distinguish it from other species, regardless of the color phase. It prefers broken, sparsely settled country.

**KIT FOX.** *Vulpes velox.* pp. **56**, 50

**Recognition:** — Head and body, 15–20 in.; tail, 9–12 in.; wt., 4–6 lb. This small, large-eared, pale *buffy-yellow* fox with a blackish spot on either side of its snout and a *black tip on* its

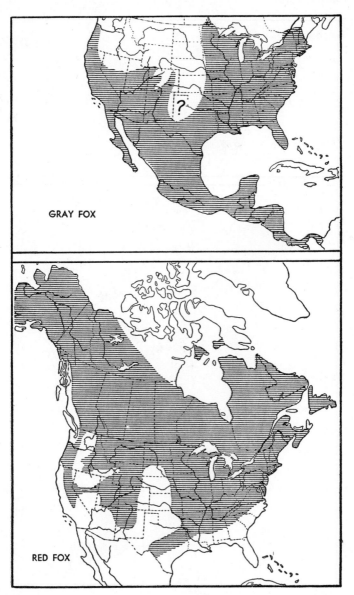

GRAY FOX

RED FOX

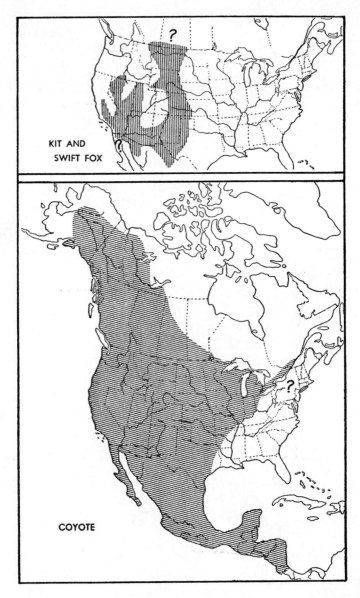

KIT AND
SWIFT FOX

COYOTE

*bushy tail* is found in the *arid* west, usually in the *low open country*.

**Similar species:** — Red Fox; white tip on tail. Gray Fox; black streak down top of tail.

**Remarks:** — Another "species," *Vulpes macrotis*, is recognized in the literature. It is the western desert representative and has larger ears.

**GRAY FOX.** *Urocyon cinereoargenteus*.                pp. **56**, 49

**Recognition:** — Head and body, 21–29 in.; tail, 11–16 in.; wt., 7–13 lb. This is the common fox throughout the brushy and wooded areas of the West and South. Its *pepper and salt* coat with buffy underfur; long, *bushy tail* with a *median black streak* down its total length, and *tipped with black*; and its rusty-yellowish sides of neck, back of ears, legs, and feet will serve to distinguish it.

**Similar species:** — Red Fox; white tip on tail. Kit Fox; black of tail only at tip. Coyote; larger, black of tail only at tip.

**Remarks:** — The Gray Foxes on the Santa Barbara Islands, California (*littoralis*), and those along the Pacific Coast (*californicus*) have been considered as separate species.

**ARCTIC FOX.** *Alopex lagopus*.                pp. **56**, 52

**Recognition:** — Head and body, 20± in.; tail, 11± in.; wt., 7–15 lb. This far northern fox lives chiefly in the *tundra* area beyond the line of tree growth. It has *short rounded ears* and heavily furred feet, as becomes an arctic mammal. There are two color phases, *blue and white*. Both phases are similar in summer, dull *brownish* to slate with yellowish white on belly, sides of neck, and flanks. In winter, the white phase is *white* throughout; the blue phase is *slate-blue* with sometimes brownish on the head and feet. No white tip on tail. On Pribilof Island they are all blue.

**Similar species:** — Red Fox; reddish yellow with white tip on tail.

**COYOTE.** *Canis latrans*.                pp. **56**, 50

**Recognition:** — Head and body, 32–37 in.; tail, 11–16 in.; wt., 20–50 lb. The Coyote looks like a medium-sized dog; it is *gray* or *reddish gray with rusty legs, feet*, and *ears*, and with a pointed nose. The throat and belly are whitish. The tail is bushier than normal in dogs, and is *held down* between the hind legs *when running*. Found in nearly every habitat, it prefers open areas. In the evening a series of high-pitched *yaps* may be heard, especially on the desert.

**Similar species:** — Wolf; larger, holds tail high when running, nose pad 1 in. or more wide. Foxes; smaller, hold tail out straight when running.

**GRAY WOLF.** *Canis lupus*.                pp. **56**, 52

**Recognition:** — Head and body, 43–48 in.; tail, 12–19 in.; height at shoulders, 26–28 in.; wt., 70–170 lb. This is the largest of our

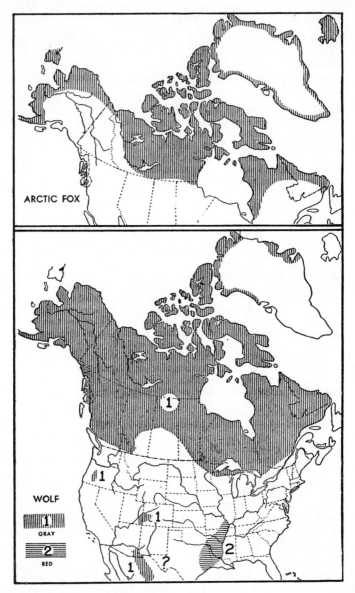

ARCTIC FOX

WOLF

1 GRAY

2 RED

wild dogs and is found only in the wilder parts of its range. Color varies from *dark gray, nearly black,* to *nearly white* in the arctic. When running, *the tail is carried high.* Its ears are more rounded and relatively smaller than are those of the Coyote. It is also more dog-like in appearance.

**Similar species:** — Coyote; smaller, carries tail low when running, nose pad less than 1 in.

**RED WOLF.** *Canis niger.*                           pp. **56**, 52
    **Recognition:** — Head and body, 42–49 in.; tail, 13–17 in.; wt., 30–80 lb. This southern wolf varies in color from a *grayish black*, with tawny muzzle, ears, and outer parts of legs, *to nearly black.* Small individuals in the light color phase are difficult to distinguish from the Coyote. They run with their *tails out behind,* not down between their legs.
    **Similar species:** — Coyote; usually smaller and yellowish gray, runs with tail between legs, nose pad 1 in. or less wide.

# Cats: Felidæ

THIS family, to which the House Cat belongs, is familiar to most people. Except for color and size, cats all look about alike. They have *short faces,* relatively small rounded ears, and *retractile claws.* They have five toes on each front foot, four on each back foot.

**JAGUAR.** *Felis onca.*                             pp. **57**, 54
    **Recognition:** — Head and body, 44–58 in.; tail, 21–26 in.; wt., 150–225 lb. This large tawny cat is uniformly spotted with black. The *spots* on the sides and back *form rosettes,* a ring of black with a small black spot in the center. The belly is white with black spots. Rare in southern United States.
    **Similar species:** — Ocelot and Margay Cat; small, spots do not form rosettes. Mountain Lion; uniform color. Bobcat; short tail.

**OCELOT.** *Felis pardalis.*                          pp. **57**, 54
    **Recognition:** — Head and body, 27–35 in.; tail, 13–15 in.; wt., 20–40 lb. This small, *spotted* cat with a long tail does not have the rosettes like the jaguar. Some of the *dark markings* are *elongate,* more nearly stripes than spots. Very rare in southern United States.
    **Similar species:** — Jaguar; larger, with rosettes. Bobcat; short tail. Margay Cat; smaller.

**MARGAY CAT.** *Felis wiedi.*                         p. 54
    **Recognition:** — Head and body, 20–23 in.; tail 14–16 in. This *small spotted* cat rarely gets into southern United States. It is a miniature of the Ocelot and is distinguished chiefly by size.

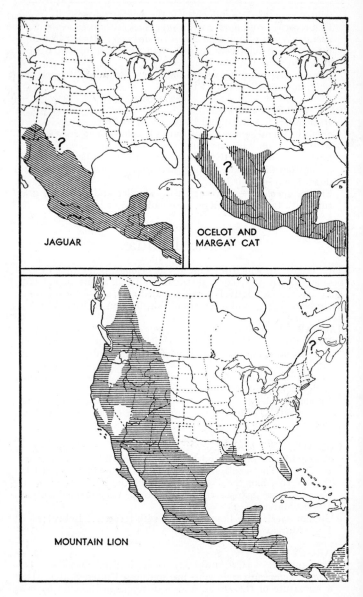

JAGUAR

OCELOT AND MARGAY CAT

MOUNTAIN LION

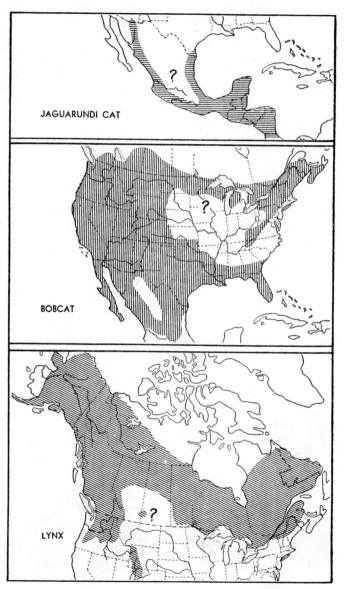

JAGUARUNDI CAT

BOBCAT

LYNX

# DOG–LIKE MAMMALS

**RED FOX**                                                    pp. *48, 49*
    *Red phase:* White tip on tail, feet black.
    *Black phase:* White tip on tail.
    *Cross phase:* Dark cross over shoulders, white tip on tail.

**GRAY FOX**                                                  pp. *51, 49*
    Black stripe down top of tail, feet rusty.

**ARCTIC FOX**                                                pp. *51, 52*
    *Blue phase:* Bluish brown.
    *White phase:* White.

**KIT FOX**                                                   pp. *48, 50*
    Black tip on tail.

**COYOTE**                                                    pp. *51, 50*
    Narrow nose pad, tail down when running.

**GRAY WOLF**                                                 pp. *51, 52*
    Broad nose pad, tail high when running.

**RED WOLF**                                                  pp. *53, 52*
    Reddish or blackish, tail high when running.

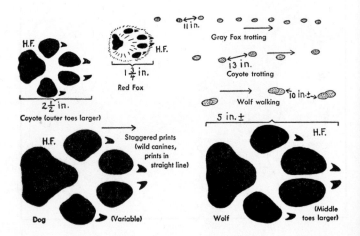

H.F.

H.F.

$1\frac{3}{4}$ in.
Red Fox

11 in.
Gray Fox trotting

13 in.
Coyote trotting

Wolf walking   10 in.±

$2\frac{1}{2}$ in.
Coyote (outer toes larger)

5 in. ±

H.F.
Staggered prints
(wild canines,
prints in
straight line)

H.F.

Dog      (Variable)      Wolf

(Middle
toes larger)

Red phase

Black phase

Cross phase

RED FOX

GRAY FOX

Blue phase

White phase

ARCTIC FOX

KIT FOX

COYOTE

GRAY WOLF

RED WOLF

LYNX

BOBCAT

Young

MOUNTAIN LION

Adult

Red
phase

Gray
phase

OCELOT

JAGUARUNDI CAT

JAGUAR

Plate 8                                                    57

# CATS

**LYNX**                                                        pp. *58*, 55
   Short tail, tip black all way around.


**BOBCAT**                                                      pp. *58*, 55
   Short tail, tip black only on top.


**MOUNTAIN LION**                                               pp. *58*, 54
   *Young:* spotted.
   *Adult:* Tan, large, long tail.


**OCELOT**                                                      pp. *53*, 54
   Small, long tail, spots and streaks.


**JAGUARUNDI CAT**                                              pp. *58*, 55
   *Red phase:* Reddish.
   *Gray phase:* Bluish gray, short legs, long tail.


**JAGUAR**                                                      pp. *53*, 54
   Large, spots in form of rosettes.

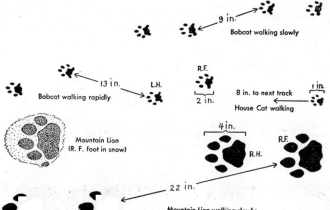

9 in. — Bobcat walking slowly

13 in. — Bobcat walking rapidly     L.H.

R.F.

2 in.     8 in. to next track     1 in.
          House Cat walking

Mountain Lion
(R. F. foot in snow)

4 in.     R.F.
          R.H.

22 in.

Mountain Lion walking slowly
(Lynx smaller, Jaguar larger)

The ground color is buffy. There are four broken dark brown stripes on the neck and one on the back. Brown spots on sides are irregular in shape; some have dark buffy centers, giving a rosette-like appearance. Belly white with dark brown spots.
Similar species: — Jaguar; larger, with rosettes. Ocelot; larger, coloration similar.

**MOUNTAIN LION.** *Felis concolor.*                    pp. **57**, 54
Recognition: — Head and body, 42–54 in.; tail, 30–36 in.; wt., 80–200 lb. This large, *tawny to grayish* cat, with *dark brown on tip of tail* and on backs of ears and sides of nose, is fast disappearing from the scene. It lives in the few wild forested areas remaining. The young are spotted. Its call is described as sounding like the scream of a woman.
Similar species: — Jaguarundi Cat; smaller.

**JAGUARUNDI CAT.** *Felis eyra.*                    pp. **57**, 55
Recognition: — Head and body, 22–30 in.; tail, 13–24 in., wt., 15–18 lb. This long-bodied, short-legged, uniform-colored (either *red* or *gray*) cat is about twice the size of an ordinary House Cat. Its tail is nearly as long as its head and body. It is extremely rare just north of the Mexican border.
Similar species: — Ocelot; spotted.

**LYNX.** *Lynx canadensis.*                    pp. **57**, 55
Recognition: — Head and body, 32–36 in.; tail, 4 in.; wt., 15–30 lb. This *bob-tailed* cat of the north country is distinguished by the short tail with a *complete black tip*, and the tufts on its ears.
Similar species: — Bobcat; tip of tail black only on top.

**BOBCAT.** *Lynx rufus.*                    pp. **57**, 55
Recognition: — Head and body, 25–30 in.; tail, 5 in.; wt., 15–30 lb. The Bobcat has a short tail that is *black only on top at the tip*. Its ear tufts are short and inconspicuous. It prefers rimrock country in the West, swamps in the East.
Similar species: — Lynx; tip of tail black all way around.

# Seals and Sea Lions: Pinnipedia

MARINE mammals with front and hind limbs developed into *flippers*. They haul out on land to rest and to give birth to young. Usually seen only *along shores*, although they may go far out to sea when in migration. Males are usually much larger than females.

# Eared Seals: Otariidæ

**CALIFORNIA SEA LION.** *Zalophus californianus.*      p. **60**
Recognition: — Head and body, males, 8 ft., females, 5½–6 ft. Along the coast and on the islands of California, from about

Monterey Bay southward, one may see this *small brown* (blackish when wet) sea lion with a *high forehead*. It has small, pointed ears and large eyes. Usually hauls out on rocky shores, sometimes on sand beaches. Its *continual honking bark* is also characteristic.

**Similar species:** — Northern Sea Lion; larger, paler, low forehead, seldom bark when not molested. Elephant Seal; much larger, no external ears, usually quiet. Guadalupe Fur Seal; forehead low, nose pointed, silvery on neck and head. Harbor Seal; spotted.

**Range:** — Pacific Coast, from Monterey Bay south.

**NORTHERN SEA LION.** *Eumetopias jubata.*               p. **60**
**Recognition:** — Head and body, male, 10½ ft., female, 8 ft. From Santa Rosa Island off southern California, northward along the Pacific Coast, one is likely to see these *large yellowish-brown* to brown sea lions hauled out on some rock or beach. The *forehead is low* and they are usually fairly *quiet* when not molested.
**Similar species:** — California Sea Lion; smaller, darker, high forehead, usually barking. Alaska Fur Seal; much smaller, reddish below, face brown. Harbor Seal; smaller, spotted.
**Range:** — Pacific Coast, Santa Rosa Island, California, northward.

**ALASKA FUR SEAL.** *Callorhinus alascanus.*               p. **60**
**Recognition:** — Head and body, males, 6 ft., females, 4 ft. These fur seals breed principally on the *Pribilof Islands* and at other localities in the Bering Sea. In winter, they may be seen as far south as California. The males are *blackish above, reddish on the belly,* and gray on the shoulders and front of the neck. The face is *brownish.* Females are gray above, reddish below.
**Similar species:** — Northern Sea Lion; larger, not reddish below. Harbor Seal; spotted.
**Range:** — Pacific Coast, south to California.

**GUADALUPE FUR SEAL.** *Arctocephalus townsendi.*
**Recognition:** — Head and body, male 5½ ft., female, 4½ ft. From San Nicolas Island south, this rare fur seal, long thought to be extinct, may still survive. It has a *pointed muzzle,* is dark brown with a *silvery grizzling of head and neck.* The sides of the snout are rusty.
**Similar species:** — California Sea Lion; larger, high forehead. Elephant Seal; much larger, male has proboscis. Harbor Seal; spotted.
**Range:** — Pacific, north to San Nicolas Island, California.

# Hair Seals: Phocidæ

**HARBOR SEAL.** *Phoca vitulina.*                         p. **60**
**Recognition:** — Head and body, 5 ft. There is no appreciable

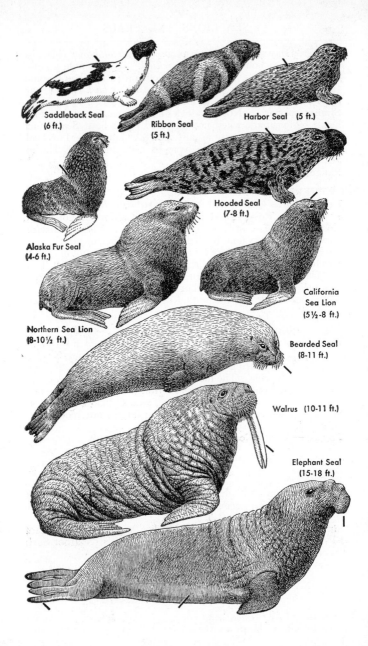

Saddleback Seal
(6 ft.)

Ribbon Seal
(5 ft.)

Harbor Seal   (5 ft.)

Alaska Fur Seal
(4-6 ft.)

Hooded Seal
(7-8 ft.)

California
Sea Lion
(5½-8 ft.)

Northern Sea Lion
(8-10½ ft.)

Bearded Seal
(8-11 ft.)

Walrus   (10-11 ft.)

Elephant Seal
(15-18 ft.)

difference in size of the sexes. This small *spotted* seal, yellowish with brown spots or brown with yellowish spots, may be seen in harbors or at mouths of rivers. It cannot rotate its hind flippers forward.

**Similar species:** — Sea Lions and Fur Seals; no spots. Elephant Seal; larger, no spots. Ringed Seal; both spots and streaks along back.

**Range:** — Pacific, Atlantic south to Carolinas, and Arctic.

**RIBBON SEAL.** *Phoca fasciata.* p. 60

**Recognition:** — Head and body, 5 ft. This small, brown seal with *bands of yellow* around its *neck*, around the *front flipper*, and around the *rump*, is known from the Aleutians and the coast of Alaska. Females are less brightly colored than males. This is a rare seal, and the only one with the above markings.

**Range:** — Pacific Coast, Alaska northward.

**RINGED SEAL.** *Phoca hispida.*

**Recognition:** — Head and body, 4½–5 ft. This dull *yellowish to brownish* seal has *dark spots* and *streaks* which are usually continuous *along the back*. Usually, there are pale buffy rings on the sides; the belly is yellowish, sometimes spotted.

**Similar species:** — Harbor Seal; no streaks.

**Range:** — Arctic, south to Labrador and the Bering Sea.

**SADDLEBACK SEAL.** *Phoca grœnlandica.* p. 60

**Recognition:** — Head and body, 6 ft. This northern seal is grayish or yellowish with a *dark brown or black face* and a dark, irregular band which crosses the shoulders and extends back along the sides, sometimes over the rump. Smaller spots may be present on feet and neck. Females less distinctly marked or without dark markings; young *yellowish white*. No other seal has the above markings.

**Range:** — Gulf of St. Lawrence north into the Arctic.

**BEARDED SEAL.** *Erignathus barbatus.* p. 60

**Recognition:** — Head and body, 8–11 ft. This seal is uniformly *grayish to yellowish*. It has a prominent *tuft* of long flattened *bristles* on *each side of the muzzle*. The prominent tufts are characteristic of this, and no other, seal. A fairly common seal on the *ice floes*.

**Range:** — From Alaska, across the polar waters to Newfoundland.

**GRAY SEAL.** *Halichœrus grypus.*

**Recognition:** — Head and body, 10–12 ft. This *large*, rare, grayish seal prefers rocky shores with strong currents. *Large size* and *plain color* characterize it.

**Range:** — Atlantic, from Nova Scotia to Greenland.

**HOODED SEAL.** *Cystophora cristata.*                              p. 60
  **Recognition:** — Head and body, 7–8 ft. In the cold waters this
  is one of the common seals. It is *dark gray to slaty black* with *paler
  sides* which are *spotted with whitish.* The young are *white.* On
  top of the head of the male is an inflatable bag. When angry,
  this is "blown up" and makes the animal appear more formidable.
  These seals are commonly seen on *floe ice.*
  **Range:** — Atlantic, Nova Scotia to Greenland.

**ELEPHANT SEAL.** *Mirounga angustirostris.*                       p. 60
  **Recognition:** — Head and body, males, 15–18 ft., females, 8–9 ft.
  On a *sand beach,* by day, these large seals may be seen sleeping.
  They feed by night. They are pale *brown to grayish,* lighter on
  the belly than on the back. Old males have large, overhanging,
  *proboscis-like snouts.* Largest of the seals where they occur.
  **Similar species:** — Sea Lions and Fur Seals; much smaller, ex-
  ternal ears, can rotate hind flippers forward.
  **Range:** — Pacific, north to Santa Barbara Islands, California.

# Walruses: Odobenidæ

**WALRUS.** *Odobenus rosmarus.*                                    p. 60
  **Recognition:** — Head and body, males, 10–11 ft., females, 7–8 ft.
  These huge seals with *two large, white tusks projecting downward
  from the mouth* may be seen in groups on the *ice.* The tusks and
  large size set them apart from all other marine mammals.
  **Range:** — Arctic waters; Bering Sea to Labrador.
  **Remarks:** — In recent literature, the Walrus on the Pacific side
  is considered a distinct species, *O. divergens.*

# Gnawing Mammals: Rodentia

THE order of rodents is made up of small to medium-size mammals.
All are characterized by having only *two incisors* (gnawing teeth)
*above* and *two below.* There is a distinct *space* between these teeth
and the grinding or cheek teeth. Most, but not all, rodents have
four toes on each front foot, five on each hind foot.
**Similar kinds:** — Rabbits and Hares. These have a small pair of
incisors immediately behind the large upper incisors, not apparent
from the outside. They also have short, cottony tails.

# Squirrels: Sciuridæ

THIS family includes a wide variety of mammals. Marmots, Woodchucks, Prairie Dogs, Ground Squirrels, Chipmunks, and Tree

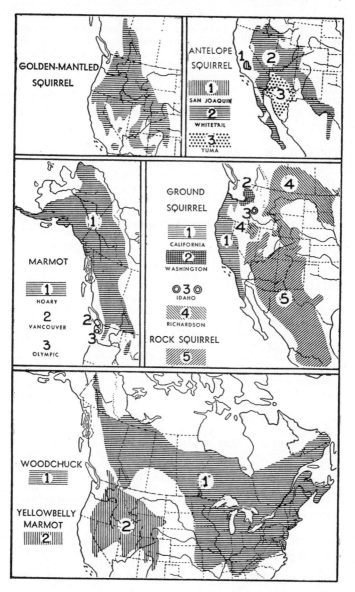

Squirrels all belong here. They have four toes on the front foot, five on the back. The tail is always covered with hair, sometimes bushy. They are all diurnal (*active during the daytime*) except the Flying Squirrels, which come out only at night. The Marmots, Ground Squirrels, Prairie Dogs, and Chipmunks all nest in burrows in the ground or beneath rocks or logs. Tree Squirrels and Flying Squirrels nest in trees. Most of the ground-living kinds have a habit of sitting up "picket pin" fashion on their haunches. This enables them to see over the low ground vegetation and avert danger.

**WOODCHUCK.** *Marmota monax.*                                pp. **72**, 63
 **Recognition:** — Head and body, 16–20 in.; tail, 4–7 in.; wt., 5–10 lb. This heavy-bodied, short-legged, *yellowish-brown to blackish-brown* animal is best known in the eastern part of its range. The belly is paler than the back. Hairs on body have a slightly *frosted* appearance. The feet are *dark brown or black.* No white, except around nose. Hibernates during winter months; prefers woodland edges and nearby open areas.
 **Similar species:** — Hoary Marmot; black and white on head and shoulders.

**YELLOWBELLY MARMOT.** *Marmota flaviventris.*   pp. **72**, 63
 **Recognition:** — Head and body, 14–19 in.; tail, 4½–9 in.; wt., 5–10 lb. The Yellowbelly Marmot is found in the higher reaches of the Rockies and Sierras, usually in rocky situations. It is heavy-bodied, *yellowish brown*, with *yellow belly* and usually *white between the eyes.* The sides of the neck have conspicuous buffy patches. The feet are light buff to dark brown, *never black.* These marmots hibernate in winter.
 **Similar species:** — Hoary Marmot; conspicuous white and black head and shoulders.

**HOARY MARMOT.** *Marmota caligata.*                     pp. **72**, 63
 **Recognition:** — Head and body, 18–21 in.; tail, 7–10 in. These *high-mountain* dwellers may be known by their *shrill whistle* or by the *black and white head and shoulders* and general grayish body washed with yellowish. The feet are *black*, and the belly is soiled whitish. Seen most commonly around *rock slides*, they hibernate in winter.
 **Similar species:** — Woodchuck and Yellowbelly Marmot; both without black and white on head and shoulders.

**OLYMPIC MARMOT.** *Marmota olympus.*                         p. 63
 **Recognition:** — Head and body, 18–21 in.; tail, 7–10 in. Found only on the *upper slopes* of the *Olympic Mountains*, this brownish-drab marmot, with white intermixed, and with brown feet, is the only one in the area.

**VANCOUVER MARMOT.** *Marmota vancouverensis.* p. 63
**Recognition:** — Head and body, 16–18 in.; tail, 8–12 in. Confined to *Vancouver Island*, this dark brown marmot is not likely to be confused with any other kind of mammal. It is the only marmot on the island.

**TOWNSEND GROUND SQUIRREL.** *Citellus townsendi.* p. 68
**Recognition:** — Head and body, 5½–7 in.; tail, 1⅛–2⅛ in. Found chiefly in the *arid valleys* of the Great Basin area, this little shorttail ground squirrel blends well with its surroundings. It is *smoke-gray* washed with *pinkish buff*, and the belly and flanks are whitish.
**Similar species:** — Washington Ground Squirrel; dappled. Whitetail Antelope Squirrel; stripes on sides, underpart of tail white. Belding Ground Squirrel; tail reddish beneath. Uinta Ground Squirrel; brownish down middle of back, black in tail. Columbian Ground Squirrel; feet and legs rufous, larger.
**Remarks:** — *C. idahoensis*, with a restricted range north of the Snake River, is included here.

**WASHINGTON GROUND SQUIRREL.** *Citellus washingtoni.*
pp. **73**, 63
**Recognition:** — Head and body, 6–7 in.; tail, 1⅛–2½ in.; wt., 221–280 gm. This small, *dappled* ground squirrel is found in the *low arid* parts of southeastern Washington and northeastern Oregon. It is *smoke-gray flecked with whitish spots*. The tail has a *blackish tip*.
**Similar species:** — Belding Ground Squirrel and Townsend Ground Squirrel; no spots. Columbian Ground Squirrel; larger, feet and legs rufous.

**IDAHO GROUND SQUIRREL.** *Citellus brunneus.* p. 63
**Recognition:** — Head and body, 6½–7¾ in.; tail, 2–2½ in. Restricted to Weiser and Payette Valleys, western Idaho, this little smoke-gray squirrel has its back distinctly *washed with cinnamon* or light brown and sprinkled with *small grayish-white spots*.
**Similar species:** — Columbian Ground Squirrel; larger, feet and legs rufous.

**RICHARDSON GROUND SQUIRREL.** *Citellus richardsoni.*
p. 63
**Recognition:** — Head and body, 7¾–9½ in.; tail, 2–4½ in. This *plains* ground squirrel, sometimes called the "Picket Pin," is drab *smoke-gray* washed with *cinnamon-buff*. The belly is pale buff or whitish and the underside of the tail is clay color, buff, or light brown. The tail is *bordered with white or buff*.
**Similar species:** — Spotted Ground Squirrel; distinct spots. Columbian Ground Squirrel; larger, rufous feet and legs. Thir-

teen-lined Ground Squirrel; stripes on body. Franklin Ground Squirrel; larger, long tail. Uinta Ground Squirrel; tail blackish mixed with buff above and below. Belding Ground Squirrel; median area of back usually brownish, tail rufous below.

**UINTA GROUND SQUIRREL.** *Citellus armatus.* p. 68
**Recognition:** — Head and body, 8¾–9 in.; tail, 2½–3¼ in. Found in the *mountains and foothills*, this small squirrel has a light brownish-gray back. The tail is *fuscous black mixed with buffy white* above and below; belly hairs tipped with pale buff.
**Similar species:** — Townsend Ground Squirrel; tail not blackish. Thirteen-lined Ground Squirrel; stripes. Richardson Ground Squirrel; tail clay-color beneath.

**BELDING GROUND SQUIRREL.** *Citellus beldingi.* p. 68
**Recognition:** — Head and body, 8–9 in.; tail, 2⅛–3 in.; wt., 172–366 gm. A medium-sized ground squirrel with upper parts *grayish*, usually washed with buff, and usually with a definite *broad brownish streak down the back*, contrasting with the sides. The tail is deep fulvous beneath, tipped with black and bordered with buff or white.
**Similar species:** — Townsend Ground Squirrel; tail not fulvous beneath. Richardson Ground Squirrel; tail pale buff or clay-color beneath. Washington Ground Squirrel; dappled above.

**COLUMBIAN GROUND SQUIRREL.** *Citellus columbianus.*
pp. **73,** 68
**Recognition:** — Head and body, 10–12 in.; tail, 3–5 in.; wt., 341–830 gm. This rather *large, bushy-tailed* ground squirrel may be distinguished from all others within its range by the *dark fulvous feet* and *legs* and the *mottled grayish upper parts.*
**Similar species:** — Townsend, Washington, and Richardson ground squirrels; none have deep fulvous feet and legs, all smaller.

**ARCTIC GROUND SQUIRREL.** *Citellus parryi.* pp. **73,** 68
**Recognition:** — Head and body, 8½–13¾ in.; tail, 3–6 in.; wt., 1–2½ lb. In the *far North*, including the *tundra* areas, lives this *large* ground squirrel. It is also found on a number of the islands off Alaska. In general, it is tawny to reddish brown or fuscous abundantly flecked with white. The feet, legs, and underside of tail are tawny.
**Similar species:** — Marmots and Woodchucks; larger, with black feet.
**Remarks:** — Included here are *Citellus kodiacensis*, from Kodiak Island, and *Citellus osgoodi* from the Yukon.

**THIRTEEN–LINED GROUND SQUIRREL.** *Citellus tridceem-lineatus.* pp. **73,** 68
**Recognition:** — Head and body, 4½–6½ in.; tail, 2½–5¼ in.;

wt., 144–243 gm. Typical of the great *prairie* region, this is the most widely ranging of the ground squirrels. The base color varies from light to dark brown. On the sides and back are *thirteen whitish stripes*, some broken into rows of spots, others more or less continuous. The belly is whitish. No other ground squirrel within its range has definite stripes on the body.
**Similar species:** — Chipmunks; stripes on sides of face. Spotted Ground Squirrel; spots, but not stripes.

## MEXICAN GROUND SQUIRREL. *Citellus mexicanus.* p. 68
**Recognition:** — Head and body, 6¾–7½ in.; tail, 4½–5 in. This is a medium-sized ground squirrel with a *long*, slightly bushy tail, the hairs of which are tipped with buff. The back and sides are snuff brown with about *nine rows of light buff spots*.
**Similar species:** — Spotted Ground Squirrel; spots indistinct and not in rows. Rock Squirrel; larger, no spots in rows.

## SPOTTED GROUND SQUIRREL. *Citellus spilosoma.* pp. **73**, 68
**Recognition:** — Head and body, 5–6 in.; tail, 2¼–3½ in.; wt., 80–95 gm. In the semi-arid *prairies*, this small grayish brown or reddish brown squirrel with *squarish spots of white or buff*, sometimes indistinct, on its back, may be seen. The tail is pencil-like, *not bushy*. The belly is whitish.
**Similar species:** — Mexican Ground Squirrel; spots distinct and in rows. Thirteen-lined Ground Squirrel; distinct stripes on body. Roundtail Ground Squirrel; no spots. Richardson Ground Squirrel; no spots.

## FRANKLIN GROUND SQUIRREL. *Citellus franklini.*
pp. **73**, 68
**Recognition:** — Head and body, 9–10 in.; tail, 5–6 in. Typical of the *prairie* is this *large, gray* squirrel with a fulvous overwash on the back and rump. The belly is nearly as dark as the back, and the tail is fairly long. Much larger and darker than any other ground squirrel in its range.
**Similar species:** — Spotted and Thirteen-lined ground squirrels; spots or stripes. Richardson Ground Squirrel; short tail, smaller.

## ROCK SQUIRREL. *Citellus variegatus.* pp. **73**, 63
**Recognition:** — Head and body, 10–11 in.; tail, 7–10 in. In the arid southwest, usually where there are *rocky areas*, this, *largest* of the ground-living squirrels within its range, may be seen foraging in the open or *sitting on top a boulder* on the watch for danger. The usual color is *grayish* (sometimes nearly black) mixed with cinnamon or brown, sometimes with head and back blackish. Tail nearly as long as head and body and slightly bushy. There is a slightly *mottled* effect over the body. Hibernates in winter. Nests beneath boulders.
**Similar species:** — Other ground squirrels; smaller with shorter tails. Prairie dogs; found only on open prairies, tails short.

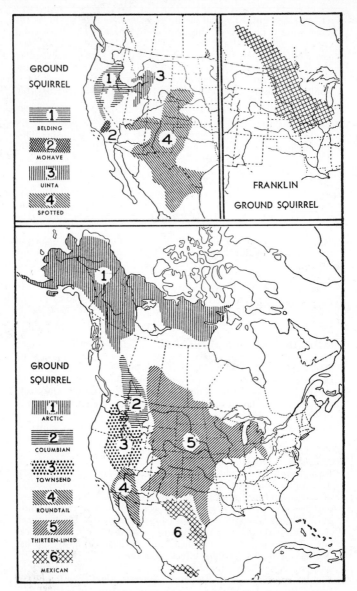

GROUND SQUIRREL

1 BELDING

2 MOHAVE

3 UINTA

4 SPOTTED

FRANKLIN GROUND SQUIRREL

GROUND SQUIRREL

1 ARCTIC

2 COLUMBIAN

3 TOWNSEND

4 ROUNDTAIL

5 THIRTEEN-LINED

6 MEXICAN

**CALIFORNIA GROUND SQUIRREL.** *Citellus beecheyi.*

pp. **73**, 63

**Recognition:** — Head and body, 9–11 in.; tail, 5–9 in. In the far west, this large ground squirrel is common in the *valleys* and *foothills;* prefers semi-open country with low vegetation. Often lives in colonies where its burrows are conspicuous on the open hillsides. The head is brownish and the body is brown flecked with buffy white or buff. Sides of *neck and shoulders whitish,* leaving a conspicuous dark triangle over the middle of the shoulders; belly buff; tail bushy. Hibernates in winter and aestivates in late summer. Found on Catalina Island also.

**Similar species:** — Other ground squirrels; all smaller with shorter, less bushy tails. Western Gray Squirrel; white belly, no buff.

**YUMA ANTELOPE SQUIRREL.** *Citellus harrisi.* pp. **88**, 63

**Recognition:** — Head and body, 6–6¼ in.; tail, 3–3¾ in. In the *arid desert* of southern Arizona this small, *pinkish-cinnamon to mouse-gray* squirrel, with a narrow *white line* on each side of the back, lives among the cactus and desert shrubs. It is the only ground squirrel in its range with *stripes.* The tail is gray above and below.

**WHITETAIL ANTELOPE SQUIRREL.** *Citellus leucurus.*

pp. **88**, 63

**Recognition:** — Head and body, 5½–6½ in.; tail, 2–3 in. This pale, pinkish-gray squirrel, with a *white line on each side of the back* and a *white undersurface to the tail,* inhabits much of the *open country* of the Southwest. When running, the tail is curled over the back, exposing the white undersurface, and all one really sees is a *white patch* going away. No other ground squirrel within its range has its color pattern.

**Similar species:** — Chipmunks; no white undertail. Mohave Ground Squirrel; no stripes.

**SAN JOAQUIN ANTELOPE SQUIRREL.** *Citellus nelsoni.*

p. 63

**Recognition:** — Head and body, 6–6½ in.; tail, 2½–3 in. In the *San Joaquin Valley,* California, this pinkish-buff squirrel, with a creamy *white line on each side* of its back and a creamy white underside of the tail, is the only ground squirrel with stripes. It curls its tail over its back when running, exposing the white undersurface.

**MOHAVE GROUND SQUIRREL.** *Citellus mohavensis.* p. 68

**Recognition:** —·Head and body, 6–6½ in.; tail, 2–3½ in. This little squirrel, found only in the *Mohave Desert,* is *cinnamon-gray* with a *short tail* that is *fuscous above and white beneath.* There are

*no stripes* on its sides. When running, it holds its tail over its back and exposes the white undersurface.
**Similar species:** — Whitetail Antelope Squirrel; white stripes on body.

## ROUNDTAIL GROUND SQUIRREL. *Citellus tereticaudus.*
p. 68
**Recognition:** — Head and body, 5¾–6½ in.; tail, 2½–4 in. This is truly a *desert* ground squirrel; *pinkish cinnamon* with a *grayish cast*, it harmonizes with its background. Usually, when seen it is sitting in the shade of some plant or post. The tail is pencil-like, not bushy. The belly is slightly paler than the back. There are *no contrasting markings*.
**Similar species:** — Antelope Squirrels; with stripes.

## GOLDEN–MANTLED SQUIRREL. *Citellus lateralis.* pp. **88**, 63
**Recognition:** — Head and body, 6–8 in.; tail, 2½–4¾ in. In the high reaches of the *western mountains*, usually in *pine forests*, this chipmunk-like ground squirrel with a *coppery head* and with a *white stripe bordered with black* on each side of its back, is a common visitor to most camps. There are no stripes on the sides of its face. The tail is relatively short and fully haired, not bushy. It lives in burrows in the ground, and it hibernates in winter.
**Similar species:** — Chipmunks; all have stripes on side of face. Chickaree, Spruce Squirrel, and Red Squirrel; no contrast between color of head and body.
**Remarks:** — *Citellus saturatus* is included here. It may be a distinct species. It is found in the Cascades of Washington and British Columbia.

## BLACKTAIL PRAIRIE DOG. *Cynomys ludovicianus.* pp. **73**, 81
**Recognition:** — Head and body, 11–13 in.; tail, 3–4 in.; wt., 2–3 lb. The presence of this inhabitant of the *short-grass prairies* is usually revealed by a group of *bare mounds*, twenty-five to seventy-five feet apart and each mound a foot or two in height. If, sitting erect on top of one of these mounds, there is a *yellowish* animal slightly smaller than a cat, it is probably a prairie dog. On closer inspection, the Blacktail Prairie Dog will be found to have the *terminal third* of its short tail *black*; its ears are small and its belly is pale buff or whitish.
**Similar species:** — Whitetail Prairie Dog; tail white, found in mountains.

## WHITETAIL PRAIRIE DOG. *Cynomys gunnisoni.* pp. **73**, 81
**Recognition:** — Head and body, 11–12 in.; tail, 1¼–2½ in.; wt., 1½–2½ lb. Usually found in *high country*, this small prairie dog is similar in general to the Blacktail Prairie Dog (see above). The tail is *white-tipped*.

**Similar species:** — Blacktail Prairie Dog; black tip on tail, low country.
**Remarks:** — Two other species, *leucurus* and *parvidens*, are recorded in the literature. Subsequent study may show them to belong to this species.

## EASTERN CHIPMUNK. *Tamias striatus.*      pp. **88,** 76

**Recognition:** — Head and body, 5–6 in.; tail, 3–4 in. In the eastern hardwood forests or semi-open brushy areas this small squirrel-like animal may be seen in daytime running with its *tail straight in the air* or sitting with bulging cheek pouches on a stump or log. Its *facial stripes* distinguish it from all other mammals over most of its range. The *side and back stripes end at the reddish rump.* In the North it usually hibernates during cold weather. It is seldom seen in trees, mostly on the ground. Its rather sharp *chuck-chuck-chuck* is often heard before the animal is seen.
**Similar species:** — Least Chipmunk; smaller and with side and back stripes continuing to base of tail. Thirteen-lined Ground Squirrel; yellowish, no stripes on face.

## ALPINE CHIPMUNK. *Eutamias alpinus.*      p. 76

**Recognition:** — Head and body, 4¼–4½ in.; tail, 2¾–3½ in.; wt., 27–45 gm. This small chipmunk lives from *timber line* down to about *8000 feet* elevation in the Sierras. The head and body are grayish, and the dark side stripes on face and body are tawny.
**Similar species:** — Yellow Pine and Colorado chipmunks; dark stripes blackish or dark brown, and/or clear white patches back of ears, larger.

## LEAST CHIPMUNK. *Eutamias minimus.*      pp. **88,** 76

**Recognition:** — Head and body, 3⅔–4½ in.; tail, 3–4½ in.; wt., 30–52 gm. This is the most widely ranging, geographically and altitudinally, of the chipmunks. As a group, they are also the *smallest* and most variable. Color ranges from a washed-out *yellowish* with pale fulvous dark stripes to a *rich grayish fulvous* with black dark stripes. The stripes continue to the *base of the tail.* When running, these little animals carry the tail *straight in the air.* They prefer brushy, semi-open areas to dense forest.
**Similar species:** — Eastern Chipmunk; body stripes terminate at reddish rump. Grayneck Chipmunk; larger, neck and shoulders gray. Yellow Pine Chipmunk; ears blackish in front, whitish behind. Panamint Chipmunk; rump gray, contrasts with color of back and sides. Townsend Chipmunk; stripes indistinct, larger. Colorado Chipmunk; ears blackish in front, white behind. Uinta Chipmunk; rump gray. Cliff Chipmunk; side stripes indistinct. Redtail Chipmunk; rump gray, tail dark rufous below.

## MEDIUM–SIZED MAMMALS

**WOODCHUCK**                                             pp. *64*, 63
    Brownish, frosted, feet blackish.

**YELLOWBELLY MARMOT**                                    pp. *64*, 63
    Belly yellow, white between eyes.

**HOARY MARMOT**                                          pp. *64*, 63
    Head and shoulders black and white.

**RINGTAIL CAT**                                          pp. *36*, 35
    Yellowish gray, long tail with rings.

**RACCOON**                                               pp. *34*, 35
    Black mask, tail with rings.

**COATI**                                                 pp. *36*, 37
    Brownish, long tail, long nose.

**BADGER**                                                pp. *48*, 47
    Grayish, white stripe on forehead, feet blackish.

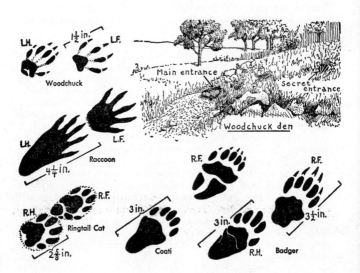

WOODCHUCK

YELLOWBELLY MARMOT

HOARY MARMOT

RINGTAIL CAT

RACCOON

COATI

BADGER

SPOTTED
GROUND
SQUIRREL

WASHINGTON
GROUND SQUIRREL

THIRTEEN-LINED
GROUND
SQUIRREL

CALIFORNI
GROUND
SQUIRREL

COLUMBIAN
GROUND
SQUIRREL

ARCTIC
GROUND
SQUIR

ROCK
SQUIRREL

FRANKLIN
GROUND
SQUIRREL

WHITETAIL PRAIRIE DOG

BLACKTAIL PRAIRIE DOG

Plate 10                                                    73

## GROUND SQUIRRELS AND PRAIRIE DOGS

**SPOTTED GROUND SQUIRREL**                     pp. *67*, 68
    Indistinct, squarish spots.

**THIRTEEN–LINED GROUND SQUIRREL**             pp. *66*, 68
    Broken stripes on sides and back.

**WASHINGTON GROUND SQUIRREL**                 pp. *65*, *63*
    Dappled, blackish tip on tail.

**COLUMBIAN GROUND SQUIRREL**                  pp. *66*, 68
    Feet and legs dark fulvous.

**CALIFORNIA GROUND SQUIRREL**                 pp. *69*, *63*
    Neck and shoulders whitish.

**ROCK SQUIRREL**                              pp. *67*, *63*
    Mottled grayish, large, rocky areas.

**ARCTIC GROUND SQUIRREL**                     pp. *66*, 68
    Feet and legs tawny.

**FRANKLIN GROUND SQUIRREL**                   pp. *67*, 68
    Dark gray, large, open prairies.

**BLACKTAIL PRAIRIE DOG**                      pp. *70*, 81
    Tip of tail black.

**WHITETAIL PRAIRIE DOG**                      pp. *70*, 81
    Tip of tail white.

Prairie dog town

**YELLOW PINE CHIPMUNK.** *Eutamias amœnus.* p. 76

　Recognition: — Head and body, 4½–5⅕ in.; tail, 3–4½ in.; wt., 37–50 gm. This chipmunk is found chiefly in the western *yellow pine forests*. Its colors are bright and the black and white (or grayish) back and side stripes are *distinct*. The underside of the tail is usually deep fulvous, as are the sides.

　Similar species: — Least Chipmunk; front of ears fulvous. Alpine Chipmunk; dark side stripes fulvous. Colorado Chipmunk; dark side stripes brown. Redtail Chipmunk; underside of tail dark rufous. Townsend, Merriam, Long-eared, and Sonoma chipmunks; larger, stripes indistinct. Uinta Chipmunk; side stripes dark brown.

**PANAMINT CHIPMUNK.** *Eutamias panamintinus.* p. 76

　Recognition: — Head and body, 4½–4⅔ in.; tail, 3½–4 in.; wt., 45–65 gm. This brightly colored chipmunk is found in the *piñon pine-juniper* belt. The head and rump are gray and the sides and back are fulvous; median line fuscous.

　Similar species: — Least Chipmunk; rump similar to back. Colorado Chipmunk; ears blackish in front, whitish behind. Charleston Mountain Chipmunk; in yellow pine belt and above. Cliff Chipmunk; no white side stripe.

**COLORADO CHIPMUNK.** *Eutamias quadrivittatus.* pp. **88**, 76

　Recognition: — Head and body, 5 in.; tail, 3⅕–4½ in.; wt., 50–65 gm. Found in the *yellow pine belt and above*, this is a common chipmunk of the western mountains. The head, rump, and sides are gray with an overwash of fulvous on the sides. The tail is fulvous beneath, tipped with black, and bordered with white or pale fulvous.

　Similar species: — Alpine Chipmunk; dark side stripes pale fulvous. Least Chipmunk; dorsal stripes continue to base of tail. Yellow Pine Chipmunk; side stripes black. Panamint Chipmunk; shoulders and sides bright fulvous, ears fulvous in front. Townsend, Merriam, Long-eared, and Cliff chipmunks; side stripes indistinct.

　Remarks: — *Eutamias adsitus*, from the Beaver Mountains, Utah, and the Kaibab Plateau, is considered by some to be a distinct species, as is also *E. callipeplus* from Mt. Pinos, California. These are included on the map with the Colorado Chipmunk.

**UINTA CHIPMUNK.** *Eutamias umbrinus.* p. 76

　Recognition: — Head and body, 5 in.; tail, 2¾–4½ in. This species is found from 7000 to 11,000 feet elevation, *above the yellow pine zone*. Characters as in the Colorado Chipmunk (see above).

　Similar species: — Least Chipmunk; front of ear fulvous. Yellow Pine Chipmunk; side stripes black.

**CHARLESTON MOUNTAIN CHIPMUNK.** *Eutamias palmeri.*
p. 76
**Recognition:** — Head and body, 5 in.; tail, 3½–4 in. Found only in yellow pines and above, *Charleston Mountains*, Nevada.

**REDTAIL CHIPMUNK.** *Eutamias ruficaudus.*                p. 76
**Recognition:** — Head and body, 5 in.; tail, 4–5 in. This *large*, brilliantly colored chipmunk lives in the *yellow pine belt and above.* The shoulders and sides are bright fulvous and the rump is gray.
**Similar species:** — Least Chipmunk; smaller, rump does not contrast with sides and head. Yellow Pine Chipmunk; underside of tail pale fulvous.

**GRAYNECK CHIPMUNK.** *Eutamias cinereicollis.*          p. 76
**Recognition:** — Head and body, 4¾–5½ in.; tail, 3⅗–4⅗ in. This chipmunk is found in the *yellow pines and above* in parts of Arizona and New Mexico. It is *dark gray* washed on the sides with fulvous and with a *pale gray neck.* The dark stripes are dark brown, the median one black.
**Similar species:** — Least Chipmunk; smaller, neck not noticeably gray. Cliff Chipmunk; side stripes indistinct.

**TOWNSEND CHIPMUNK.** *Eutamias townsendi.*       pp. **88**, 76
**Recognition:** — Head and body, 5⅓–6 in.; tail, 3⅘–5 in.; wt., 70–123 gm. This large, *dark* chipmunk, found on the humid Pacific Coast, has dull yellowish or grayish light stripes along its sides and back. The dark stripes are blackish. The backs of the ears are fuscous in front, gray behind. Prefers *heavy forests.*
**Similar species:** — Least, Yellow Pine, and Colorado chipmunks; smaller, with stripes distinct and contrasting with body colors. Long-eared Chipmunk; large white patch behind ear, black line below ear. Sonoma Chipmunk; backs of ears one color.
**Remarks:** — *Eutamias alleni,* in Marin County, California, is considered by some as a distinct species. It is here included on the distribution map with *townsendi.*

**SONOMA CHIPMUNK.** *Eutamias sonomæ.*                p. 76
**Recognition:** — Head and body, 4⅘–5½ in.; tail, 4–5 in. This *large dark* chipmunk is found chiefly in *open or brushy areas* on warm slopes. Backs of the ears are uniform in color and body stripes are *indistinct,* the light ones being yellowish.
**Similar species:** — Yellow Pine Chipmunk; stripes bright, black and white. Townsend Chipmunk; backs of ears bicolor, fuscous in front and gray behind.

**LONG–EARED CHIPMUNK.** *Eutamias quadrimaculatus.* p. 76
**Recognition:** — Head and body, 5⅕–5½ in.; tail, 4–4½ in.; wt.,

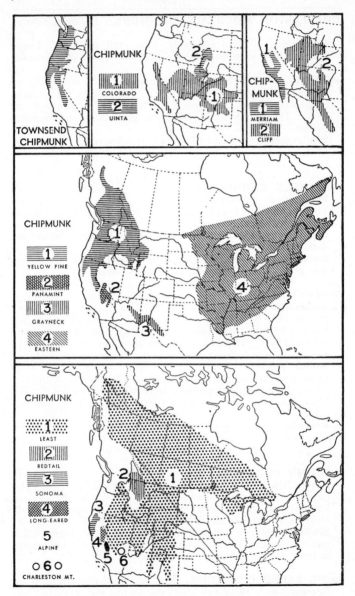

TOWNSEND CHIPMUNK

CHIPMUNK

1 COLORADO

2 UINTA

CHIP-MUNK

1 MERRIAM

2 CLIFF

CHIPMUNK

1 YELLOW PINE

2 PANAMINT

3 GRAYNECK

4 EASTERN

CHIPMUNK

1 LEAST

2 REDTAIL

3 SONOMA

4 LONG-EARED

5 ALPINE

6 CHARLESTON MT.

73–105 gm. This *large, high-Sierra* chipmunk is grayish or tawny with fairly distinct body stripes. Behind each ear is a large, clearly defined *white patch*. The dark stripe below the ear is black.

Similar species: — Yellow Pine and Colorado chipmunks; smaller, stripes distinct. Townsend and Merriam chipmunks; stripe below ear brownish.

**MERRIAM CHIPMUNK.** *Eutamias merriami.* pp. **88**, 76
**Recognition:** — Head and body, 5½ in.; tail, 4–5½ in.; wt., 53–88 gm. In the *foothills* and *brushy areas* lives this large, grayish chipmunk with *indistinct stripes*. It occasionally gets into the lower edge of the pines.
Similar species: — Yellow Pine and Colorado chipmunks; distinct white stripes. Long-eared Chipmunk; black stripe under ear, white patch back of ear.

**CLIFF CHIPMUNK.** *Eutamias dorsalis.* pp. **88**, 76
**Recognition:** — Head and body, 5 in.; tail, 3⅘–4½ in. In the *piñon pine-juniper*, and lower edge of the yellow pine belts, we find this *gray* chipmunk with a fairly distinct dark stripe down the middle of the back. The other stripes are *faint and indistinct*.
Similar species: — Least, Colorado, Grayneck, and Uinta chipmunks; all with distinct dark and light stripes.

**RED SQUIRREL.** *Tamiasciurus hudsonicus.* pp. **88**, 79
**Recognition:** — Head and body, 7–8 in.; tail, 4–6 in.; wt., 120–250 gm. Primarily an inhabitant of the *evergreen forests,* this *noisy* little squirrel is usually heard before seen. Its *ratchet-like call* reveals its presence, usually sitting on a branch ten to twenty feet above ground. It is fairly uniformly *yellowish or reddish*, paler on the back in winter (with ear tufts), a *black line* along side in summer, and has a whitish belly. The tail is bushy. Smallest of the tree squirrels in its range.
Similar species: — Eastern Gray Squirrel; gray or black. Fox Squirrel; larger, no black line on side in summer, no ear tufts in winter.

**CHICKAREE.** *Tamiasciurus douglasi.* pp. **88**, 79
**Recognition:** — Head and body, 7 in.; tail, 5–6 in. This *noisy* little squirrel of the *evergreen forests* of the west, known by some as "Douglas Squirrel," is a counterpart of the Red Squirrel. It is dark, *reddish olive* brown, grayer in winter, with a *rusty-reddish belly*. There is a distinct *black line* along each side in summer, absent or indistinct in winter.
Similar species: — Western Gray Squirrel; gray with white belly, larger.

**SPRUCE SQUIRREL.** *Tamiasciurus fremonti.* p. 79
**Recognition:** — Head and body, 8 in.; tail, 5–6 in. In the *spruce*

*forests* of the southern Rocky Mountain states, this small squirrel adds life and beauty. It is grayish yellow with a *black line along the side* in summer, paler in winter.

**Similar species:** — Arizona Gray Squirrel; gray. Tassel-eared Squirrel; gray sides, reddish down middle of back, tail white or gray. Apache Fox Squirrel; belly ochraceous.

**WESTERN GRAY SQUIRREL.** *Sciurus griseus.* pp. **89**, 79

**Recognition:** — Head and body, 12 in.; tail, 10–12 in. This *large gray* tree squirrel inhabits the *oak and pine* areas within its range. Its large *bushy tail, white belly,* and *dusky feet* will serve to distinguish it from similar kinds within its range.

**Similar species:** — California Ground Squirrel; tail not noticeably bushy, shoulders blackish. Chickaree; belly yellowish or rusty.

**EASTERN GRAY SQUIRREL.** *Sciurus carolinensis.* pp. **89**, 79

**Recognition:** — Head and body, 8–10 in.; tail, 7¾–10 in.; wt., ¾–1½ lb. Primarily a squirrel of the *eastern hardwoods,* the Eastern Gray Squirrel also enters the lower edge of the pine forests. Its general *grayish* color, washed with fulvous in summer, and *bushy tail bordered with white-tipped hairs* will usually serve to distinguish this squirrel. Black squirrels (a melanistic color phase) are common in some parts of its range.

**Similar species:** — Red Squirrel; small, reddish. Eastern Fox Squirrel; yellowish, tail bordered with fulvous-tipped hairs, or with distinct white or black markings, or steel gray all over.

**ARIZONA GRAY SQUIRREL.** *Sciurus arizonensis.* p. 79

**Recognition:** — Head and body, 10–11 in.; tail, 10–12 in. The common tree squirrel in the oak and pine belts of the *mountains* of southeastern Arizona. This large *gray* squirrel is sometimes washed with yellowish on the back, and has a *white belly* and *tail-fringe.*

**Similar species:** — Spruce Squirrel; reddish. Tassel-eared Squirrel; prominent tufts on ears. Apache Fox Squirrel; yellowish.

**TASSEL–EARED SQUIRREL.** *Sciurus aberti.* pp. **89**, 79

**Recognition:** — Head and body, 11–12 in.; tail, 8–9 in. This most colorful of our tree squirrels inhabits the *conifer forests* of the southern Rocky Mountain states. The tail is either *all white* or *white beneath* and broadly bordered with white; the belly is either *white or black;* prominent black, or blackish, *ear tufts* are present. The sides are gray and the back is deep fulvous. This is the only squirrel with the above markings.

**Remarks:** — Some authors consider the squirrels north of the Grand Canyon, *Sciurus kaibabensis,* as distinct species. They have *all-white tails.*

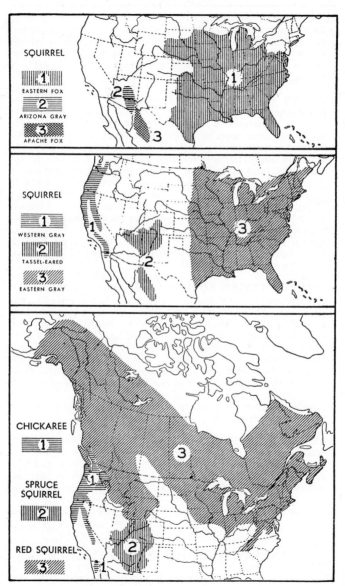

SQUIRREL

1 — EASTERN FOX
2 — ARIZONA GRAY
3 — APACHE FOX

SQUIRREL

1 — WESTERN GRAY
2 — TASSEL-EARED
3 — EASTERN GRAY

CHICKAREE

1

SPRUCE SQUIRREL

2

RED SQUIRREL

3

**APACHE FOX SQUIRREL.** *Sciurus apache.*                    p. 79
   **Recognition:** — Head and body, 11 in.; tail, 11 in.  Barely enter-
ing the United States in the mountains of southeastern Arizona
and southwestern New Mexico is this large, *yellowish-brown*,
slightly *grizzled* squirrel with an *ochraceous belly*.  It is the only
tree squirrel in the area with the above characters.

**EASTERN FOX SQUIRREL.** *Sciurus niger.*              pp. **89**, 79
   **Recognition:** — Head and body, 10–15 in.; tail, 9–14 in.; wt.,
1⅕–3 lb.  Wherever there are nut trees in the East there are fox
squirrels.  Over most of its extensive range, the Eastern Fox
Squirrel is *rusty* yellowish with a pale *yellow to orange belly*, and
with the bushy tail *bordered with fulvous-tipped hairs*.  In the
Southeast, the body may be variously grizzled with mixtures of
yellow, white, and black, and the head more or less black with
white on the nose and ears.  In a small area on the Atlantic
Coast, Delaware, Maryland, and adjoining parts of Virginia,
West Virginia, and Pennsylvania, they may be pure steel-gray
with no fulvous.
   **Similar species:** — Red squirrel; smaller, white belly.  Eastern
Gray Squirrel; smaller, gray with slight overwash of fulvous
and with white border to tail.

**SOUTHERN FLYING SQUIRREL.** *Glaucomys volans.* pp. **89**, 81
   **Recognition:** — Head and body, 5½–6 in.; tail, 3½–4½ in.; wt.,
50–70 gm.  Flying squirrels sleep during the day and come out to
feed at *deep dusk*.  They are seldom seen.  The thick glossy fur is
*olive brown* above, *white below*.  A folded layer of *loose skin along
each side* of the body, from the front to the hind leg, is found in no
other mammals here considered.  When outstretched, this skin
supports the body as the animal glides from tree to tree.  Hairs
of the belly are *white to their bases*.  They prefer extensive forests
with large trees.
   **Similar species:** — Northern Flying Squirrel; larger, hairs of
belly lead-color at bases.

**NORTHERN FLYING SQUIRREL.** *Glaucomys sabrinus.* p. 81
   **Recognition:** — Head and body, 5½–6 in.; tail, 4⅛–5½ in.; wt.,
75–125 gm.  Characters similar to those for the Southern Flying
Squirrel except that it is slightly larger and the belly hairs are
*white only at the tips, lead-color at the bases*.  Prefers conifers mixed
with hardwoods.
   **Similar species:** — Southern Flying Squirrel; belly hairs white to
bases.

# Pocket Gophers: Geomyidæ

MEMBERS of this family are small to medium-sized; they have
external *cheek pouches* (pockets) which are fur-lined and reversible,

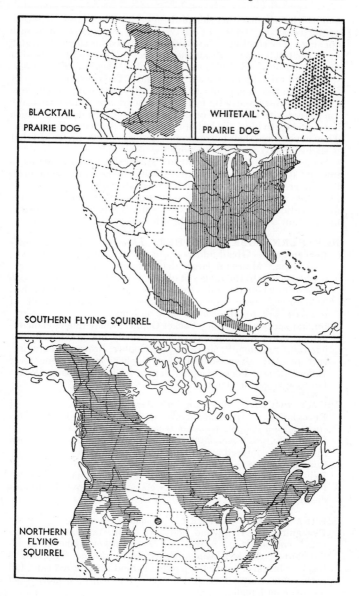

and which open on either side of the mouth. Their large, yellowish incisor (gnawing) teeth are *always exposed* in front of the mouth opening. The front claws are large and curved for efficient digging tools, the tail is *always shorter than the head and body* and is naked or scantily haired. Eyes and ears are small. They all are true *burrowers* and are seldom seen above ground. Their presence is easily detected by the *mounds* of earth which they push out as they excavate their subterranean tunnels. The mounds are characteristically *fan-shaped* with an indication of the position of the opening, which is a round earth plug, the last of the dirt to be pushed to the surface. They never leave their burrows open for long. They prefer soil that is slightly moist and easy to work.

Some of the kinds are difficult to distinguish without resorting to internal structures. Rarely are two kinds found in the same field, but the general ranges of some interdigitate with one another. If in doubt, specimens should be sent to some museum for positive identification. Color varies from nearly white to nearly black, mostly they are some shade of brown.

**NORTHERN POCKET GOPHER.** *Thomomys talpoides.* p. 83
    **Recognition:** — Head and body, 5–6½ in.; tail, 1¾–3 in.; wt., 75–130 gm. Males are larger than females. This gopher, where it occurs close to the ranges of others, is usually found in the *high mountains* where the soil is thin. It is *grayish*, sometimes washed with brown; nose brown or blackish; black patches back of rounded ears; usually *ten mammae* on female.
    **Similar species:** — Valley Pocket Gopher; where ranges come together, lower foothills and valleys, usually not grayish, female has eight mammae. Sierra Pocket Gopher; brown, not grayish, ears pointed. Townsend Pocket Gopher; larger, along river valleys. Giant Pocket Gopher; larger, lowlands. Plains Pocket Gopher; larger, lowlands.

**PIGMY POCKET GOPHER.** *Thomomys umbrinus.* p. 83
    **Recognition:** — Head and body, 4⅜–5 in.; tail, 2–2⅖ in. This small pocket gopher, *yellowish brown* to deep *chestnut* in color, is found only in the *mountains*. Other pocket gophers with which it might be confused are usually found in the valleys.
    **Similar species:** — Valley Pocket Gopher; larger, lowlands. Bailey Pocket Gopher; females with eight mammae. Mexican Pocket Gopher; lowlands, larger, yellow, deep groove down middle of each incisor.

**SIERRA POCKET GOPHER.** *Thomomys monticola.* p. 83
    **Recognition:** — Head and body, 5⅜–6 in.; tail, 2–3 in. This small, *mummy-brown to yellowish-brown* pocket gopher is an inhabitant of the *high mountains* within its range. The nose is black or blackish as are the patches behind the pointed ears; tail with some white; feet and wrists often white; usually *eight mammae* on female.

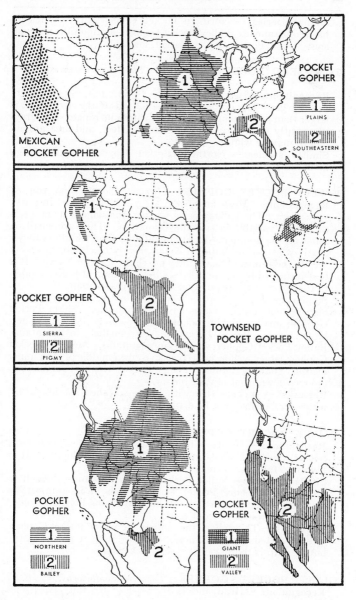

Similar species:—Northern Pocket Gopher; grayish, female has ten mammae. Valley Pocket Gopher; low foothills and valleys. Giant Pocket Gopher; larger, lowlands.

## TOWNSEND POCKET GOPHER. *Thomomys townsendi.*

p. 83

**Recognition:**— Head and body, 7–7½ in.; tail, 2–3⅘ in.; wt., 240–290 gm. This occupant of the *deep soils* of the *river valleys* is larger than any other pocket gopher within its range. It is grayish, faintly washed with buff. The tail, feet, and area around mouth may be white.

**Similar species:**— Northern Pocket Gopher; smaller, high mountains. Valley Pocket Gopher; smaller, brownish.

## VALLEY POCKET GOPHER. *Thomomys bottæ.* pp. 104, 83

**Recognition:**— Head and body, 4⅘–7 in.; tail, 2–3¾ in.; wt., 71–235 gm. The Valley Pocket Gopher, throughout its range, is extremely variable in size and coloration. They are small on some of the southern desert mountains, large in the valleys; nearly white in the Imperial Desert, nearly black along parts of the Pacific Coast. Usually they are some shade of brown. It is best identified by where it lives. Below, differences given apply to that part of the population where ranges overlap.

**Similar species:**— Northern Pocket Gopher; smaller, grayish, high in mountains, females have ten mammae. Sierra Pocket Gopher; smaller, high in mountains. Townsend Pocket Gopher; larger, gray. Pigmy Pocket Gopher; smaller, in mountains. Bailey Pocket Gopher; smaller, in mountains. Mexican Pocket Gopher; larger, yellow, a deep groove down middle of each upper incisor (gnawing tooth). Plains Pocket Gopher; larger, two grooves down front of each incisor.

**Remarks:**— Included herewith is the so-called species *fulvus*, which may or may not be distinct.

## BAILEY POCKET GOPHER. *Thomomys baileyi.* p. 83

**Recognition:**— Head and body, 6 in.; tail, 2½ in. This *foothills* pocket gopher is similar to the Valley Pocket Gopher. It is tawny to fulvous. Females have *eight* mammae.

**Similar species:**— Valley Pocket Gopher; lowlands, difficult to distinguish. Pigmy Pocket Gopher; high in mountains, six mammae. Mexican Pocket Gopher and Plains Pocket Gopher; prominent grooves in front teeth.

**Remarks:**— This may be the same as the Valley Pocket Gopher, but is treated separately here. Included with it on the distribution map is the so-called species *lachuguilla*.

## GIANT POCKET GOPHER. *Thomomys bulbivorus.* p. 83

**Recognition:**— Head and body, 7¾–8½ in.; tail, 3¼–3⅗ in.

This large, sooty-brown pocket gopher has a restricted distribution in the rich-soiled *Willamette Valley*, Oregon. It is by far the *largest* pocket gopher in Oregon.

**Similar species:** — Sierra and Northern pocket gophers; both smaller and both mountain dwellers.

**PLAINS POCKET GOPHER.** *Geomys bursarius.* pp. **104**, 83
**Recognition:** — Head and body, 5½–9 in.; tail 2–4½ in. This large pocket gopher, found chiefly in the *central plains* states, prefers good *deep soil*. In farming areas, alfalfa and other hay fields are preferred to those under constant cultivation. Color varies from yellowish tawny in the west to browns and finally nearly black in Illinois. Spotted and albino individuals are fairly common. It may be distinguished from other pocket gophers by the *two distinct grooves* down the front of each incisor (gnawing tooth).
**Similar species:** — Bailey, Northern, and Valley pocket gophers; one indistinct groove near inside and on front of each incisor. Mexican Pocket Gopher; one distinct groove in middle (front) of each incisor.
**Remarks:** — At least five species have been recognized under the genus. To separate some of them would be impossible for anyone but a specialist. All are included on the one distribution map here. The species are: *bursarius, lutescens, breviceps, arenarius,* and *personatus.*

**SOUTHEASTERN POCKET GOPHER.** *Geomys tuza.* p. 83
**Recognition:** — Head and body, 6½–8 in.; tail, 3–4 in. In the southeastern states this animal is usually known as a *salamander*. It is the only mammal in its area which has *fur-lined external cheek pouches.*
**Remarks:** — In current literature two species, *tuza* in Georgia and *floridanus* in Florida, are usually recognized. They are treated together on the distribution map.

**MEXICAN POCKET GOPHER.** *Cratogeomys castanops.*
pp. **104**, 83
**Recognition:** — Head and body, 7¼–8 in.; tail, 3–4 in. This *large, yellowish* pocket gopher prefers areas of deep soil. It may be distinguished from other pocket gophers by the distinct, *single groove down the middle* (front) *of each incisor* (gnawing tooth).
**Similar species:** — Bailey, Pigmy, and Valley pocket gophers; smaller, an indistinct groove down front of each incisor near inside of tooth. Plains Pocket Gopher; two grooves on front of each incisor tooth.

# Pocket Mice, Kangaroo Mice, and Kangaroo Rats: Heteromyidæ

MEMBERS of this family are mostly *small* with *fur-lined cheek pouches* which open on either side of the mouth. The front feet are *weak* and the hind feet and legs are *strong* and well developed. The tail is generally as long as or longer than the head and body. All are adapted for arid or semi-arid conditions. They burrow into the ground for nest sites. Usually they prefer pliable, *sandy soil*. All are nocturnal — they sleep during the day.

Pocket Mice include the smallest members of this family. They vary from pale yellowish to dark gray, with paler belly, but *never* have striking color patterns on the face or body. The tail is never swollen along its middle.

Kangaroo Rats all have *long tails* with *tufts* on the ends, distinct *facial markings*, and extremely long hind legs.

Kangaroo Mice are small, silky-haired members of this group. The tail is *swollen* along its middle, smaller at base and tip, and is *never crested* with long hairs at the tip. The head is large for the animal.

## MEXICAN POCKET MOUSE. *Liomys irroratus*. pp. 104, 92

**Recognition:** — Head and body, 4–5 in.; tail, 4–5 in. This large pocket mouse barely enters the *Brownsville* area of Texas. Here it is likely to be found along the edges of fields. It is dark gray above, white on belly, and has a pale yellow line along the side. The hair on the rump is *stiff and spine-like*.

**Similar species:** — Merriam Pocket Mouse; smaller, yellowish, fur silky. Hispid Pocket Mouse; yellowish, tail shorter than head and body.

## WYOMING POCKET MOUSE. *Perognathus fasciatus*. p. 92

**Recognition:** — Head and body, 2⅖ in.; tail, 2½ in. Found on the plains, this is one of the *silky* pocket mice — the fur is soft. It is *olive gray* with pale *yellow spots on the ears* and a yellow wash along the sides.

**Similar species:** — Plains and Silky pocket mice; yellowish above or with yellow patches behind ears, smaller. Hispid Pocket Mouse; larger, fur coarse.

## PLAINS POCKET MOUSE. *Perognathus flavescens*. p. 92

**Recognition:** — Head and body, 2¼–2¾ in.; tail 2–2⅖ in.; wt., 10 gm. On the prairies, preferably where the soil is *sandy*, this small *pale yellowish* pocket mouse, with *white belly*, may be found. There are no clear yellow patches behind the ears.

**Similar species:** — Wyoming Pocket Mouse; gray. Merriam

and Silky pocket mice; clear yellow patches behind ears. Bailey and Hispid pocket mice; larger.

**MERRIAM POCKET MOUSE.** *Perognathus merriami.* p. 92
**Recognition:** — Head and body, 2¼–2¾ in.; tail, 1½–2 in.; wt., 5–7 gm. This is an inhabitant of the *open plains*, chiefly where the soil is *sandy*. Its soft, silky fur is rich *fulvous* sprinkled with dark hairs on the back, and with yellow patches behind the ears. The belly is *white*. It is difficult to distinguish this from the Silky Pocket Mouse on external characters alone.
**Similar species:** — Plains Pocket Mouse; no patches behind ears. Silky Pocket Mouse; less richly colored, difficult to distinguish. Other pocket mice; distinctly larger and with coarse pelage.

**SILKY POCKET MOUSE.** *Perognathus flavus.* pp. **104**, 92
**Recognition:** — Head and body, 2–2½ in.; tail, 1¾–2¼ in.; wt., 7–10 gm. In the prairie region where the soil is sandy, this small, soft-furred pocket mouse holds forth. Its upper parts are *pale yellow* faintly to heavily sprinkled with black hairs. There is a clear *yellow patch behind each ear* and the belly is *white*. The tail is usually slightly *shorter than the head and body*.
**Similar species:** — Wyoming (dark gray) and Plains pocket mice; no yellow patches behind ears. Merriam Pocket Mouse; more richly colored, difficult to distinguish. All other pocket mice; tail over 2½ in.

**APACHE POCKET MOUSE.** *Perognathus apache.* pp. **104**, 92
**Recognition:** — Head and body, 2⅘–3⅕ in.; tail, 2⅗–3 in. The soft fur of this inhabitant of some of our sparsely populated West is *buff*, slightly sprinkled with black. The belly is *white*.
**Similar species:** — Silky Pocket Mouse; tail less than 2½ in. Arizona Pocket Mouse; similar, slightly larger. Other pocket mice; larger and with long hairs toward tip of tail.

**ARIZONA POCKET MOUSE.** *Perognathus amplus.* p. 92
**Recognition:** — Head and body, 3 in.; tail, 3⅕–3¾ in. This is typically a *desert* pocket mouse. Its *pinkish-buff* coloration, sparsely sprinkled with black hairs on the back, and *white belly* fit it to its surroundings. The fur is *soft and silky*. The tail is *longer than the head and body*.
**Similar species:** — Silky Pocket Mouse; smaller, tail less than 2½ in. Apache and Little pocket mice; smaller. Bailey, Rock, and Desert pocket mice; all larger and with long hairs toward tip of tail.

**LITTLE POCKET MOUSE.** *Perognathus longimembris.* p. 92
**Recognition:** — Head and body, 2½–2⅘ in.; tail, 2–3½ in.; wt., 6–10 gm. In the valleys and on the slopes below the piñon pine-juniper belt, where the soil is *sandy* and covered with a *desert*

# SQUIRRELS WITH STRIPES

**RED SQUIRREL**                                          pp. *77*, 79
    *Winter:* Ear tufts.
    *Summer:* Black line along side.

**CHICKAREE**                                             pp. *77*, 79
    *Winter:* Ear tufts.
    *Summer:* Black line along side.

**CLIFF CHIPMUNK**                                        pp. *77*, 7⁶
    Indistinct dark line down middle of back.

**COLORADO CHIPMUNK**                                     pp. *74*, 7⁶
    Stripes distinct, bright color.

**LEAST CHIPMUNK**                                        pp. *71*, 7⁶
    *West:* Pale, grayish, small.
    *East:* Stripes on face, back stripes to base of tail.

**EASTERN CHIPMUNK**                                      pp. *71*, 7⁶
    Stripes end at reddish rump.

**TOWNSEND CHIPMUNK**                                     pp. *75*, 7⁶
    Dark brownish, stripes indistinct.

**MERRIAM CHIPMUNK**                                      pp. *77*, 7⁶
    Stripes indistinct.

**YUMA ANTELOPE SQUIRREL**                                pp. *69*, 63
    Pinkish gray, white stripes on body.

**WHITETAIL ANTELOPE SQUIRREL**                           pp. *69*, 63
    Tail white beneath, white stripes on body.

**GOLDEN–MANTLED SQUIRREL**                               pp. *70*, 63
    Coppery head, stripes on body.

Chipmunk, front feet not together

$1\frac{5}{8}$ in.

6-12 in. to next print

Chipmunk at food cache

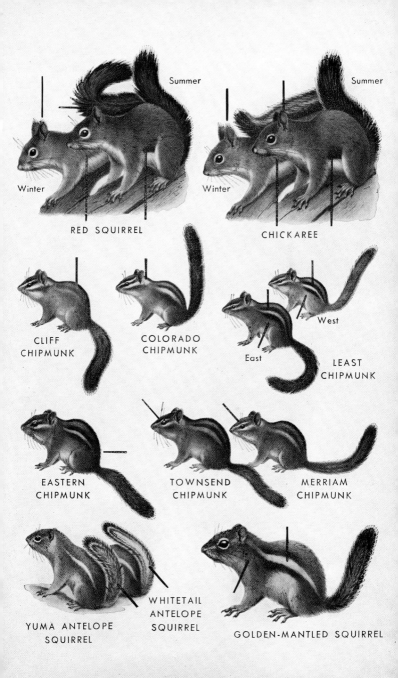

Summer

Winter

RED SQUIRREL

Summer

Winter

CHICKAREE

CLIFF
CHIPMUNK

COLORADO
CHIPMUNK

West

East

LEAST
CHIPMUNK

EASTERN
CHIPMUNK

TOWNSEND
CHIPMUNK

MERRIAM
CHIPMUNK

YUMA ANTELOPE
SQUIRREL

WHITETAIL
ANTELOPE
SQUIRREL

GOLDEN-MANTLED SQUIRREL

EASTERN GRAY
SQUIRREL

Summer

Winter

WESTERN GRAY SQUIRREL

SOUTHERN
FLYING
SQUIRREL

TASSEL-EARED
SQUIRREL
South of Grand Canyon

North of Grand Canyo

South

North

East

EASTERN FOX SQUIRREL

Plate 12                                                      89

## TREE SQUIRRELS

**WESTERN GRAY SQUIRREL**                           pp. *78*, 79
    Bushy tail, feet dusky.


**EASTERN GRAY SQUIRREL**                           pp. *78*, 79
    *Winter:* White behind ears.
    *Summer:* Tail bordered with white.


**SOUTHERN FLYING SQUIRREL**                        pp. *80*, 81
    Loose skin between front and hind legs.


**TASSEL–EARED SQUIRREL**                           pp. *78*, 79
    Ears tufted except late summer.
    *South of Grand Canyon:* Tail white beneath.
    *North of Grand Canyon:* Tail all white.


**EASTERN FOX SQUIRREL**                            pp. *80*, 79
    *South:* Head blackish, body grayish.
    *North:* Rusty, tail bordered with fulvous.
    *East:* Steel gray, no fulvous.

Leaf nest of
Tree Squirrel

Flying Squirrel gliding
from den-tree hole

Gray Squirrel
bounding

2¼ in.

Fox Squirrel,
H. F. 2⅞ in.

(Front feet paired)

Red Squirrel
H. F. 1¾ in.

24 in.

*pavement* of small pebbles, one finds this *soft-furred, buffy* to gray-ish buff pocket mouse. The belly is white. Difficult to distin-guish from the San Joaquin Pocket Mouse, but the ranges, for the most part, are distinct.

**Similar species:** — Arizona Pocket Mouse; larger, tail longer. San Joaquin Pocket Mouse; confined to San Joaquin Valley, California. Great Basin Pocket Mouse; larger, dark olive gray. All other pocket mice; larger, long hairs toward tip of tail. Dark Kangaroo Mouse; brownish, tail swollen in middle. Pale Kan-garoo Mouse; whitish, tail swollen in middle.

## SAN JOAQUIN POCKET MOUSE. *Perognathus inornatus.*

p. 92

**Recognition:** — Head and body, 2½–3⅕ in.; tail, 2⅘–3 in. This soft-haired, buffy pocket mouse is confined to the *San Joaquin Valley*, California. The only other pocket mouse of similar size and coloration with which this mouse might be confused is the Little Pocket Mouse whose range is mostly to the east and south of the San Joaquin Valley.

**Similar species:** — White-eared Pocket Mouse; in pine zone. California Pocket Mouse; dark olive brown.

## GREAT BASIN POCKET MOUSE. *Perognathus parvus.*

pp. **104**, 92

**Recognition:** — Head and body, 2½–3 in.; tail, 3¼–4 in.; wt., 20–30 gm. This olive-gray mouse, washed with fulvous, usually, on the belly, is found in the *piñon* and *yellow pine* belts. Its fur is soft, and its tail, paler below than above, is not particularly bushy on the end.

**Similar species:** — Little Pocket Mouse; smaller, buffy. Long-tail and Desert pocket mice; tail with long hairs, distinctly bushy near tip. Kangaroo Mice; belly white.

## WHITE–EARED POCKET MOUSE. *Perognathus alticolus.*

p. 92

**Recognition:** — Head and body, 3–3⅖ in.; tail, 3–3⅗ in. This soft-haired, *white-eared* pocket mouse is found in the *pine belt* in the San Bernardino Mountains and those of southwestern Kern County, California. In the *tree yucca belt* at Walker Pass, it is known as *P. xanthonotus.*

**Similar species:** — San Joaquin Pocket Mouse; ears not white, below pines. California and San Diego pocket mice; fur harsh, usually below pines.

## LONGTAIL POCKET MOUSE. *Perognathus formosus.*

pp. **104**, 92

**Recognition:** — Head and body, 3⅕–3⅘ in.; tail, 3⅘–4⅘ in.; wt., 16–25 gm. This *gray, soft-haired* pocket mouse with a long *tail*, which is conspicuously *crested with long hairs* on its terminal

one-third, and with a white belly, prefers *rocky slopes* of the low desert.
**Similar species:** — Little Pocket Mouse; yellowish, tail not crested. Great Basin Pocket Mouse; tail not crested. Bailey Pocket Mouse; larger, yellowish admixture of hairs. Desert Pocket Mouse; yellowish. San Diego and Spiny pocket mice; rump with long, spine-like hairs.

**BAILEY POCKET MOUSE.** *Perognathus baileyi.* pp. **104**, 92
**Recognition:** — Head and body, 3⅗–4⅕ in.; tail, 4⅖–5⅗ in.; wt., 30 gm. This is the *largest* of the *soft-haired* pocket mice with crested tails. It is in general grayish with a good sprinkling of yellowish hairs. The belly and underside of tail are white, and the tail has a distinct *crest* of long hairs on its *terminal one-third.* It is found primarily on the *low deserts.*
**Similar species:** — Longtail Pocket Mouse; smaller, no yellowish mixture. Hispid Pocket Mouse; tail not crested. Desert Pocket Mouse; smaller, yellow. Rock Pocket Mouse; smaller. San Diego, California, and Spiny pocket mice; smaller, all have spine-like hairs on rump. All other pocket mice; no crest on tail.

**DESERT POCKET MOUSE.** *Perognathus penicillatus.* p. 92
**Recognition:** — Head and body, 3–3⅘ in.; tail, 3½–4⅘ in.; wt., 14–32 gm. Found only on the *low desert* where the soil is sandy, this pale *yellowish*-brown to yellowish-gray pocket mouse has a *crested tail* which is *longer than the head and body.* The hair is slightly harsh, but there are *no rump spines.*
**Similar species:** — Bailey Pocket Mouse; larger, gray. Longtail Pocket Mouse; slate-gray. Rock Pocket Mouse; rocky situations. San Diego, Spiny, and Nelson pocket mice; spine-like hairs on rump. All other pocket mice; no crest on tail.

**ROCK POCKET MOUSE.** *Perognathus intermedius.* pp. **104**, 92
**Recognition:** — Head and body, 3–3⅘ in.; tail, 3⅕–4 in. On old *lava flows and rocky slopes,* this desert dweller may be found. It is usually *gray* sprinkled with fulvous, but on some of the lava areas it is nearly *black.* The tail is *crested.* Some have indistinct spine-like hairs on the rump.
**Similar species:** — Desert Pocket Mouse; on sandy soils. Bailey Pocket Mouse; larger. All other pocket mice within its range; no crest on tail.

**NELSON POCKET MOUSE.** *Perognathus nelsoni.* p. 92
**Recognition:** — Head and body, 3⅗ in.; tail, 4–4½ in. This pocket mouse is found in a limited area in the *Great Bend* region of Texas. The *crested tail* is longer than the head and body. The hispid fur, with *spine-like hairs on the rump,* is grizzled fulvous and light brown. It is similar to the Rock Pocket Mouse, and probably belongs to the same species. No other pocket mouse within its range has spine-like hairs on the rump.

POCKET MOUSE

1 SAN JOAQUIN
2 DESERT

POCKET MOUSE

1 SAN DIEGO
2 MERRIAM

POCKET MOUSE

1 GREAT BASIN
2 WYOMING
3 WHITE-EARED
4 ARIZONA

POCKET MOUSE

1 LONGTAIL
2 SILKY

POCKET MOUSE

1 LITTLE
2 APACHE
3 PLAINS
4 NELSON

POCKET MOUSE

1 ROCK
2 MEXICAN

BAILEY POCKET MOUSE

POCKET MOUSE

1 CALIFORNIA
2 SPINY
3 HISPID

**SAN DIEGO POCKET MOUSE.** *Perognathus fallax.* p. 92
**Recognition:** — Head and body, 3½ in.; tail, 3–4⅘ in. This dark pocket mouse, *rich brown* flecked *with* deep *fulvous*, is found on the *low desert* and *foothills* of southern California. It has definite *spine-like hairs on the rump.* The belly is white and there is a deep fulvous line along each side. The tail is crested.
**Similar species:** — California Pocket Mouse; similar, and difficult to distinguish, usually found in chaparral or live-oak belt; not on low desert. Spiny Pocket Mouse; pale yellowish. All other pocket mice; no spine-like hairs on rump.

**CALIFORNIA POCKET MOUSE.** *Perognathus californicus.* pp. **104**, 92
**Recognition:** — Head and body, 3⅕–3⅗ in.; tail, 4–5⅘ in. This is the common pocket mouse along the coast of the southern part of California. It is rather dark *brownish gray* flecked *with fulvous.* The tail is *longer than the head and body*, and is *crested.* There are spine-like hairs on the rump.
**Similar species:** — San Diego Pocket Mouse; difficult to distinguish, usually found lower on desert. Other pocket mice in range; no rump spines.

**SPINY POCKET MOUSE.** *Perognathus spinatus.* p. 92
**Recognition:** — Head and body, 3–3⅗ in.; tail, 3–4½ in. This *pale, yellowish* pocket mouse, mixed with light brown, is found on the *hot desert* of southeastern California. It has a *long, crested tail* and distinct *spine-like hairs on its rump.*
**Similar species:** — San Diego Pocket Mouse; dark brownish. All other pocket mice within its range; no spines on rump.

**HISPID POCKET MOUSE.** *Perognathus hispidus.* pp. **104**, 92
**Recognition:** — Head and body, 4½–5 in.; tail, 3½–4½ in. This is primarily a *prairie* pocket mouse. Its hair is *harsh* and grizzled brownish. *Large size and non-crested tail shorter than head and body* will distinguish this pocket mouse.
**Similar species:** — Mexican Pocket Mouse; not noticeably yellowish, tail as long as or longer than head and body. Other pocket mice; either very much smaller or with crested tail.

# Kangaroo Rats: Heteromyidæ (in part)

KANGAROO rats prefer *arid* or *semi-arid* country and soil that is easily worked. They have extremely *long hind legs* and small front legs and front feet. The belly is always *white*, and the upper parts vary from a pale yellow to dark-brownish. The *long tail* usually is dark above and below with side stripes of white, and with a crest of long hairs on the terminal one-fifth or more. There are *facial markings* of white and usually black. On most of them, a definite *white band crosses the thigh region* and joins the tail. Variation is mostly in intensity of coloration, not pattern.

**HEERMANN KANGAROO RAT.** *Dipodomys heermanni.*

pp. **105**, 96

**Recognition:** — Head and body, 4–5 in.; tail, 6½–8½ in.; wt., 50–94 gm. This medium-sized kangaroo rat may have either four or five toes on each hind foot, normally it has four. The tip of the tail may be white or dusky. The species is difficult to characterize on external characters — the skull must be examined for certain identification in some parts of its range. It occurs in the *low valleys* and in the *live oak* and *pine* areas.

**Similar species:** — Giant Kangaroo Rat; larger, head and body over 5 in., five toes. Santa Cruz Kangaroo Rat; dark brownish, not yellowish, five toes. Big-eared Kangaroo Rat; tail heavily crested. Fresno Kangaroo Rat; tail not more than 6 in.

**MORRO BAY KANGAROO RAT.** *Dipodomys morroensis.* p. 96

**Recognition:** — Head and body, 4½–5 in.; tail, 6½–7½ in.; wt., 60–80 gm. Restricted to a small sandy area in the immediate vicinity of *Morro Bay*, less than a township in size, this *darkest* of the kangaroo rats also has the smallest geographic range. There is *no* sharp, conspicuous white band across outer side of flank.

**Similar species:** — Santa Cruz Kangaroo Rat; a white band across outer flank.

**MOHAVE KANGAROO RAT.** *Dipodomys mohavensis.* p. 96

**Recognition:** — Head and body, 5 in.; tail, 6–7 in.; wt., 65–86 gm. This kangaroo rat has *five toes on each hind foot.* It inhabits the low areas of the *Mohave Desert*, California. The dark stripe beneath the tail tapers to a point near the tip of the tail.

**Similar species:** — Pacific Kangaroo Rat; dark tail stripe, beneath, continues to tip of tail. Merriam Kangaroo Rat; smaller, four toes on hind foot. Desert Kangaroo Rat; pale yellowish, tail with white tip, four toes on hind foot.

**PANAMINT KANGAROO RAT.** *Dipodomys panamintinus.* p. 96

**Recognition:** — Head and body, 5 in.; tail, 6⅗–7⅗ in.; wt., 64–94 gm. This kangaroo rat is found chiefly where there are *yuccas* or scattered *piñon pines*, not in sagebrush or greasewood. There are *five toes* on each hind foot.

**Similar species:** — Great Basin Kangaroo Rat; chiefly in sagebrush and greasewood. Ord Kangaroo Rat; smaller, tail not more than 6 in. Merriam Kangaroo Rat; smaller, four toes on hind foot. Desert Kangaroo Rat; larger, pale, no black markings, four toes on hind foot.

**STEPHENS KANGAROO RAT.** *Dipodomys stephensi.* p. 96
**Recognition:** — Head and body, 5½ in.; tail, 6½–7⅕ in.; wt., 75 gm. This *five-toed* kangaroo rat is found only in the *San Jacinto Valley*, California.
**Similar species:** — Pacific Kangaroo Rat; difficult to distinguish without the skull. Merriam Kangaroo Rat; smaller, four toes on hind foot.

**GIANT KANGAROO RAT.** *Dipodomys ingens.* pp. **105**, 96
**Recognition:** — Head and body, 5⅗–6 in.; tail, 7–8 in.; wt., 105 gm. This is the *largest* of the kangaroo rats *in its area.* It has *five toes on each hind foot.* It occupies the semi-arid southwestern border of the San Joaquin Valley and the Carrizo Plain and Cuyama Valley, California.
**Similar species:** — Heermann, Fresno (four-toed), Pacific, and Santa Cruz kangaroo rats; all with head and body less than 5½ in.

**BANNERTAIL KANGAROO RAT.** *Dipodomys spectabilis.* pp. **105**, 96
**Recognition:** — Head and body, 5–6 in.; tail, 7–9 in. Most spectacularly marked of any of the kangaroo rats, this *large, four-toed* species has a *prominent white tip on its tail.* The narrow white side stripes on the tail end about two-thirds the distance to the tip; there is then a black band followed by the white tip.
**Similar species:** — Ord Kangaroo Rat; smaller, no white tip to tail. Merriam Kangaroo Rat; smaller, no white tip to tail.

**TEXAS KANGAROO RAT.** *Dipodomys elator.* p. 96
**Recognition:** — Head and body, 6 in.; tail, 8 in. This large, *four-toed* kangaroo rat, with a *white tip* on the end of its tail, has a limited range in Texas and Oklahoma.
**Similar species:** — Ord Kangaroo Rat; no white tip on tail.

**MERRIAM KANGAROO RAT.** *Dipodomys merriami.* pp. **105**, 96
**Recognition:** — Head and body, 4 in.; tail, 5–6⅖ in.; wt., 33–47 gm. This is the *smallest* of the kangaroo rats. It has *four toes* on each hind foot. Color varies from pale yellowish to dark brownish above.
**Similar species:** — Ord Kangaroo Rat; five toes, or, ventral tail stripe broad at base and tapers to point near tip of tail. Bannertail and Desert kangaroo rats; larger, white tip on tail. Other species; five toes on each hind foot.

**FRESNO KANGAROO RAT.** *Dipodomys nitratoides.* p. 96
**Recognition:** — Head and body, 3⅗–4 in.; tail, 4⅘–6 in.; wt., 28–52 gm. By its *small size* and *four toes* on each hind foot, this inhabitant of the *San Joaquin Valley*, California, may be distinguished from other kangaroo rats.

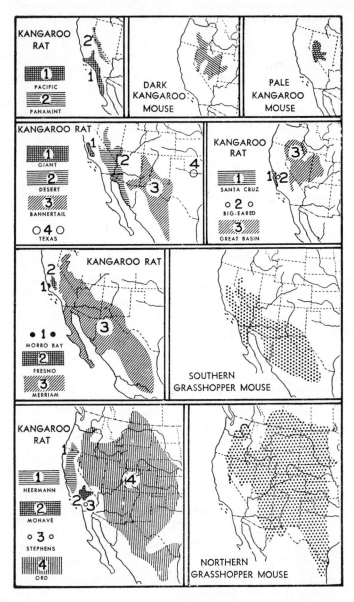

KANGAROO RAT
1 PACIFIC
2 PANAMINT

DARK KANGAROO MOUSE

PALE KANGAROO MOUSE

KANGAROO RAT
1 GIANT
2 DESERT
3 BANNERTAIL
○ 4 ○ TEXAS

KANGAROO RAT
1 SANTA CRUZ
○ 2 ○ BIG-EARED
3 GREAT BASIN

KANGAROO RAT
● 1 ● MORRO BAY
2 FRESNO
3 MERRIAM

SOUTHERN GRASSHOPPER MOUSE

KANGAROO RAT
1 HEERMANN
2 MOHAVE
○ 3 ○ STEPHENS
4 ORD

NORTHERN GRASSHOPPER MOUSE

**Similar species:** — Heermann Kangaroo Rat; larger, tail more than 6 in. Other kangaroo rats; five toes.

**ORD KANGAROO RAT.** *Dipodomys ordi.* pp. **105**, 96

**Recognition:** — Head and body, 4–4½ in.; tail, 5–6 in.; wt., 39–65 gm. This is the most widely distributed of the kangaroo rats. It is often found on rather hard soils. It may have either four or five toes on each hind foot. The *dark tail stripes are broader* than the white ones, and the ventral one *tapers to a point* near the tip of the tail. The lower incisors (gnawing teeth) are rounded, not flat across the front.

**Similar species:** — Panamint Kangaroo Rat; tail more than 6 in. Merriam Kangaroo Rat; always four toes, light tail stripes broader than dark ones. Great Basin Kangaroo Rat; lower incisors flat and chisel-like. Texas, Bannertail, and Desert kangaroo rats; white tip on tail.

**PACIFIC KANGAROO RAT.** *Dipodomys agilis.* pp. **105**, 96

**Recognition:** — Head and body, 4⅗–5 in.; tail, 6⅕–8 in.; wt., 45–76 gm. This is the common kangaroo rat of the Pacific Coast of southern California. It has *five toes* on each hind foot.

**Similar species:** — Merriam and Fresno kangaroo rats; smaller, four-toed. Giant Kangaroo Rat; larger. Mohave Kangaroo Rat; dark ventral stripe tapers to point near tip of tail. Stephens Kangaroo Rat; difficult to distinguish without skull.

**SANTA CRUZ KANGAROO RAT.** *Dipodomys venustus.* p. 96

**Recognition:** — Head and body, 4⅘–5⅕ in.; tail, 7–8 in.; wt., 80–90 gm. Along a narrow strip of the Pacific Coast of California, this *five-toed, richly colored* kangaroo rat may be found. It has *large ears.*

**Similar species:** — Morro Bay Kangaroo Rat; no white band across outer side of flank. Heermann Kangaroo Rat; yellowish, not dark brown above. Giant Kangaroo Rat; head and body more than 5½ in.

**BIG-EARED KANGAROO RAT.** *Dipodomys elephantinus.* pp. **105**, 96

**Recognition:** — Head and body, 5 in.; tail, 7–8 in.; wt., 79–90 gm. This handsome, *big-eared* kangaroo rat is found on the *chaparral slopes* of the *southern* end of the *Gabilan Range,* California. The end of the tail is heavily crested with long hairs.

**Similar species:** — Heermann Kangaroo Rat; tail not heavily crested, may have only four toes.

**GREAT BASIN KANGAROO RAT.** *Dipodomys microps.* p. 96

**Recognition:** — Head and body, 4–5 in.; tail, 5⅗–7⅓ in.; wt., 48–90 gm. Usually in the *sagebrush* or *greasewood* habitats, rarely where there are piñon pines or on the low open flats, one finds this medium-sized kangaroo rat. In some, the insides of the cheek pouches are blackish. The lower incisors (gnawing teeth) are flat across the front.

**Similar species:** — Panamint Kangaroo Rat; chiefly in yucca and piñon pine habitats. Merriam Kangaroo Rat; small, four toes. Ord Kangaroo Rat; lower incisors rounded, not flat. Desert Kangaroo Rat; pale, white-tipped tail.

**DESERT KANGAROO RAT.** *Dipodomys deserti.*    pp. **105**, 96
  **Recognition:** — Head and body, 5–6½ in.; tail, 7–8½ in.; wt., 82–140 gm. This pale, *yellowish, four-toed* desert species is found only where there is *soft sand*, usually dunes. There are *no* dark markings except just in front of the white tail tip where there may be a dusky band. By its *large size, pale coloration*, and *white tip on tail* this species may be distinguished.
  **Similar species:** — No other species within its range has a white tip on the tail.

# Kangaroo Mice: Heteromyidæ (in part)

**DARK KANGAROO MOUSE.** *Microdipodops megacephalus.* p. 96
  **Recognition:** — Head and body, 2⅘–3 in.; tail, 2⅜–4 in.; wt., 10–17 gm. This *small, brownish or blackish* kangaroo mouse usually has the bases of the hairs lead color and the tip of tail blackish. The tail is *swollen* in the middle. They prefer sandy soils.
  **Similar species:** — Pale Kangaroo Mouse; whitish or light buffy upper parts. Great Basin Pocket Mouse; belly washed with fulvous, tail not swollen in middle. Little Pocket Mouse; yellowish.

**PALE KANGAROO MOUSE.** *Microdipodops pallidus.* pp. **105**, 96
  **Recognition:** — Head and body, 3 in.; tail, 3–4 in.; wt., 10–16 gm. Where the sand is *fine* and there is some plant cover, this *whitish* or *pale buff* mouse is at home. The hairs of the belly and underside of the tail are *white to the bases.* The tail is *swollen* in the middle; there is no black tip.
  **Similar species:** — Dark Kangaroo Mouse; brownish or blackish, tail with blackish tip. Great Basin Pocket Mouse; olive brown. Little Pocket Mouse; yellowish.

# Beaver: Castoridæ

THE BEAVER is the largest North American rodent. *Rich brown* in color, it has a scaly tail which is *shaped like a paddle* (flat from top to bottom). Found only along streams and lakes.

**BEAVER.**   *Castor canadensis.*                          pp. **132**, 111

   **Recognition:** — Head and body, 25–30 in.; tail, 9–10 in.; wt., 30–60 lb.  A stick and mud *dam across a stream* or a large *conical house* of similar material at the edge of a lake, and stumps of small trees in the vicinity, showing tooth marks, will reveal the presence of the beaver.  A loud report, as the beaver slaps the surface of the water with its broad flat tail, will also indicate its presence.

   **Similar species:** — River Otter; tail covered with fur.  Muskrat; smaller, tail slender and flattened from side to side.

# Mice, Rats, Voles, Lemmings: Cricetidæ

THIS family includes small to medium-sized rodents.  Most of them have four toes on the front foot, some have five, and all have five toes on the hind foot.  The tails are rarely bushy, mostly covered with short hair.  The mice and rats have large ears and eyes and long tails, voles and lemmings have short tails, small ears and eyes, and usually long fur on the body.  They live mostly on and in the ground, some in trees, in part, and some in rocky situations.

# Grasshopper Mice: Cricetinæ (in part)

THESE mice are inhabitants chiefly of the *prairies* and southwest *desert* areas.  They are either *gray* or *pinkish cinnamon* above, white beneath.  The fur is short.  The only mice that they might be confused with are members of the genus *Peromyscus* (p. 102).  The *short, white-tipped* tail will usually be sufficient to distinguish the grasshopper mouse.

**NORTHERN GRASSHOPPER MOUSE.** *Onychomys leucogaster.*
                                              pp. **120**, 96

   **Recognition:** — Head and body, 4–5 in.; tail, 1–2⅖ in.; wt., 24–40 gm.  This is a stocky, heavy-bodied, *gray* or *pinkish-cinnamon* mouse with a relatively *short, white-tipped tail.*

   **Similar species:** — Southern Grasshopper Mouse; smaller, tail usually more than one-half length of head and body, low valleys.

**SOUTHERN GRASSHOPPER MOUSE.** *Onychomys torridus.*
                                              p. 96

   **Recognition:** — Head and body, 3½–4 in.; tail, 1⅗–2 in.; wt., 20–25 gm.  In the *low valleys* where the ground vegetation is not

too sparse, one is likely to find this *grayish* or *pinkish cinnamon,* white-bellied mouse. The tip of the tail is *white.*
**Similar species:** — Northern Grasshopper Mouse; larger, usually above valley floors where the two overlap.

# Harvest Mice: Cricetinæ (in part)

THESE small brown mice prefer rather dense low vegetation. Externally, they resemble a house mouse. One certain way to distinguish them from all other small brownish mice is to part the lips and examine the upper front teeth. If each of these has a distinct *groove* running down the front, lengthwise, it is probably a harvest mouse. Other mice having grooved teeth have either external cheek pouches, extremely long scaly tails, or tails less than an inch.

**EASTERN HARVEST MOUSE.** *Reithrodontomys humulis.* pp. **120**, 101
**Recognition:** — Head and body, $2\frac{3}{5}$–3 in.; tail, $1\frac{4}{5}$–$2\frac{1}{2}$ in. This *rich brown* mouse, with belly and under side of tail slightly paler than back, is the only kind of harvest mouse over most of its range.
**Similar species:** — Fulvous Harvest Mouse; white belly, longer tail.

**PLAINS HARVEST MOUSE.** *Reithrodontomys montanus.* p. 101
**Recognition:** — Head and body, $2\frac{1}{5}$–3 in.; tail, 2–$2\frac{3}{5}$ in. This is a *pale grayish* mouse, faintly *washed with fulvous* and often with an indistinct dark area down the middle of the back. The belly, feet, and underside of the tail are white.
**Similar species:** — Western Harvest Mouse; may be difficult to distinguish, tail usually more than $2\frac{1}{2}$ in. Fulvous Harvest Mouse; tail more than 3 in.

**WESTERN HARVEST MOUSE.** *Reithrodontomys megalotis.* pp. **120**, 101
**Recognition:** — Head and body, $2\frac{4}{5}$–3 in.; tail, $2\frac{1}{3}$–$3\frac{1}{5}$ in. This wide-ranging harvest mouse is found from the Great Lakes to the Pacific Coast. In color, they range from *pale gray,* slightly washed with fulvous, to *rich brown.* The belly and underside of the tail range from white to deep gray. Occurs on Catalina Island and Santa Cruz Island, California.
**Similar species:** — Plains Harvest Mouse; may be difficult to distinguish, tail usually less than $2\frac{1}{2}$ in. Salt Marsh Harvest Mouse; belly rusty. Fulvous Harvest Mouse; bright fulvous sides, tail usually more than $3\frac{1}{3}$ in.

**SALT MARSH HARVEST MOUSE.** *Reithrodontomys raviventris.* pp. **120**, 101

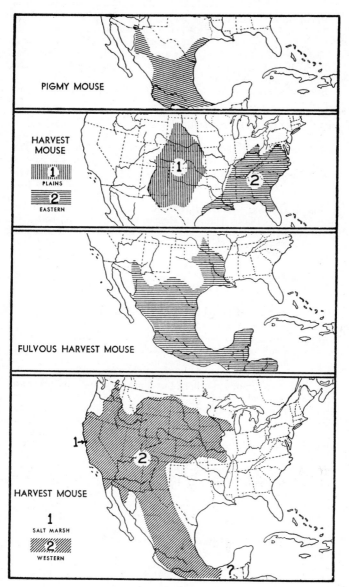

PIGMY MOUSE

HARVEST
MOUSE

1
PLAINS

2
EASTERN

FULVOUS HARVEST MOUSE

HARVEST MOUSE

1
SALT MARSH

2
WESTERN

**Recognition:** — Head and body, $2\frac{3}{5}$–$3\frac{1}{5}$ in.; tail, $2\frac{1}{5}$–$3\frac{2}{5}$ in. This *rich brown* mouse is washed with deep *fulvous*, especially on the belly. The tail is about the same color all around. It is found only in the *salt marshes* around San Francisco Bay, San Pablo Bay, Suisun Bay, and the lower San Joaquin and Sacramento rivers, California.
**Similar species:** — Western Harvest Mouse; belly gray, not rusty.

**FULVOUS HARVEST MOUSE.** *Reithrodontomys fulvescens.* pp. **120**, 101
**Recognition:** — Head and body, $2\frac{4}{5}$–$3\frac{1}{5}$ in.; tail, $3\frac{1}{3}$–4 in. This is the most strikingly colored as well as the *largest* of the harvest mice here considered. It is *grayish brown* with *bright fulvous along the sides* and with a *white belly*. The tail is paler below than above.
**Similar species:** — Eastern Harvest Mouse; smaller, dark brown, gray belly. Plains Harvest Mouse; short tail, less than 3 in. Western Harvest Mouse; sides not bright fulvous, tail usually 3 in. or less.

# White-footed or Deer Mice: Cricetinæ (in part)

THESE medium-sized mice all have *white feet*, usually white bellies and some shade of brown or fulvous backs. The tails are relatively *long*, as long as head and body, in many of them. They are nocturnal, live in woods, prairies, rocks, and occasionally around buildings. Most are ground-dwellers, but some of them nest in trees and are quite arboreal.
**Similar species:** — Grasshopper mice; short tail with white tip. Harvest mice; grooves down front of upper gnawing teeth. Rice Rat; fur of belly woolly, tail long and scantily haired with scales showing through.

**PIGMY MOUSE.** *Baiomys taylori.* pp. **120**, 101
**Recognition:** — Head and body, 2–$2\frac{1}{2}$ in.; tail, $1\frac{3}{5}$–$1\frac{4}{5}$ in. This, *smallest* of our mice, is a *dark brown or blackish* animal with the belly slightly paler than the back. It has somewhat the appearance of a young house mouse, but the tail is *paler below than above* and is covered with short hairs.
**Similar species:** — House Mouse; tail naked, larger. Harvest mice; front teeth grooved.

**CACTUS MOUSE.** *Peromyscus eremicus.* pp. **121**, 108
**Recognition:** — Head and body, $3\frac{1}{5}$–$3\frac{3}{5}$ in.; tail, $3\frac{4}{5}$–$4\frac{2}{5}$ in

This longtail, *pale gray* mouse, faintly washed with fulvous, prefers low *arid* regions where cactus abounds. Its belly is whitish and its thinly-haired tail is faintly bicolor.

**Similar species:** — California Mouse; larger, tail more than 5 in. Canyon Mouse; tail with tuft of long hairs at tip. Deer Mouse; tail well haired and distinctly bicolor. White-footed Mouse; tail relatively shorter. Brush Mouse; tail with long hairs toward tip. White-ankled Mouse; head and body smaller, difficult to distinguish. Piñon Mouse; huge ears, foothills. Rock Mouse; huge ears, tail well haired.

**CALIFORNIA MOUSE.** *Peromyscus californicus.* pp. **121**, 108

**Recognition:** — Head and body, $3\frac{4}{5}$–$4\frac{3}{5}$ in.; tail, 5–$5\frac{4}{5}$ in. This is the *largest* mouse *of this genus* here considered. It is *dark brown* with a *blackish tail;* feet and belly are whitish. Size alone will serve to distinguish this species; tail, 5 in. or more. Found in the *chaparral* and *live oak* areas.

**Similar species:** — Cactus Mouse, Canyon Mouse, Deer Mouse, Brush Mouse, and Piñon Mouse; all with tail under 5 in.

**CANYON MOUSE.** *Peromyscus crinitus.* pp. **121**, 106

**Recognition:** — Head and body, 3–$3\frac{2}{5}$ in.; tail, $3\frac{1}{2}$–$4\frac{1}{3}$ in. In *rocky canyons* throughout its range, this longtail, *buffy-gray to buff* mouse may be found. The fur is long and lax, and the *well-haired tail* has a slight *tuft* on the end. The belly and underside of tail are whitish.

**Similar species:** — Cactus Mouse; tail not tufted. California Mouse; tail more than 5 in. Deer Mouse; tail less than $3\frac{1}{2}$ in. Brush Mouse; brown. Piñon and Rock mice; ears huge, nearly an inch high, head and body more than $3\frac{1}{2}$ in.

**DEER MOUSE.** *Peromyscus maniculatus.* pp. **121**, 106

**Recognition:** — Head and body, $2\frac{4}{5}$–4 in.; tail, 2–5 in.; wt., 10–35 gm. This is the most widely distributed and the most variable of the members of this genus. In the prairie region they are seldom found in woods; in the northern forests they prefer the woods. Color ranges from pale grayish buff to deep reddish brown. The tail is always *sharply bicolor*, white below, dark above. It is often difficult to distinguish from similar species.

**Similar species:** — Cactus Mouse; tail not sharply bicolor, scantily haired. California Mouse; larger. Canyon Mouse; tail longer than head and body, fur long and lax. White-footed Mouse; in south, tail not distinctly bicolor, in the northeast forests, difficult to distinguish, tail less than $3\frac{3}{5}$ in. Cotton Mouse; dark brown, head and body larger. Brush and White-ankled mice; tail as long as, or longer than, head and body. Piñon and Rock mice; huge ears, nearly an inch high. Golden Mouse; head and body uniform cinnamon.

# POCKET MICE, JUMPING MICE, POCKET GOPHERS

(Fur-lined cheek pouches or with long hind legs and tails)

**SILKY POCKET MOUSE**                              pp. *87*, 9²
    Small, yellowish, soft fur, tail not crested.

**APACHE POCKET MOUSE**                             pp. *87*, 9²
    Yellowish, tail more than two and one-half inches.

**ROCK POCKET MOUSE**                               pp. *91*, 9²
    Tail crested, gray to black, usually grizzled.

**CALIFORNIA POCKET MOUSE**                         pp. *93*, 9²
    Spine-like hairs on rump.

**LONGTAIL POCKET MOUSE**                           pp. *90*, 9²
    Medium size, soft fur, tail long and crested.

**GREAT BASIN POCKET MOUSE**                        pp. *90*, 9²
    Olive gray, soft fur.

**HISPID POCKET MOUSE**                             pp. *93*, 9²
    Fur coarse, yellowish, tail medium, not crested.

**BAILEY POCKET MOUSE**                             pp. *91*, 9²
    Large, fur soft, tail crested.

**MEXICAN POCKET MOUSE**                            pp. *86*, 9²
    Dark gray, spine-like hairs on rump.

**MEADOW JUMPING MOUSE**                            pp. *139*, 138
    Long tail, large hind feet, no pouches.

**WOODLAND JUMPING MOUSE**                          pp. *139*, 138
    White tip on tail.

**PLAINS POCKET GOPHER**                            pp. *85*, 83
    Two grooves down front of each upper incisor.

**MEXICAN POCKET GOPHER**                           pp. *85*, 83
    One groove down middle front of each upper incisor.

**VALLEY POCKET GOPHER**                            pp. *84*, 83
    *Three color phases:*
    One indistinct groove near inside front of each incisor.

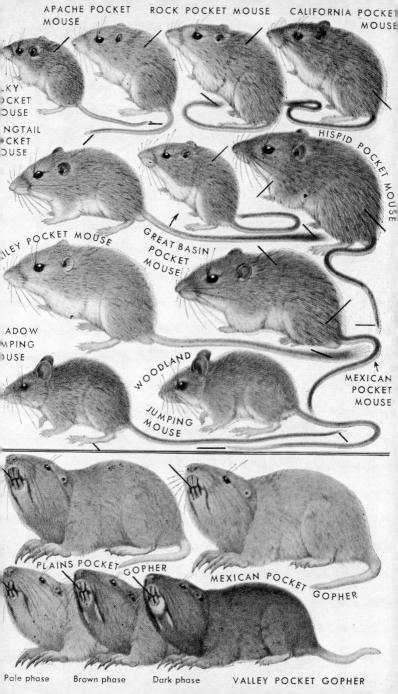

APACHE POCKET MOUSE

ROCK POCKET MOUSE

CALIFORNIA POCKET MOUSE

SILKY POCKET MOUSE

LONGTAIL POCKET MOUSE

HISPID POCKET MOUSE

VALLEY POCKET MOUSE

GREAT BASIN POCKET MOUSE

MEADOW JUMPING MOUSE

WOODLAND JUMPING MOUSE

MEXICAN POCKET MOUSE

PLAINS POCKET GOPHER

MEXICAN POCKET GOPHER

Pale phase        Brown phase        Dark phase        VALLEY POCKET GOPHER

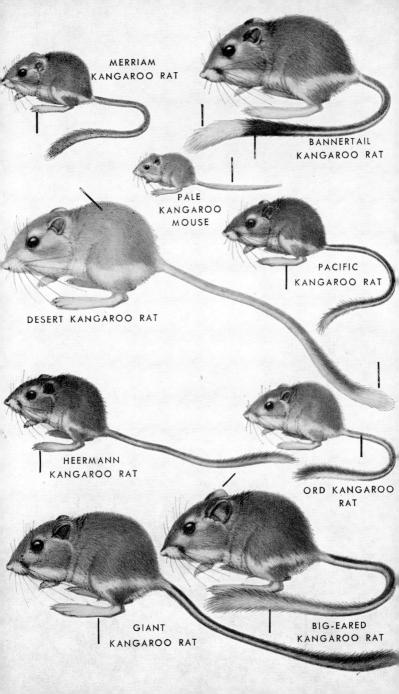

MERRIAM
KANGAROO RAT

BANNERTAIL
KANGAROO RAT

PALE
KANGAROO
MOUSE

PACIFIC
KANGAROO RAT

DESERT KANGAROO RAT

HEERMANN
KANGAROO RAT

ORD KANGAROO
RAT

GIANT
KANGAROO RAT

BIG-EARED
KANGAROO RAT

Plate 14                                                    105

# KANGAROO RATS AND MICE

(Fur-lined cheek pouches, deserts)

**MERRIAM KANGAROO RAT**                              pp. *95*, *96*
   Small, four toes on hind foot.


**BANNERTAIL KANGAROO RAT**                           pp. *95*, *96*
   White tip on tail, black in front of white.


**PALE KANGAROO MOUSE**                               pp. *98*, *96*
   Tail swollen in middle, not crested.


**DESERT KANGAROO RAT**                               pp. *98*, *96*
   Large, pale, no black on tail, white tip.


**PACIFIC KANGAROO RAT**                              pp. *97*, *96*
   Five toes on hind foot.


**HEERMANN KANGAROO RAT**                             pp. *94*, *96*
   Normally four toes on hind foot, valleys and foothills.


**ORD KANGAROO RAT**                                  pp. *97*, *96*
   Dark tail stripe broader than white one.


**GIANT KANGAROO RAT**                                pp. *95*, *96*
   Large, five toes on hind foot.


**BIG–EARED KANGAROO RAT**                            pp. *97*, *96*
   Large ears, end of tail heavily crested.

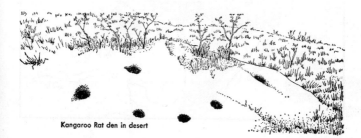

Kangaroo Rat den in desert

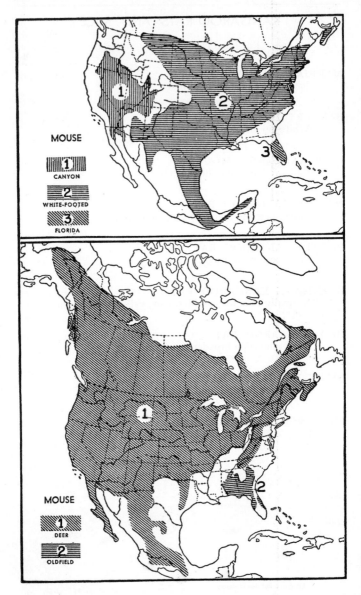

MOUSE

1 CANYON
2 WHITE-FOOTED
3 FLORIDA

MOUSE

1 DEER
2 OLDFIELD

**SITKA MOUSE.** *Peromyscus sitkensis.*
**Recognition:** — Head and body, 4⅓–4½ in.; tail, 4–4½ in. This longtail, white-footed mouse is found on the following islands: Baranof, Chichagof, and Forrester, off Alaska; Prevost, Queen Charlotte group, and Pine Island, British Columbia.

**OLDFIELD MOUSE.** *Peromyscus polionotus.* pp. **121**, 106
**Recognition:** — Head and body, 3⅖–3⅘ in.; tail, 1⅗–2⅖ in. This small, shorttail, *whitish* to *pale-cinnamon* mouse is found along the *sand beaches* or in *old fields* within its range.
**Similar species:** — White-footed, Cotton, and Florida mice; dark brown or with tail more than 2⅖ in. Golden Mouse; bright cinnamon over head and body, tail, 3 in. or more.

**WHITE-FOOTED MOUSE.** *Peromyscus leucopus.* pp. **121**, 106
**Recognition:** — Head and body, 3⅗–4⅕ in.; tail, 2⅖–4 in.; wt., 12–31 gm. This mouse prefers *woods* or *brushy areas* over most of its range. The belly and feet are white and the upper parts are pale to rich reddish brown. The tail is usually shorter *than the head and body.* In parts of its range it is difficult to distinguish from other species.
**Similar species:** — Cactus Mouse; tail scantily haired. Deer Mouse; always sharply bicolored tail, in northeast forests difficult to distinguish, tail more than 3⅗ in. Oldfield Mouse; tail less than 2⅖ in. Cotton Mouse; slightly larger, difficult to distinguish. Cactus and White-ankled mice; hairs distinctly longer on terminal one inch of tail. Piñon and Rock mice; ears nearly an inch high. Golden Mouse; head and body rich cinnamon.

**COTTON MOUSE.** *Peromyscus gossypinus.* p. 108
**Recognition:** — Head and body, 3⅗–4⅗ in.; tail, 2⅘–3⅗ in. This mouse prefers the *wooded areas* within its range. It is *dark brown* with a slight fulvous mixture above, whitish below. The tail may or may not be bicolored.
**Similar species:** — Deer Mouse; smaller. Oldfield Mouse; pale, tail less than 2½ in. White-footed Mouse; slightly smaller, difficult to distinguish. Golden Mouse; bright cinnamon. Florida Mouse; larger, sandy ridges.

**BRUSH MOUSE.** *Peromyscus boylei.* pp. **121**, 108
**Recognition:** — Head and body, 3⅗–4⅕ in.; tail, 3⅗–4⅖ in. This mouse characteristically inhabits the *chaparral* areas of arid or semi-arid regions. In color, it ranges from *grayish brown* to fairly *dark brown*, and is washed with *fulvous* on the sides. The *well-haired tail* is about as long as the head and body, often slightly longer.
**Similar species:** — Cactus Mouse; tail scantily haired. California Mouse; large, tail over 5 in. Canyon Mouse; pale gray or

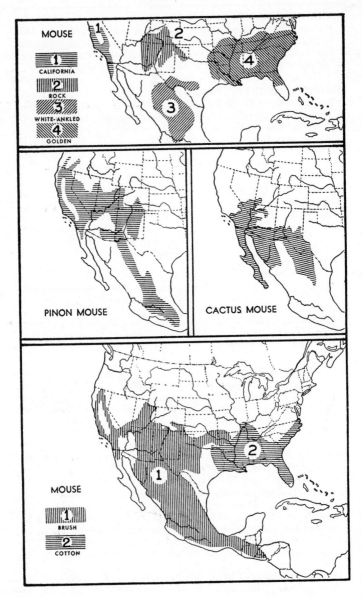

MOUSE

1 CALIFORNIA
2 ROCK
3 WHITE-ANKLED
4 GOLDEN

PINON MOUSE

CACTUS MOUSE

MOUSE

1 BRUSH
2 COTTON

buffy. Deer and White-footed mice; tail shorter than head and body. White-ankled Mouse; head and body slightly smaller, ankles white, difficult to distinguish. Piñon and Rock mice; ears nearly an inch high, in California some may be difficult to distinguish. Golden Mouse; bright cinnamon.

**WHITE-ANKLED MOUSE.** *Peromyscus pectoralis.* p. 108

**Recognition:** — Head and body, $3\frac{2}{5}$ in.; tail, $3\frac{4}{5}$–$4\frac{2}{5}$ in. This *pale grayish* mouse is found only in the *Big Bend* area, Texas. The tail is *longer* than the head and body, and the ankles are *white.*

**Similar species:** — Cactus Mouse; tail scantily haired, ankles dusky. Deer Mouse and White-footed Mouse; tail shorter than head and body. Brush Mouse; ankles dusky, difficult to distinguish.

**PIÑON MOUSE.** *Peromyscus truei.* pp. **121**, 108

**Recognition:** — Head and body, $3\frac{3}{5}$–4 in.; tail, $3\frac{2}{5}$–$4\frac{4}{5}$ in., wt., 20–30 gm. This *large-eared* mouse, *grayish brown*, heavily washed with fulvous, is characteristic of the lower slopes of the mountains where there are *rocks* and *piñon pines, junipers*, or their equivalents. The tail runs from slightly shorter to slightly longer than the head and body; it is *distinctly bicolored.*

**Similar species:** — Cactus Mouse; tail not hairy, low desert. California Mouse; tail over 5 in. Canyon Mouse; pale gray or buff, smaller. Deer and White-footed mice; ears small, less than $\frac{1}{2}$ in. high; Brush Mouse; ears smaller, less than $\frac{3}{4}$ in. high, in California some are difficult to distinguish. Rock Mouse; difficult to distinguish.

**ROCK MOUSE.** *Peromyscus nasutus.* p. 108

**Recognition:** — Head and body, $3\frac{3}{5}$–4 in.; tail, $3\frac{3}{5}$–$4\frac{2}{5}$ in. The Rock Mouse is very similar to the Piñon Mouse, is intermediate between that and the Brush Mouse, and is difficult to distinguish even in the museum. See Piñon Mouse for characters and similar species.

**GOLDEN MOUSE.** *Peromyscus nuttalli.* pp. **121**, 108

**Recognition:** — Head and body, $3\frac{2}{5}$–$3\frac{4}{5}$ in.; tail 3–$3\frac{3}{5}$ in. This handsome, bright *golden-cinnamon* mouse, with *white belly*, builds its nest, *a round ball* of soft plant materials, *in vines, bushes, or trees.* The nest is 4–6 or more in. in diameter and up to 10 ft. above ground. The mouse is primarily *arboreal* in habits.

**Similar species:** — No other mouse has the striking golden coloration of this one. Others found within its range are: Deer, Old-field, White-footed, Cotton, Brush, and Florida mice.

**FLORIDA MOUSE.** *Peromyscus floridanus.* p. 106

**Recognition:** — Head and body, $4\frac{2}{5}$–5 in.; tail, $3\frac{1}{5}$–$3\frac{4}{5}$ in. This *large* mouse is found only on the *sand ridges* where it occupies burrows of other animals.

**Similar species:** — Oldfield Mouse; smaller, pale gray or buffy. Cotton Mouse; smaller, woods. Golden Mouse; bright cinnamon.

# Rice Rats: Cricetinæ (in part)

**RICE RAT.** *Oryzomys palustris.*                    pp. **121**, 111

**Recognition:** — Head and body, 4¾–5⅛ in.; tail, 4⅓–7⅛ in. The Rice Rat prefers *grasses and sedges* in moist conditions, near water. It is *grayish brown* or fulvous brown with *gray or fulvous* (Rio Grande Valley) belly. The *long, scaly tail* is slightly paler below than above and the feet are *whitish*. It is nocturnal. The fur is short and not grizzled.

**Similar species:** — Cotton Rat; fur long and grizzled, tail black above. Norway and Black rats, tail not paler below. Other kinds; smaller.

**Remarks:** — The Rice Rat at Brownsville, Texas, is considered distinct and is known as *Oryzomys couesi.*

# Cotton Rats: Cricetinæ (in part)

COTTON RATS are found usually where there is *tall grass* or similar vegetation and where conditions are moist. They are medium-sized rats with grayish brown to blackish brown fur *heavily grizzled* with pale buff. The finely haired tail is blackish above, pale below, and is shorter than head and body. The feet are gray, and the ears are nearly concealed by the long fur. They are active day and night.

**HISPID COTTON RAT.** *Sigmodon hispidus.*          pp. **124**, 111

**Recognition:** — Head and body, 5–8 in.; tail, 3–5 in.; wt., 80–240 gm. This species is grizzled buff and black above, *whitish below*, pale in West and dark in East. Found in *low* country.

**Similar species:** — Least Cotton Rat; buff belly. Yellownose Cotton Rat; yellowish around nose. Rice Rat; tail scaly and as long as head and body.

**LEAST COTTON RAT.** *Sigmodon minimus.*               p. 111

**Recognition:** — Head and body, 5–6 in.; tail, 4 in. This is a *mountain* rat and may be distinguished by its grizzled black and pale buff upper parts and *buff belly*.

**Similar species:** — Hispid Cotton Rat; gray belly. Yellownose Cotton Rat; gray belly.

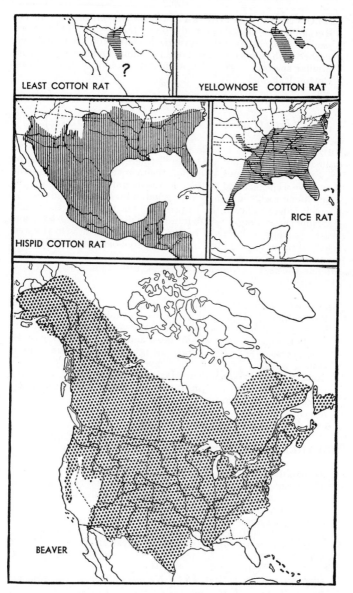

LEAST COTTON RAT

YELLOWNOSE COTTON RAT

HISPID COTTON RAT

RICE RAT

BEAVER

**YELLOWNOSE COTTON RAT.** *Sigmodon ochrognathus.* p. 111
　**Recognition:** — Head and body, 6 in.; tail, 4½ in. This rat is a *foothills* or *mountain* form. It is grizzled buffy and blackish above, washed with *fulvous* on *nose*, face, and rump, and has a *gray belly*.
　**Similar species:** — Hispid Cotton Rat; no buff on nose. Least Cotton Rat; buff belly.

# Woodrats: Cricetinæ (in part)

THE WOODRATS, also known as "Packrats," are about the size of ordinary house rats, but are easily distinguished from the latter by the *hairy*, not scaly, tail. Further, their ears are *larger* and usually they have *white* feet and bellies. In the mountains they are usually found along rock cliffs where their small piles of sticks and rubbish on rock ledges indicate their presence. On the plains they build stick and cactus houses two to four feet in diameter at the base, and nearly as high, in clumps of cactus, yucca, or brush. On the west coast, their nests (houses) may be in live-oak trees. They are nocturnal; seldom seen by day.
**Similar species:** — Norway and Black rats; tails scaly, not covered with hair.

**EASTERN WOODRAT.** *Neotoma floridana.*　　pp. **125**, 113
　**Recognition:** — Head and body, 8–9 in.; tail, 6–8 in. This is a large, *grayish brown* woodrat with *white or grayish belly* and with the tail, which is *shorter* than head and body, *white or gray beneath, brown above.* In the East, along *cliffs;* in the plains it nests among *yuccas.*
　**Similar species:** — Southern Plains Woodrat; steel gray, not washed with brown. Bushytail Woodrat; tail squirrel-like. Norway and Black rats; tail scaly.
　**Remarks:** — The northeastern woodrat is currently recognized as a distinct species, *Neotoma magister.*

**SOUTHERN PLAINS WOODRAT.** *Neotoma micropus.*
　　　　　　　　　　　　　　　　　　　　　　　　pp. **125**, 113
　**Recognition:** — Head and body, 7½–8½ in.; tail, 5½–6½ in. This large plains rat is *steel gray* above, gray on belly, and *white on throat and breast.* The feet are *white*, and the tail is blackish above, gray below.
　**Similar species:** — Whitethroat Woodrat; back mixed with fulvous. Desert Woodrat; smaller, throat hairs not white at bases, back with fulvous mixture. Mexican Woodrat; throat hairs slate at bases.

**WHITETHROAT WOODRAT.** *Neotoma albigula.* pp. **125**, 113
　**Recognition:** — Head and body, 7½–8½ in.; tail, 5½–7⅛ in

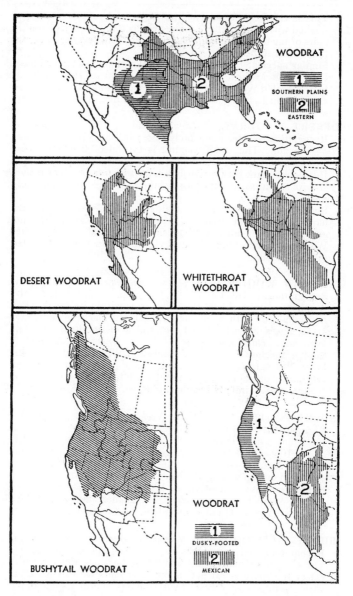

WOODRAT

1 SOUTHERN PLAINS

2 EASTERN

DESERT WOODRAT

WHITETHROAT WOODRAT

BUSHYTAIL WOODRAT

WOODRAT

1 DUSKY-FOOTED

2 MEXICAN

This is chiefly an animal of the *plains* and *valleys*. It is *gray* washed with *fulvous* above. The belly is *white or grayish* and the hairs of the throat are *white to their bases*. The feet are *white;* the tail is whitish below, brown above.
**Similar species:** — Southern Plains Woodrat; steel gray above. Desert and Mexican woodrats; hairs of throat slate at bases. Dusky-footed Woodrat; tail blackish above, hind feet dusky near ankles. Bushytail Woodrat; tail squirrel-like, high mountains.

**DESERT WOODRAT.** *Neotoma lepida.* pp. **125**, 113
**Recognition:** — Head and body, 5⅘–7 in.; tail, 4⅓–6⅖ in.; wt., 95–160 gm. This small woodrat is typical of the low, *cactus-covered*, arid regions. Its houses are found in clumps of cactus. It is pale to dark *gray* variously *washed with fulvous*. The belly is *grayish to fulvous*, and the bases of the hairs are everywhere *slate-color*.
**Similar species:** — Southern Plains and Whitethroat woodrats; hairs of throat white to bases. Mexican Woodrat; tail white, not gray, below, difficult to distinguish without skull. Dusky-footed Woodrat; larger, hind feet dusky above. Bushytail Woodrat; tail squirrel-like.

**MEXICAN WOODRAT.** *Neotoma mexicana.* pp. **125**, 113
**Recognition:** — Head and body, 6½–7¾ in.; tail, 6–6½ in. This woodrat occupies chiefly the *rocky areas* within its range. It is normally *gray* with a *fulvous wash*, nearly black on some lava areas, has a grayish-white belly, and a distinctly bicolor tail, *white below, blackish above.*
**Similar species:** — Southern Plains and Whitethroat woodrats; hairs of throat white to bases, valleys and plains. Desert Woodrat; hardly distinguishable without skull, tail less sharply bicolor. Bushytail Woodrat; tail squirrel-like.

**DUSKY-FOOTED WOODRAT.** *Neotoma fuscipes.* pp. **125**, 113
**Recognition:** — Head and body, 7⅗–9 in.; tail 6⅘–8⅔ in. A tree-going woodrat, this species often builds houses in the live oaks. It is *grayish brown above, grayish to whitish below.* The tail may be slightly paler below than above, and the hind feet are sprinkled on top with *dusky* hairs. It is a large rat.
**Similar species:** — Whitethroat Woodrat, hind feet white above, usually smaller. Desert Woodrat; smaller, hind feet white. Bushytail Woodrat; tail squirrel-like, hind feet white.

**BUSHYTAIL WOODRAT.** *Neotoma cinerea.* pp. **125**, 113
**Recognition:** — Head and body, 7–9⅔ in.; tail, 5⅕–7⅗ in.; wt., 320–585 gm. Usually not found below the pines, this is a woodrat of the *rimrock*. It gets about over cliffs with ease. Color varies from *pale gray* washed with fulvous to *nearly black* above.

It may be distinguished from all other woodrats by its *long bushy, squirrel-like tail.*

**Similar species:** — Whitethroat, Desert, Mexican, and Dusky-footed woodrats; all have short-haired tails which taper toward tip.

## Bog Lemmings: Microtinæ (in part)

THESE vole-like mammals, about five inches in total length and with *short tails,* usually less than an inch long, characteristically inhabit *wet bogs and meadows* where there is a thick mat of ground vegetation. They are active by day as well as by night. Their long, grizzled, brownish-gray fur nearly conceals the short ears. Superficially they are easily confused with the voles, but a close inspection of the front surfaces of the upper gnawing teeth will reveal a *shallow groove* near the outer edge of each tooth.

**SOUTHERN BOG LEMMING.** *Synaptomys cooperi.* pp. **124**, 116

**Recognition:** — Head and body, 3⅖–4⅖ in.; tail, ⅗–⅞ in.; wt., 15–40 gm. As described above.

**Similar species:** — Redback Vole; tail more than an inch, red down middle of back. Meadow Vole; tail more than an inch. Yellownose Vole; yellow nose. Prairie Vole; front teeth not grooved. Pine Vole; not grizzled, uniform auburn color.

**NORTHERN BOG LEMMING.** *Synaptomys borealis.* p. 116

**Recognition:** — Head and body, 4–4⅗ in.; tail, ⅘–1 in. As described above.

**Similar species:** — Brown Lemming; soles of feet hairy, teeth not grooved. Collared Lemming; tawny band across throat, summer, or white, winter. Other voles; front teeth not grooved and/or tail more than an inch.

## Lemmings: Microtinæ (in part)

THESE are the common small rodents of the *far north.* They have dense, long fur and *small ears and tail.* They are the most brilliantly colored of the small arctic rodents. The collared lemmings are the only small rodents that turn white in winter.

**BROWN LEMMING.** *Lemmus trimucronatus.* pp. **124**, 116

**Recognition:** — Head and body, 4½–5½ in.; tail, ⅘–1+ in. Characteristically a *tundra* mammal, but also found south of timber line, is this *brown-rumped, grayish-headed* lemming. By

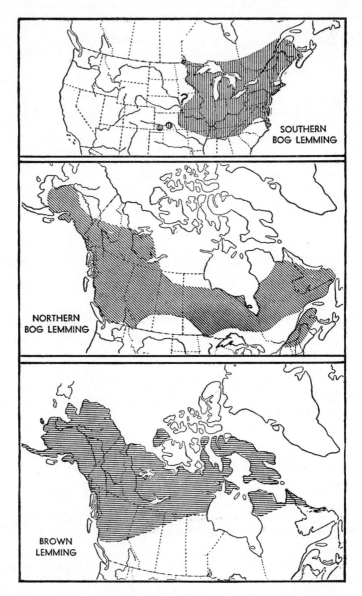

SOUTHERN
BOG LEMMING

NORTHERN
BOG LEMMING

BROWN
LEMMING

its extremely *long reddish fur* and *short tail*, it may be distinguished from other small rodents.

**Similar species:** — Collared Lemming; dark median stripe down back. Northern Bog Lemming; grayish brown, incisors grooved. Voles and Phenacomys; tail more than an inch.

**HUDSON BAY COLLARED LEMMING.** *Dicrostonyx hudsonius.* p. 118

**Recognition:** — Head and body, 5 in.; tail, ⅖ in. Found on the *tundra* east of Hudson Bay, this bundle of *buffy gray* fur is the common rodent. A *dark stripe* extends along the middle of the back in summer. The ears and tail barely show through the long fur, which is *white in winter*. The third and fourth claws on the front feet are greatly enlarged especially in winter.

**Similar species:** — Brown Lemming; no dark back stripe. Northern Bog Lemming; uniform grayish brown, teeth grooved. Ungava Phenacomys and voles; tail more than an inch.

**GREENLAND COLLARED LEMMING.** *Dicrostonyx grœnlandicus.* pp. **124**, 118

**Recognition:** — Head and body, 4–5½ in.; tail, ⅖–⅘ in. See Hudson Bay Collared Lemming for description. This lemming occupies the *tundra* west and north of Hudson Bay and a strip in Greenland.

**Similar species:** — Brown Lemming; no dark streak down back, brown in winter. All voles; tail more than an inch.

**UNALASKA COLLARED LEMMING.** *Dicrostonyx unalascensis.* p. 118

**Recognition:** — Head and body, 6 in.; tail, ½ in. This, *largest* of the collared lemmings, is dull *buffy brown* with a *dark stripe* down the back. It does not turn white in winter. Known only from *Unalaska* and *Umnak* Islands, Alaska.

# Phenacomys: Microtinæ (in part)

THESE rare vole-like rodents are inhabitants of grassy areas within the *cold forested regions* of Canada and the *high mountaintops* of western United States. They occur where people seldom go and they are not likely to be encountered by the average person. Most of them are ground-living, have relatively *short tails*, and rather *long, soft, grizzled grayish brown fur*. The belly is pale grayish. The Tree Phenacomys is quite different; it has a relatively long blackish tail which contrasts with the bright rufous body. It is arboreal to some extent.

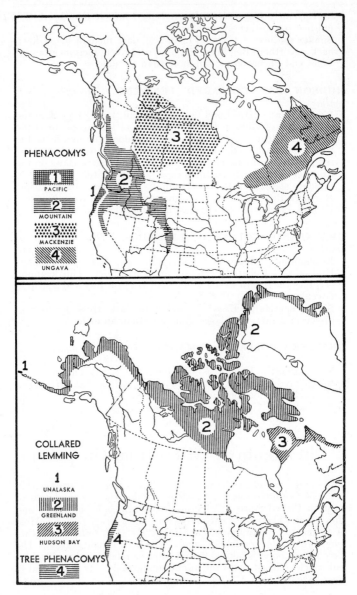

PHENACOMYS

1 PACIFIC
2 MOUNTAIN
3 MACKENZIE
4 UNGAVA

COLLARED LEMMING

1 UNALASKA
2 GREENLAND
3 HUDSON BAY

TREE PHENACOMYS
4

**MOUNTAIN PHENACOMYS.** *Phenacomys intermedius.* pp. **124**, 118

**Recognition:** — Head and body, 4⅕–4⅖ in.; tail, 1–1⅔ in. Found on scattered *mountaintops* in open *grassy parks*, this phenacomys is *grayish brown* with *white* feet and *silvery* belly. The short tail is bicolor.

**Similar species:** — Mountain Vole; tail usually longer, difficult to distinguish. Longtail Vole; tail more than 2 in. Others; not found near mountaintops or measurements differ.

**UNGAVA PHENACOMYS.** *Phenacomys ungava.* p. 118

**Recognition:** — Head and body, 3½–4⅗ in.; tail, 1⅛–1½ in. This bright *chestnut-brown* phenacomys has a *yellowish nose.* The belly is grayish, sometimes tinged with buff. The tail is bicolor.

**Similar species:** — Yellownose Vole; tail more than 1½ in. Redback Vole; nose not yellow. Others; tail under an inch.

**MACKENZIE PHENACOMYS.** *Phenacomys mackenziei.* p. 118

**Recognition:** — Head and body, 4⅕–4⅔ in.; tail, 1⅕–1⅖ in. In *strips of forest*, along *low grassy glades*, this rather pale, grayish-brown phenacomys with a *yellowish face* and a bicolor tail makes its home.

**Similar species:** — Yellow-cheeked Vole; head and body more than 5 in. Tundra Vole; yellowish. Longtail Vole; tail over 2 in. Meadow Vole; face not yellowish. Prairie Vole; face not yellowish. Redback Voles; back reddish. Others; tail less than an inch.

**PACIFIC PHENACOMYS.** *Phenacomys albipes.* p. 118

**Recognition:** — Head and body, 3⅘–4⅖ in.; tail, 2½–2⅘ in. This dark, *rich brown* phenacomys lives along *small streams* in the humid forests.

**Similar species:** — Mountain Vole; high mountain meadows. Townsend and Longtail voles; head and body over 4½ in. Oregon Vole; tail under 2 in. California Redback Vole; back chestnut. Tree Phenacomys; reddish with black tail.

**TREE PHENACOMYS.** *Phenacomys longicaudus.* pp. **124**, 118

**Recognition:** — Head and body, 4–4⅓ in.; tail, 2⅖–3⅓ in. This bright *reddish brown* phenacomys with a *blackish, well-haired tail* spends much of its time in *trees*, where it builds its nest among the branches. Color and size serve to distinguish this species from all others in the area.

**Remarks:** — Authors have considered those phenacomys in Oregon as a distinct species, *Phenacomys silvicola.*

## SMALL MICE

**EASTERN HARVEST MOUSE**                    pp. *100*, 101
  Grooves down front of upper incisors.


**WESTERN HARVEST MOUSE**                    pp. *100*, 101
  Uniform brownish, belly paler, grooved incisors.


**SALT MARSH HARVEST MOUSE**                 pp. *100*, 101
  Belly fulvous, salt marshes.


**FULVOUS HARVEST MOUSE**                    pp. *102*, 101
  Sides fulvous, tail long, teeth grooved.


**HOUSE MOUSE**                              pp. *137*, 136
  Tail scaly, incisors smooth.


**PIGMY MOUSE**                              pp. *102*, 101
  Small, dark grayish brown, incisors smooth.


**NORTHERN GRASSHOPPER MOUSE**               pp. *99*, 96
  *Two color phases:* Tail short with white tip.

Harvest Mouse
and nest

EASTERN HARVEST MOUSE

WESTERN HARVEST MOUSE

SALT MARSH HARVEST MOUSE

FULVOUS HARVEST MOUSE

HOUSE MOUSE

PIGMY MOUSE

Cinnamon phase                                    Gray phase

NORTHERN GRASSHOPPER MOUSE

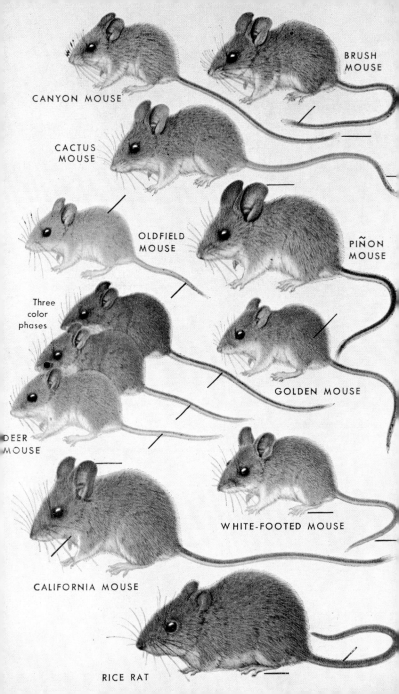

CANYON MOUSE

BRUSH MOUSE

CACTUS MOUSE

OLDFIELD MOUSE

PIÑON MOUSE

Three color phases

GOLDEN MOUSE

DEER MOUSE

WHITE-FOOTED MOUSE

CALIFORNIA MOUSE

RICE RAT

Plate 16                                                    121

# MICE WITH LONG TAILS

### (Usually with white bellies and feet)

**CANYON MOUSE**                                    pp. *103*, 106
    Tuft on end of long **tail.**

**BRUSH MOUSE**                                     pp. *107*, 108
    Tail well haired.

**CACTUS MOUSE**                                    pp. *102*, 108
    Tail slightly haired, desert.

**OLDFIELD MOUSE**                                  pp. *107*, 106
    Small, pale, tail short and bicolor.

**PIÑON MOUSE**                                     pp. *109*, 108
    Large ears.

**GOLDEN MOUSE**                                    pp. *109*, 108
    Rich golden brown, nests in trees and vines.

**DEER MOUSE**                                      pp. *103*, 106
    *Three color phases:* Tail bicolor.

**WHITE–FOOTED MOUSE**                              pp. *107*, 106
    Tail shorter than head and body.

**CALIFORNIA MOUSE**                                pp. *103*, 108
    Large with large ears.

**RICE RAT**                                        pp. *110*, 111
    Whitish feet, scaly tail, near water.

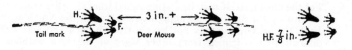

H. → ← 3 in. + →    H.F. ⅞ in.
Tail mark   F.   Deer Mouse

# Redback Voles: Microtinæ (in part)

THESE small forest rodents, 5–6 in. in overall length, usually have long soft fur which is *gray on the sides* and *reddish down the back*. In the southern part of the range they may be deep brown with little if any contrast between sides and back. The belly is always *gray or silvery*, and the tail is *bicolor*.

**BRITISH COLUMBIA REDBACK VOLE.** *Clethrionomys caurinus.*                                                                p. 123

**Recognition:** — Head and body, 4 in.; tail, 1⅝ in. Along a strip of coast opposite Vancouver Island, this chestnut-backed, gray-sided vole may be found on the *forest floors*. The combination of *short tail, red back*, and *gray sides* will set it off from all other small rodents in the area.

**WRANGELL ISLAND REDBACK VOLE.** *Clethrionomys wrangeli.*                                                                p. 123

**Recognition:** — Head and body, 4⅖ in.; tail 1½ in. On *Wrangell* and *Revillagigedo* islands, Alaska, this small vole may at once be distinguished by its deep *chestnut back* and *gray sides*.

**TUNDRA REDBACK VOLE.** *Clethrionomys dawsoni.*    p. 123

**Recognition:** — Head and body, 4⅖ in.; tail 1⅓ in. Extending northward beyond the limit of tree growth, into the tundra, this small vole may be distinguished from others of the area by its *bright reddish back* and *buffy sides and belly*.

**ST. LAWRENCE ISLAND REDBACK VOLE.** *Clethrionomys albiventer.*                                                                p. 123

**Recognition:** — Head and body, 4⅔ in.; tail, 1⅕–1½ in. Living among the *boulders* on *St. Lawrence Island*, Bering Sea, this vole may be distinguished by its *brown back* and *gray sides*.

**BOREAL REDBACK VOLE.** *Clethrionomys gapperi.* pp. 124, 123

**Recognition:** — Head and body, 3⅔–4⅔ in.; tail, 1⅕–2 in.; wt., 15–40 gm. Throughout most of the *forested* area of Canada and in the *mountains* of the United States, where it is moderately *damp and cool*, this *ground-dwelling* vole may be found. In the North and East there are two color phases, a red and a gray. For the most part, it may be distinguished from all other voles of its area by the *reddish back* and *gray sides*, but in the North and East, the gray phase may not have a reddish back and may be difficult to distinguish from other voles of the area without recourse to the skull.

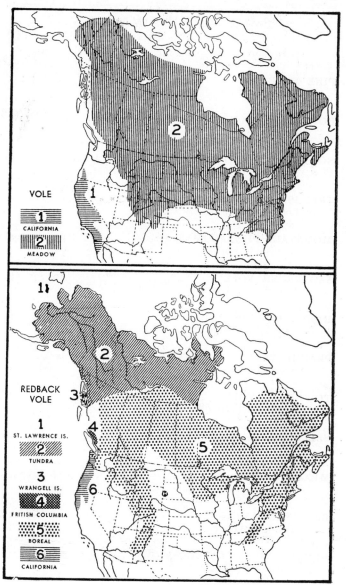

VOLE

**1**
CALIFORNIA

**2**
MEADOW

REDBACK
VOLE

1
ST. LAWRENCE IS.

**2**
TUNDRA

3
WRANGELL IS.

**4**
BRITISH COLUMBIA

**5**
BOREAL

**6**
CALIFORNIA

# SMALL VOLE-LIKE MAMMALS

(With short tails and long fur, nearly concealing ears)

**PINE VOLE**                                    pp. *135*, 134
    Auburn, soft fur, short tail.

**BOREAL REDBACK VOLE**                          pp. *122*, 123
    Reddish down middle of back.

**SOUTHERN BOG LEMMING**                         pp. *115*, 116
    Short tail, upper incisors grooved in front.

**TREE PHENACOMYS**                              pp. *119*, 118
    Long tail, reddish body.

**MOUNTAIN PHENACOMYS**                          pp. *119*, 118
    Grayish, incisors smooth.

**SAGEBRUSH VOLE**                               pp. *135*, 134
    Pale grayish, sagebrush.

**HISPID COTTON RAT**                            pp. *110*, 111
    Grizzled fur, large size.

**PRAIRIE VOLE**                                 pp. *131*, 130
    Short tail, smooth incisors, grayish, prairies.

**TOWNSEND VOLE**                                pp. *129*, 128
    Large, blackish tail, dusky feet.

**YELLOWNOSE VOLE**                              pp. *131*, 128
    Yellowish on nose.

**MEADOW VOLE**                                  pp. *126*, 123
    Brownish gray, long tail.

**BROWN LEMMING**                                pp. *115*, 116
    Reddish, short tail.

**GREENLAND COLLARED LEMMING**                   pp. *117*, 118
    Dark stripe down back.

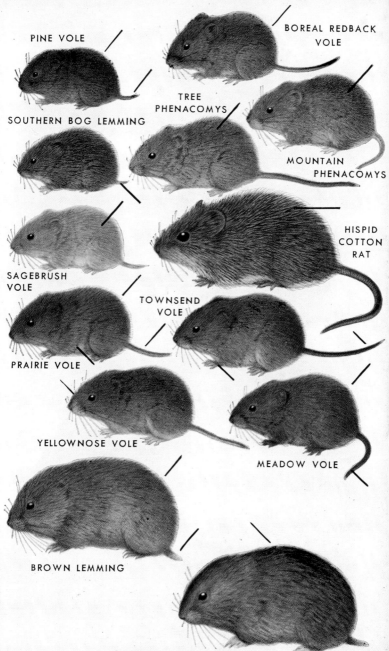

PINE VOLE

BOREAL REDBACK VOLE

TREE PHENACOMYS

SOUTHERN BOG LEMMING

MOUNTAIN PHENACOMYS

SAGEBRUSH VOLE

HISPID COTTON RAT

TOWNSEND VOLE

PRAIRIE VOLE

YELLOWNOSE VOLE

MEADOW VOLE

BROWN LEMMING

GREENLAND COLLARED LEMMING

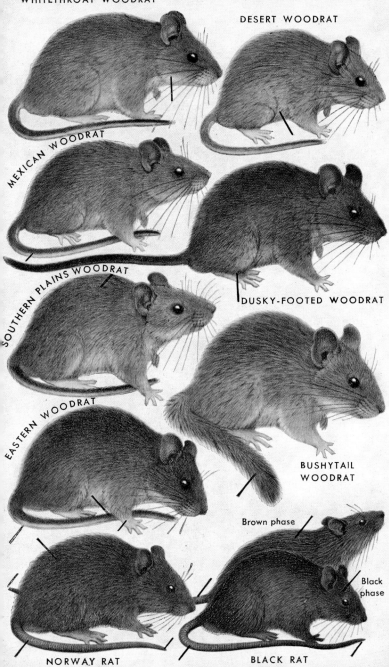

WHITETHROAT WOODRAT

DESERT WOODRAT

MEXICAN WOODRAT

SOUTHERN PLAINS WOODRAT

DUSKY-FOOTED WOODRAT

EASTERN WOODRAT

BUSHYTAIL WOODRAT

Brown phase

Black phase

NORWAY RAT

BLACK RAT

Plate 18                                           125

## WOODRATS AND OTHERS

**WHITETHROAT WOODRAT**                    pp. *112*, 113
  Hairs of throat white to skin.


**DESERT WOODRAT**                         pp. *114*, 113
  Grayish belly, hairs slate near skin, desert.


**MEXICAN WOODRAT**                        pp. *114*, 113
  Tail white below, rocky areas.


**DUSKY–FOOTED WOODRAT**                   pp. *114*, 113
  Feet dusky.


**SOUTHERN PLAINS WOODRAT**                pp. *112*, 113
  Gray, no fulvous.


**BUSHYTAIL WOODRAT**                      pp. *114*, 113
  Tail squirrel-like.


**EASTERN WOODRAT**                        pp. *112*, 113
  Feet and belly whitish, tail haired.


**NORWAY RAT**                             pp. *137*, 136
  Brownish, tail scaly and shorter than head and body.


**BLACK RAT**                              pp. *137*, 136
  *Brown phase:* Tail longer than head and body, scaly.
  *Black phase:* Blackish.

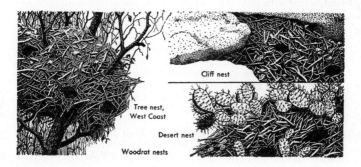

Cliff nest

Tree nest,
West Coast

Desert nest

Woodrat nests

**CALIFORNIA REDBACK VOLE.** *Clethrionomys californicus.* p. 123

**Recognition:** — Head and body, 4⅓ in.; tail, 2–2⅕ in. In the *forests* of the humid coast of Washington, Oregon, and northern California, this *dark sepia* vole harmonizes with its surroundings. The back is *dark chestnut*, but does not contrast strikingly with the sides. The belly is *buffy* or *soiled whitish* and the feet may be *whitish or dusky.*

**Similar species:** — Mountain Vole; high mountain meadows, grayish. California Vole; grayish brown. Townsend, Richardson, and Longtail voles; head and body 4½ in. or more. Oregon Vole; tail less than two inches. Mountain Phenacomys; high mountains, tail less than two inches. Pacific and Tree Phenacomys; tail more than 2⅕ inches.

# Voles, Muskrats: Microtinæ (in part)

THROUGHOUT Canada and Alaska and in all but three of the United States (Mississippi, Alabama, and Florida) where there is good *grass cover*, one is likely to encounter one or more kinds of voles. Their presence may be detected by *narrow runways*, one to two inches wide, through the matted grasses. Small piles of brownish droppings and short pieces of grass stems along these runways are further evidence. In a few places, these voles are found among rocks or on forest floors where there is no grass. In areas of winter snow, their *round openings* to the surface of the snow also reveal their presence. They are active by day as well as by night. Mostly, they are *brownish gray* with *long fur*, *small ears*, and relatively *short tails*, always less than head and body length. They have small, black, bead-like eyes.

**Similar species:** — Bog Lemmings; gnawing teeth have grooves down their front surfaces, tail always less than an inch. Lemmings; brightly colored. Phenacomys; difficult to distinguish as a group, see special accounts. Redback Voles; usually have reddish backs contrasting with pale sides. Pine Voles; not grizzled, auburn, tail less than an inch. Sage Brush Vole; pale gray, no brown, tail less than an inch.

**MEADOW VOLE.** *Microtus pennsylvanicus.* pp. 124, 123

**Recognition:** — Head and body, 3½–5 in.; tail, 1⅖–2⅗ in.; wt., 20–70 gm. The most widely distributed of the voles, this species varies from a gray, faintly washed with brown, in the west, to dark brown in the east. The belly is *silvery to slightly buffy or dark gray*, and the tail is *bicolor*. The fur is *long* and usually has a *grizzled* appearance.

**Similar species:** — Mountain Vole; high mountain meadows, characters not distinct. Tundra Vole; yellowish. Alaska Vole; above timberline, tail under 1⅕ in. Longtail Vole; tail over 2 in.

Yellow-cheeked and Yellownose voles; nose yellow. Richardson Vole; head and body more than 5½ in. Prairie Vole; tail usually less than 1⅖ in. Redback Vole; back reddish, sides pale grayish or tail blackish. Phenacomys; pale gray, tail usually under 1⅖ in. Others; tail under an inch.

**Remarks:** — The vole on Newfoundland and Penguin Island may be a distinct species, *M. terraenovae;* that on Muskeget Island, Massachusetts, *M. breweri;* and the one, probably extinct, on Gull Island, off Long Island, New York, *M. nesophilus.*

**MOUNTAIN VOLE.** *Microtus montanus.* p. 128

**Recognition:** — Head and body, 4–5½ in.; tail, 1⅕–2⅗ in.; wt., 30–85 gm. This *grayish-brown to blackish* vole, usually with *dusky feet,* is found primarily in the *valleys* of the mountainous Great Basin area.

**Similar species:** — Oregon Vole; dark brown, not grizzled. Richardson Vole; head and body 5½ in. or more. Prairie Vole; low prairies. Longtail Vole; tail usually longer, may be difficult to distinguish. Mexican Vole; belly yellowish, not white. Meadow Vole; usually not in mountains, difficult to distinguish. California Vole; usually in low valleys and flats, difficult to distinguish. Townsend Vole; tail black. Mountain Phenacomys; near tops of mountains, difficult to distinguish.

**CALIFORNIA VOLE.** *Microtus californicus.* p. 123

**Recognition:** — Head and body, 4¾–5⅔ in.; tail, 1⅗–2⅘ in. This is a *grayish brown* (blackish toward the coast, reddish in the desert) vole with *bicolor tail* and *pale feet* that contrast with the color of the back. Found from seashore to high in the mountains, usually in grassy meadows.

**Similar species:** — Mountain Vole; feet dusky, high mountain meadows. Townsend Vole; tail blackish, feet dusky. Longtail Vole; mostly above foothills, tail usually longer, may be difficult to distinguish. Oregon Vole; dark brown, fur short, not grizzled. Redback Vole; back reddish, sides buffy. Mountain Phenacomys; high mountains, tail usually under 1⅗ in. Pacific Phenacomys; rich brown. Tree Phenacomys; reddish, tail black.

**TUNDRA VOLE.** *Microtus oeconomus.* p. 128

**Recognition:** — Head and body, 5 in.; tail, 1⅗ in. This vole, an inhabitant of the *tundra,* is *dull brown* washed with buffy or fulvous. The belly is *grayish* and the tail is *bicolor.* Its fairly uniform color above, and size, will distinguish it from most other small rodents in the area.

**Similar species:** — Yellow-cheeked Vole; large, nose yellow. Meadow Vole; not yellowish. Alaska Vole; tail under 1⅖ in. Longtail Vole; tail over 2 in. Redback Vole; back reddish. Mackenzie Phenacomys; gray. Lemmings; tail under an inch.

**Remarks:** — Several species of this group of voles have been

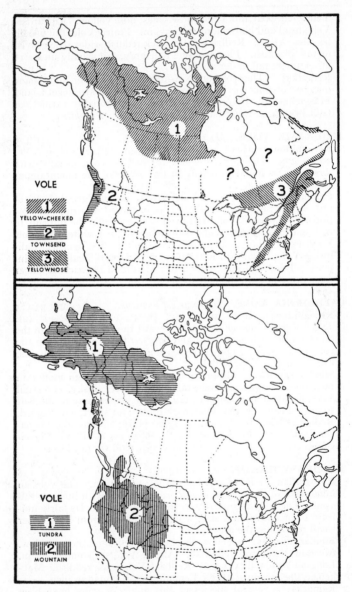

VOLE

1 YELLOW-CHEEKED

2 TOWNSEND

3 YELLOWNOSE

VOLE

1 TUNDRA

2 MOUNTAIN

described from the mainland and islands off Alaska. Included here are *M. macfarlani* and *M. yakutatensis* from Mackenzie and Alaska, respectively. From the islands are the following: *M. kadiacensis*, Kodiak Island; *M. unalascensis*, Unalaska and Popof Islands: *M. sitkensis*, Baranof Island; *M. elymocetes*, Montague Island; *M. amakensis*, Amak Island. All the above are closely related and may be recognized by the island on which they occur.

## ALASKA VOLE. *Microtus miurus.* p. 130
**Recognition:** — Head and body, 4–5 in.; tail, 1–1⅓ in. This shorttail, *buffy* vole occupies areas *above timberline*. It may be distinguished from all other voles by *small size* and *tail under 1⅓ in.*

**Remarks:** — Included within the general range given for the Alaska Vole are *M. andersoni*, *M. cantator*, and *M. muriei*. Closely related island species are: *M. innuitus*, St. Lawrence and Big Punuk islands; *M. abbreviatus*, Hall and St. Matthew islands.

## TOWNSEND VOLE. *Microtus townsendi.* pp. 124, 128
**Recognition:** — Head and body, 4¾–6⅖ in.; tail, 2–3 in. This large, *blackish brown* vole with *gray belly*, *blackish tail*, and *dusky feet*, is usually found near *water* in the low country. Its ears project well above the fur. It is found also on San Juan and Shaw islands, Washington, and Bowen and Vancouver islands, British Columbia. It may be distinguished from all others by size and color.

## LONGTAIL VOLE. *Microtus longicaudus.* p. 130
**Recognition:** — Head and body, 4½–5⅛ in.; tail, 2–3½ in.; wt., 37–58 gm. This is a rather *large* vole with a *long tail*. Its fur is *dark gray washed with brown or blackish* and the feet are *soiled whitish*. The tail is *bicolor*. Often found in rather *dry situations* far from water.

**Similar species:** — Mexican, Prairie, Oregon, Alaska, and Tundra voles; all have tail under 2 in. Meadow Vole; tail usually under 2 in., may be difficult to distinguish. California Vole; mostly in foothills and valleys, tail usually shorter, but may be difficult to distinguish. Mountain Vole; belly whitish, sometimes difficult. Townsend Vole; large, black tail. Richardson Vole; head and body more than 5½ in. Phenacomys; either reddish with black tail or with tail under two inches. Redback voles; back reddish, sides gray or buffy. Others; tail less than 2 in.

## MEXICAN VOLE. *Microtus mexicanus.* p. 130
**Recognition:** — Head and body, 4 in.; tail 1⅛ in. This *small*, *brownish* vole is found chiefly in the *semi-arid mountainous* parts of New Mexico and Arizona. Its feet are *dusky* and its tail is *short*.

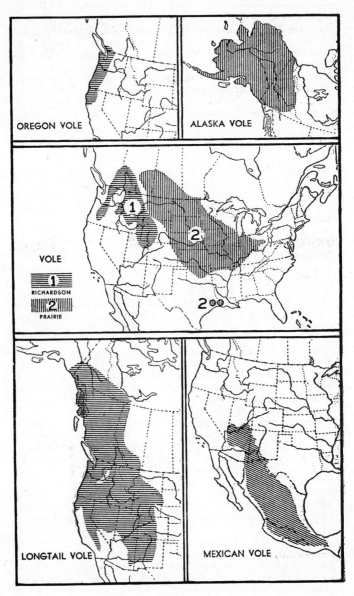

OREGON VOLE

ALASKA VOLE

VOLE

1
RICHARDSON

2
PRAIRIE

LONGTAIL VOLE

MEXICAN VOLE

**Similar species:** — Mountain Vole; belly whitish. Longtail Vole; tail 2 in. or more. Redback Vole; back red, sides gray.

**YELLOW-CHEEKED VOLE.** *Microtus xanthognathus.* p. 128
**Recognition:** — Head and body, 6⅖–7 in.; tail, 1⅘–2 in. This large, yellow-nosed, dull brown vole may be distinguished from all other voles in the area by *size,* relative *length of tail,* and *yellow nose.*

**YELLOWNOSE VOLE.** *Microtus chrotorrhinus.* pp. **124**, 128
**Recognition:** — Head and body, 4½–4⅘ in.; tail, 1⅘–2 in. This medium-sized, *grayish-brown* vole may be distinguished by the rich *yellow nose.* It is often found in *rocky situations.*
**Similar species:** — Meadow Vole, Pine Vole, Redback Vole, Bog Lemming, and Brown Lemming; none with grayish brown body and rich yellow nose. Ungava Phenacomys; tail under 1⅘ in.

**RICHARDSON VOLE.** *Microtus richardsoni.* p. 130
**Recognition:** — Head and body, 5⅗–6½ in.; tail, 2⅖–3⅗ in. This is the *largest* of voles within its range. It is dull *grayish brown* with a *pale gray belly* and a *bicolor tail.* By its large size it may be recognized.
**Similar species:** — Oregon Vole; tail under 2 in. Longtail, Mountain, and Meadow voles; head and body under 5½ in. Redback Vole; back reddish, sides buffy. Others; tail less than 2 in.

**PRAIRIE VOLE.** *Microtus ochrogaster.* pp. **124**, 130
**Recognition:** — Head and body, 3½–5 in.; tail, 1⅕–1⅗ in.; wt., 20–40 gm. In the extensive *prairie* region, this is the typical vole. It is *grayish to blackish brown* with a good mixture of fulvous-tipped hairs — darkest in the South and East, palest in the Northwest. The tail is *short* for a vole and the belly is either *whitish or fulvous.*
**Similar species:** — Meadow Vole; tail usually more than 1⅗ in., sometimes difficult to distinguish. Longtail Vole; tail 2 in. or more. Mountain Vole and Mountain Phenacomys; in mountains. Redback Vole; in forest, back red. Sagebrush Vole; ash-gray. Pine Vole; auburn, tail one inch or less. Bog Lemming; grooved incisors.

**OREGON VOLE.** *Microtus oregoni.* p. 130
**Recognition:** — Head and body, 4 in.; tail, 1⅕–1⅗ in. This small, *brown, short-haired* vole spends much of its time in *underground tunnels,* which it makes just beneath the surface. The tail is *bicolor,* and the belly is *silvery.*
**Similar species:** — California and Mountain voles; fur grizzled, long. Townsend, Longtail, and Richardson voles; tail 2 in. or more, grizzled. Pacific and Tree phenacomys; tail more than 2 in. Mountain Phenacomys; near mountaintops, gray.

# SOME ODD MAMMALS

Muskrat houses in marsh

Tree cut by Beaver

**FLORIDA WATER RAT**                                pp. *135*, 134
  Round tail, water.

**MUSKRAT**                                          pp. *135*, 134
  Scaly tail flattened on sides, water.

**APLODONTIA**                                       pp. *137*, 136
  No apparent tail, moist situations.

**NUTRIA**                                           p. *139*
  Long round tail, scantily haired, water.

**ARMADILLO**                                        pp. *163*, 162
  Covered with armor plate.

**VIRGINIA OPOSSUM**                                 pp. *1*, 2
  Naked tail, white face.

**BEAVER**                                           pp. *99*, 111
  Tail scaly, flattened on top and bottom.

**PORCUPINE**                                        pp. *142*, 143
  Long sharp spines on body and tail.

**PECCARY**                                          pp. *151*, 154
  Pig-like, three toes on hind foot.

Muskrat walking. Tail mark. R.F. R.H. 3 in.± Beaver, 4 in. ± between tracks. Hind covers front. 3-6 in.

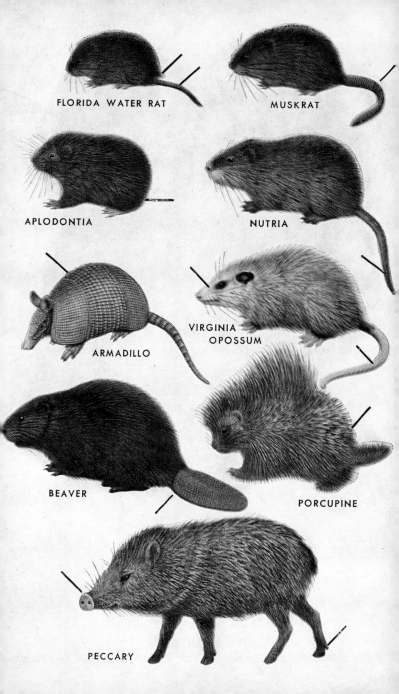

FLORIDA WATER RAT

MUSKRAT

APLODONTIA

NUTRIA

ARMADILLO

VIRGINIA
OPOSSUM

BEAVER

PORCUPINE

PECCARY

Winter

Summer

**WHITETAIL JACKRABBIT**

Winter

Summer

**SNOWSHOE HARE**

**BLACKTAIL JACKRABBIT**

**ANTELOPE JACKRABBIT**

**EUROPEAN HARE**

Winter

Summer

**ARCTIC HARE**

Plate 20                                                    133

## JACKRABBITS AND HARES

**WHITETAIL JACKRABBIT**                                    pp. *145*, 144
    *Winter:* White, large.
    *Summer:* Tail white above and below.


**SNOWSHOE HARE**                                           pp. *145*, 144
    *Winter:* White, hairs dark at bases, large hind feet.
    *Summer:* Brown, large hind feet.


**BLACKTAIL JACKRABBIT**                                    pp. *147*, 146
    Black on top of tail and rump, ears tipped black.


**ANTELOPE JACKRABBIT**                                     pp. *147*, 146
    Whitish on hips, ears huge.


**EUROPEAN HARE**                                           pp. *145*, 144
    Large, black on top of tail, open areas.


**ARCTIC HARE**                                             pp. *145*, 144
    *Winter:* Hairs white to skin.
    *Summer:* Tail white.

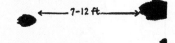

L.H.

L.F.

2¾ in. ±

Jackrabbit

7–12 ft.

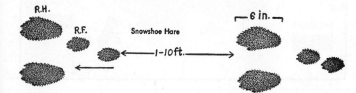

R.H.

R.F.

Snowshoe Hare

6 in.

1–10 ft.

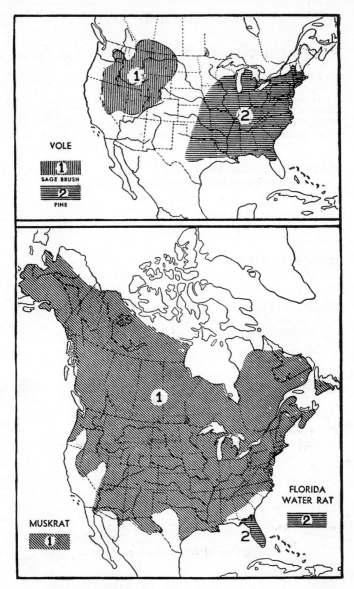

VOLE

1 SAGE BRUSH

2 PINE

MUSKRAT 1

FLORIDA WATER RAT 2

**SAGEBRUSH VOLE.** *Lagurus curtatus.* pp. **124**, 134
**Recognition:** — Head and body, $3\frac{4}{5}$–$4\frac{1}{2}$ in.; tail, $\frac{3}{5}$–$1\frac{1}{8}$ in.; wt., 22–30 gm. An extremely pale, *ash-gray* vole with *whitish belly and feet*, and a tail which usually is *less than an inch*. If found living in *sagebrush*, it is without doubt this species. It is palest of the voles, also the one found in the driest places.
**Similar species:** — Prairie Vole; dark gray, tail more than $1\frac{1}{8}$ in. Other voles; tail longer, not found in sagebrush.

**PINE VOLE.** *Pitymys pinetorum.* pp. **124**, 134
**Recognition:** — Head and body, $2\frac{4}{5}$–$4\frac{1}{5}$ in.; tail, $\frac{2}{3}$–1 in.; wt., 20–35 gm. This handsome little vole is rarely found in the pines, as the name would imply, but is more characteristic of the eastern *deciduous forest*. Its *auburn fur is thick and soft* and does not have the scattered long guard hairs found in most other voles. The ears are small and the tail is *short*.
**Similar species:** — Meadow Vole; grizzled, tail longer. Yellow-nose Vole; gray with yellow nose. Prairie Vole; grizzled. Red-back Vole; tail longer. Bog Lemming; grizzled, incisors grooved.
**Remarks:** — The Pine Vole west of the Mississippi River is considered a distinct species, *P. nemoralis*, also the one in Florida, *P. parvulus*.

**FLORIDA WATER RAT.** *Neofiber alleni.* pp. **132**, 134
**Recognition:** — Head and body, 8 in.; tail, 5 in. In the *marshes* of Florida and extreme southeastern Georgia one is likely to find this small, *roundtail* edition of the muskrat. Its *rich brown fur*, with *coarse guard hairs* over the dense underfur, and size, will distinguish it from any other water-living rodent in the area.

**MUSKRAT.** *Ondatra zibethica.* pp. **132**, 134
**Recognition:** — Head and body, 10–14 in.; tail, 8–11 in.; wt., 2–4 lb. Water is essential for this *large* rodent; however, during spring and autumn movements they are sometimes found two or three miles from water. They have *dense, rich brown fur* overlaid with coarse guard hairs. The belly is *silvery*. The long, *naked*, black tail is *flattened from side to side*. The tail alone is sufficient to distinguish the muskrat from all other mammals. Their presence in marshes may be detected by the *conical houses*, two to three feet above water, which are built of marsh vegetation.
**Remarks:** — The Muskrat on Newfoundland may be a distinct species, *O. obscura*.

# Old World Rats and Mice: Muridæ

THESE include the Norway Rat, Black Rat, and House Mouse, none of which commonly occurs far from man-made structures. They

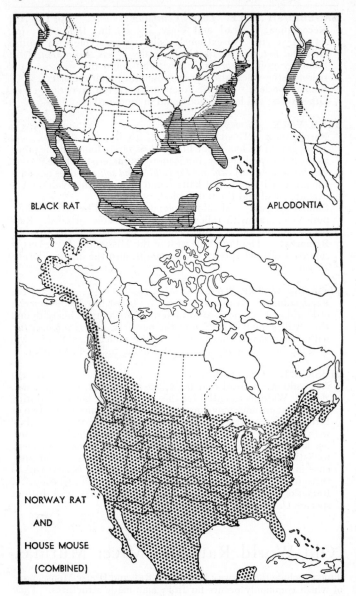

BLACK RAT

APLODONTIA

NORWAY RAT

AND

HOUSE MOUSE

(COMBINED)

are *dull grayish brown to black with long naked tails* fairly uniform in color.

**NORWAY RAT.** *Rattus norvegicus.* pp. **125**, 136
**Recognition:** — Head and body, 7–10 in.; tail, 5–8 in.; wt., 190–290 gm. Primarily an inhabitant of *cities* and *farm yards*, this rat may be distinguished by its *grayish brown* color and rather *long scaly tail.* The belly is grayish, not white.
**Similar species:** — Woodrats; belly and feet usually white, tail covered with hair. Black Rat; tail longer than head and body.

**BLACK RAT.** *Rattus rattus.* pp. **125**, 136
**Recognition:** — Head and body, 7 in., tail, 9 in. There are two color phases, *brown* and *black*, in this species. The belly may be grayish, but *never white.* The *naked* tail is *longer* than the head and body. Found chiefly around *buildings*, it is rare in the North, common in the extreme South.
**Similar species:** — Norway Rat; tail shorter than head and body.

**HOUSE MOUSE.** *Mus musculus.* pp. **120**, 136
**Recognition:** — Head and body, $3\frac{1}{5}$–$3\frac{3}{5}$ in.; tail, $2\frac{4}{5}$–$3\frac{4}{5}$ in.; wt., 12–24 gm. This small, *grayish brown* mouse with *grayish or buffy belly*, and with a *naked tail* which is about the *same color above and below*, is found chiefly in or near *buildings.* The fur is fairly short.
**Similar species:** — White-footed and Deer mice; white belly. Voles; short, haired tail. Harvest Mice; grooved incisors. Jumping Mice; white belly.

# Aplodontia: Aplodontiidæ

**APLODONTIA.** *Aplodontia rufa.* pp. **132**, 136
**Recognition:** — Head and body, 12–17 in.; tail, 1–$1\frac{1}{5}$ in. Usually in *moist* situations, this brown rodent, the size of a small house cat, makes extensive *burrows* in the moist earth. Its ears and eyes are relatively *small.* By size, color, and apparent lack of a tail, it may be distinguished from all other mammals in the area.

# Jumping Mice: Zapodidæ

MEMBERS of this family are rather small to *medium-sized* mice with extremely *long tails* and *large hind feet.* They are *yellowish to orange* along the sides, darker on the back, and have *white bellies;* the small ears are narrowly *edged with buff or white.* There are no external

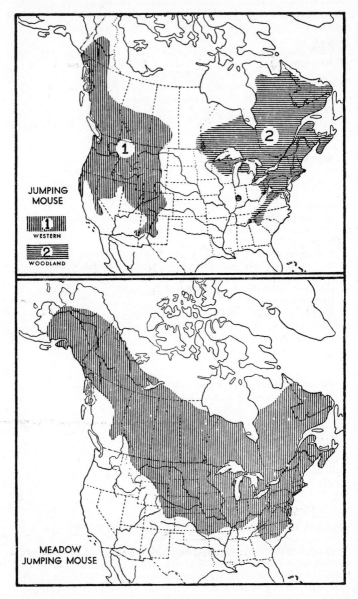

JUMPING
MOUSE

1
WESTERN

2
WOODLAND

MEADOW
JUMPING MOUSE

᠁heek pouches. The upper front teeth have *grooves* down their front surfaces. They prefer damp meadows and forests, and hibernate during the winter.

**Similar species:** — Pocket Mice and Kangaroo Rats; external cheek pouches.

**MEADOW JUMPING MOUSE.** *Zapus hudsonius.* pp. **104, 138**
    **Recognition:** — Head and body, 3–3⅛ in.; tail, 4–5⅘ in.; wt., 15–25 gm. If seen jumping through the grass, these *olive-yellow* mice might be mistaken for frogs. On close inspection, the *two tone body* and the *long*, scantily haired tail, plus the *large hind feet*, will serve to distinguish this from most other small mammals.
    **Similar species:** — Woodland Jumping Mouse; white tip on tail. Western Jumping Mouse; in mountains, head and body over 3⅛ in.

**WESTERN JUMPING MOUSE.** *Zapus princeps.*          p. 138
    **Recognition:** — Head and body, 3½–4 in.; tail, 4½–6⅛ in.; wt., 17–37 gm. Except in the far north and far west, this is chiefly a *mountain* species. Its *yellowish sides, darker back, white* (or buffy) *belly, long tail, large hind feet*, and no external cheek pouches set this species apart from most other small rodents.
    **Similar species:** — Meadow Jumping Mouse; head and body less than 3½ in., not in mountains.
    **Remarks:** — Various species names have been applied to local populations within the range here given for *princeps*. Some of these may prove to be distinct, but mostly they are difficult to distinguish and are treated as one for our purposes.

**WOODLAND JUMPING MOUSE.** *Napæozapus insignis.*
                                            pp. **104,** 138
    **Recognition:** — Head and body, 3–4 in.; tail, 5–6⅛ in.; wt., 19–27 gm. In the *deep forests*, usually not far from water, this handsome jumping mouse resides. With *bright yellowish sides, brownish back*, and *white belly*, combined with *large hind feet* and a *long white-tipped tail*, it should not be mistaken for any other mammal within its size range.
    **Similar species:** — Meadow Jumping Mouse; no white tip on tail.

# Nutrias: Capromyidæ

**NUTRIA.** *Myocastor coypus.*          p. **132**
    **Recognition:** — Head and body, 22–25 in.; tail, 12–17 in., wt., 15–18 lb. This *large, brownish*, South American rodent has been released in several places in this country, as a possible fur animal. It is probably most numerous in the marshes of *Louisiana* and *Oregon*. They are reported from as far north as Michigan in the

## COTTONTAILS AND PIKAS

Pika and haystack
in rockslide

**PIGMY RABBIT**                                      pp. *151*, 143
    Small, pale, short ears, desert brush.

**BRUSH RABBIT**                                     pp. *150*, 146
    Small, inconspicuous tail, ears short, brush.

**PIKA**                                             pp. *142*, 143
    Small, no apparent tail, rounded ears, rock slides.

**DESERT COTTONTAIL**                                pp. *150*, 146
    Pale grayish, ears large.

**MOUNTAIN COTTONTAIL**                              pp. *147*, 146
    Grayish, mountains.

**EASTERN COTTONTAIL**                               pp. *147*, 146
    Feet whitish, nape patch rusty and distinct.

**MARSH RABBIT**                                     pp. *150*, 146
    Fur coarse, marshes.

**SWAMP RABBIT**                                     pp. *150*, 146
    Feet rusty, fur coarse.

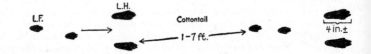

L.F.      L.H.      Cottontail          4 in.±
                1-7 ft.

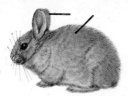

PIGMY RABBIT

BRUSH RABBIT

PIKA

DESERT COTTONTAIL

MOUNTAIN COTTONTAIL

EASTERN
COTTONTAIL

MARSH RABBIT

SWAMP RABBIT

BARREN GROUND CARIBOU

WOODLAND CARIBOU

MUSKOX

ELK

MOOSE

Plate 22                                                    141

## NORTHERN BIG GAME MAMMALS

**BARREN GROUND CARIBOU**                     pp. *159*, 160
    Small antlers, whitish.

**WOODLAND CARIBOU**                          pp. *159*, 160
    Brownish, white on rump and neck and above hoofs.

**MUSKOX**                                    pp. *161*, 160
    Long shaggy fur reaches nearly to ground.

**ELK**                                       pp. *151*, 154
    Neck chestnut brown, rump patch yellowish white.

**MOOSE**                                     pp. *155*, 154
    Palmate antlers, long snout, no white.

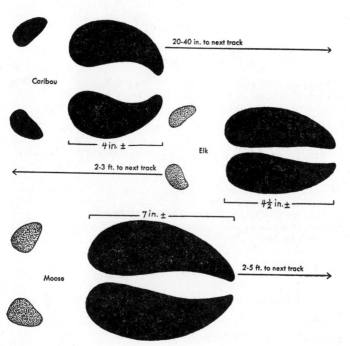

central states.  The *long, round tail is scantily haired.*  Found only near water.
**Similar species:** — Beaver and Muskrat; flattened, naked tails.

# Porcupines: Erethizontidæ

LARGE, *blackish* rodents, size of small dog, with most of body, especially the rump and tail, *thickly set with long sharp spines.*

**PORCUPINE.**  *Erethizon dorsatum.*                               pp. 132, 143
   **Recognition:** — Head and body, 18–22 in.; tail, 7–9 in.; wt., 10–28 lb.  Trees are essential to the porcupine, a *heavy-bodied, short-legged*, clumsy animal that may be seen lumbering through the forest or hunched into what appears to be a large black ball high in a tree.  Trees with the tops barked indicate the presence of porcupines nearby.  It is the only North American mammal with *long sharp quills.*

# Pikas, Hares, and Rabbits: Lagomorpha

# Pikas: Ochotonidæ

SMALL, *rat-size*, grayish to buffy or brownish, with short broad, rounded ears and *no visible tail.*  Found only in the *rock slides* and near timberline in the high mountains.

**PIKA.**  *Ochotona princeps.*                               pp. 140, 143
   **Recognition:** — Head and body, 6½–8½ in.; wt., 105–130 gm.  Small piles of *fresh hay* in the *rock slides*, high in the mountains, mean that pikas are around.  One of these *grayish* to *buffy* or *brownish* mammals may be sitting hunched up on a boulder of nearly the same color.  A series of peculiar short squeaks is further evidence.  There is *no visible tail.*  They are active during daytime, inactive at night.  The only other mammals likely to be seen in similar situations during daytime are marmots.  They are much larger and have short, bushy tails.
   **Remarks:** — The Pika in Alaska and the Yukon has been designated as a distinct species, *O. collaris.*

# Hares and Rabbits: Leporidæ

MEMBERS of this family usually have *long ears, long hind legs*, soft fur, and a *short cottony tail, white below.*

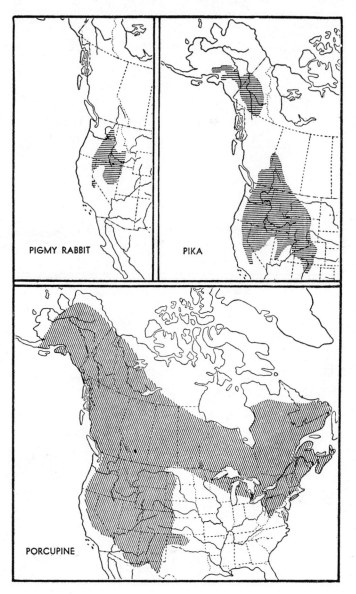

PIGMY RABBIT

PIKA

PORCUPINE

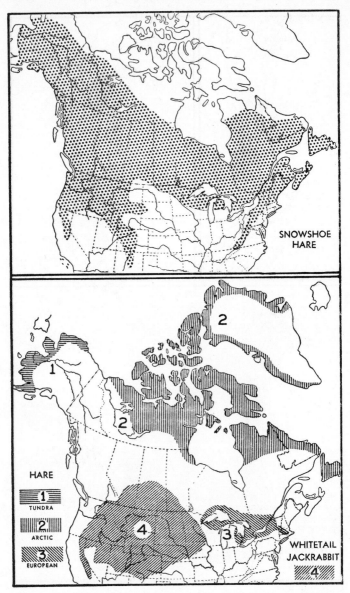

SNOWSHOE
HARE

HARE

1
TUNDRA

2
ARCTIC

3
EUROPEAN

4

WHITETAIL
JACKRABBIT

4

**ARCTIC HARE.** *Lepus arcticus.*                    pp. **133**, 144
  **Recognition:** — Head and body, 17–24 in.; ear 3¾–4¼ in., wt.,
  6–12 lb. A truly *arctic* mammal, this large hare occupies the
  barren grounds. In Ellesmere Land, northern Baffin Land, and
  Greenland, these hares remain *white throughout the year;* else-
  where they are *gray or brown in summer,* but the tail remains
  *white.* In winter the fur is *white to the base.*
  **Similar species:** — Snowshoe Hare; tail brown in summer, fur
  not white to base in winter, smaller.

**TUNDRA HARE.** *Lepus othus.*                           p. 144
  **Recognition:** — Head and body, 20–24 in.; ear 3¾–4¼ in.; wt.,
  9–10 lb. This is the western representative of the Arctic Hare
  and probably should be in the same species. It turns *brown in
  summer,* but the *tail remains white.* In winter the fur is *white to*
  the *skin.*
  **Similar species:** — Snowshoe Hare; head and body less than 20
  in., tail brown in summer, fur not white to skin in winter.

**WHITETAIL JACKRABBIT.** *Lepus townsendi.*        pp. **133**, 144
  **Recognition:** — Head and body, 18–22 in.; ear, 5–6 in.; wt., 5–8
  lb. On our northern *plains* and in the *western mountains,* this is
  the largest of the hares. It is *brownish gray* in summer, *white or
  pale gray* in winter. The tail is nearly always *white above and
  below.* It prefers open country.
  **Similar species:** — Snowshoe Hare; dark brown in summer,
  smaller, prefers forests. Blacktail Jackrabbit; top of tail black.
  Cottontails; smaller, do not turn white in winter.

**SNOWSHOE HARE.** *Lepus americanus.*              pp. **133**, 144
  **Recognition:** — Head and body, 13–18 in.; ear, 3½–4 in.; wt.,
  2–4 lb. Forests and swamps of the *colder regions* harbor this
  *large-footed* hare that turns *white* in winter. In summer it is *dark
  brown.* The white of winter is only on the tips of the hairs; beneath these is a yellowish band. Its ears are relatively small for
  a hare.
  **Similar species:** — Arctic and Tundra hares; tail always white,
  fur white to skin in winter. Whitetail Jackrabbit; tail always
  white, larger, long ears. Cottontails; brownish throughout year,
  feet usually whitish, nape patch rusty. Blacktail Jackrabbit;
  black stripe down rump and on top of tail, open areas. European Hare; larger, top of tail black, open areas.

**EUROPEAN HARE.** *Lepus europæus.*                pp. **133**, 144
  **Recognition:** — Head and body, 25–27 in.; ear, 5 in. This large,
  introduced hare prefers *open country.* It is *brownish gray,* and
  does not turn white in winter. Within its present range, it is by
  far the largest member of its group and may easily be distinguished by size alone.

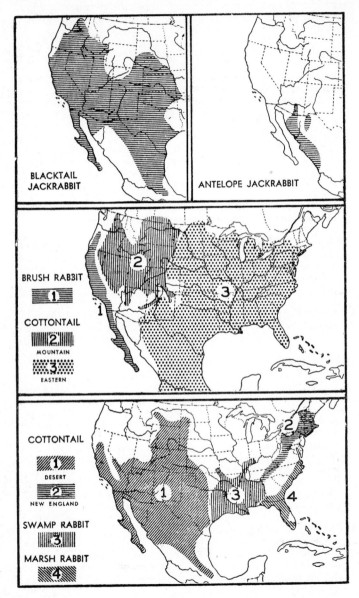

BLACKTAIL
JACKRABBIT

ANTELOPE JACKRABBIT

BRUSH RABBIT
**1**

COTTONTAIL
**2**
MOUNTAIN

**3**
EASTERN

COTTONTAIL
**1**
DESERT

**2**
NEW ENGLAND

SWAMP RABBIT
**3**

MARSH RABBIT
**4**

Similar species: — Snowshoe Hare; smaller, no black on top of tail, swamps. Cottontails; smaller, tail not black on top.

## ANTELOPE JACKRABBIT. *Lepus alleni.* pp. **133**, 146

Recognition: — Head and body, 19–21 in.; ear 7–8 in. A bounding white flash among the mesquite, giant cactus, and other desert vegetation, or a pair of *huge ears, without black* on them, erect and supported by a relatively small head, may be your introduction to this large, long-legged hare of the desert. Its pale, *whitish sides and hips* will serve for identification.

Similar species: — Blacktail Jackrabbit; brown on sides and hips, ear tips bordered with blackish. Cottontails; smaller, brown, small ears.

Remarks: — The population in extreme southern New Mexico may be of a distinct species, *L. gaillardi.*

## BLACKTAIL JACKRABBIT. *Lepus californicus.* pp. **133**, 146

Recognition: — Head and body, 17–21 in.; ear, 6–7 in.; wt., 3–7 lb. Throughout the *grasslands* and *open areas* of the West this is the common jackrabbit. In early morning and early evening they are most active, and then may be seen feeding on green vegetation, if present. Their grayish-brown bodies, *large black-tipped ears*, and the *black streak* on the top of the tail will serve to distinguish them from all near relatives.

Similar species: — Antelope Jackrabbit; white sides, no black on ears. Whitetail Jackrabbit; usually no black on top of tail, whitish in winter. Snowshow Hare; tail not black, white in winter, forests. Cottontails; much smaller, ears not black-tipped. Swamp Rabbit; no black on ears or tail, smaller.

## EASTERN COTTONTAIL. *Sylvilagus floridanus.* pp. **140**, 146

Recognition: — Head and body, 14–17 in.; ear, 2½–3 in.; wt., 2–4 lb. Heavy brush or strips or patches of forest are essential for this common cottontail. It may feed and nest in the open, but always heavy cover must be near by. It is most commonly seen during morning and evening. Its *white cottony tail,* as it bounds away, will reveal its identity.

Similar species: — Desert Cottontail; smaller, not in forests, ears longer. New England Cottontail; rusty nape patch pale or absent, reddish in summer, mountains. Swamp and Marsh rabbits; no distinct rusty nape patch, feet not pale whitish. Snowshoe Hare; larger, dark brown in summer, white in winter. European Hare and Jackrabbits; larger, ears longer, open areas.

Remarks: — The cottontails of the high mountains of central New Mexico (*S. cognatus*) and of the higher parts of the Davis, Chinati, and Chisos Mountains, Texas (*S. robustus*), are considered distinct species.

## MOUNTAIN COTTONTAIL. *Sylvilagus nuttalli.* pp. **140**, 146

Recognition: — Head and body, 12–14 in.; ear, 2⅕–2⅗ in.; wt.,

## OTHER BIG GAME MAMMALS

Whitetail Deer

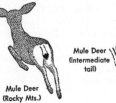

Mule Deer
(Rocky Mts.)

Mule Deer
(intermediate
tail)

Mule Deer
(Pacific Coast)

**PRONGHORN**                                              pp. *159*, *162*
    White bands on throat, whitish rump patch.

**MULE DEER**                                              pp. *155*, *158*
    *Northwest Pacific Coast:* Winter. Black on top of tail.
    *Rocky Mountains:* Winter. Large ears, whitish rump,
        black-tipped tail.
    *Head in Velvet* (Summer).

**WHITETAIL DEER**                                         pp. *155*, *158*
    *Winter, male:* Large white tail, antlers branch from main
        beam.
    *Summer, female:* Reddish coat, large white tail.
    *Fawn:* Spotted, white tail.

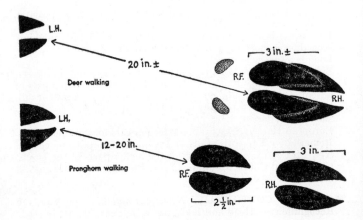

PRONGHORN

MULE DEER

Northwest Pacific Coast: Winter

Rocky Mountains: Winter

Head in velvet: Summer

Summer, female

Fawn

Winter, male

WHITETAIL DEER

MOUNTAIN GOAT

Gray phase

WHITE
SHEEP

Black phase

BIGHORN
SHEEP

WHITE SHEEP
White phase

BISON

Plate 24                                                    149

# BIG GAME MAMMALS

(With true horns)

**MOUNTAIN GOAT**                                    pp. *163*, 160
    White, horns black and smooth, beard.

**WHITE SHEEP**                                      pp. *161*, 162
    *Gray phase:* Grayish.
    *Black phase:* Blackish.

**BIGHORN SHEEP**                                    pp. *161*, 162
    Massive horns, whitish rump.

**WHITE SHEEP**                                      pp. *161*, 162
    *White phase:* Massive, yellowish horns.

**BISON**                                            pp. *161*, 160
    Hump over shoulders, massive head.

About 15 in. to next track

Mountain Goat

3 in. ±

About 15 in. to next track

Bighorn Sheep

3 in. ±

5 in. ±

3 ft. or less to next track

Bison

1½–3 lb. In the *mountains* of the West lives this *grayish* cottontail, washed with *pale yellowish*. It is usually not found below
the pines. Over most of its range, it is the only cottontail.
**Similar species:** — Desert Cottontail; valleys and low deserts,
ears longer. Snowshoe Hare; brown or white, not gray. Pigmy
Rabbit; smaller, low *desert*. Jackrabbits; larger, long ears.

**NEW ENGLAND COTTONTAIL.** *Sylvilagus transitionalis.* p. 146
   **Recognition:** — Head and body, 17 in.; ear, 2½ in. Found primarily in the *open forests*, this mountain cottontail is *reddish* in
summer and sprinkled with white to give it a *reddish-gray* appearance in winter. The nape patch, back of ears, is *pale, small, or
absent*. There is a *dark patch* between the ears.
   **Similar species:** — Eastern Cottontail; lower areas, distinct
rusty nape patch. Snowshoe Hare; feet brown in summer, white
all over in winter. European Hare; larger, top of tail black.

**DESERT COTTONTAIL.** *Sylvilagus auduboni.*     pp. 140, 146
   **Recognition:** — Head and body, 12–15 in.; ear, 3–4 in.; wt.,
1⅖–2¾ lb. This is the common cottontail of the *valleys* and
*arid* southwest. They require some brushy cover, but it is usually rather sparse. They are *pale grayish washed with yellowish*
over much of the body.
   **Similar species:** — Brush Rabbit; dark brown, smaller, shorter
ears, heavy brush. Mountain Cottontail; mountains, ears
shorter. Eastern Cottontail; larger, ears shorter. Snowshoe
Hare; high in mountains, dark brown or white. Jackrabbits;
larger, open areas. Pigmy Rabbit; smaller, heavy brush.

**BRUSH RABBIT.** *Sylvilagus bachmani.*          pp. 140, 146
   **Recognition:** — Head and body, 11–13 in.; ear, 2–2⅗ in.; wt.,
1¼–1⅘ lb. This *small brown* rabbit is found only where there is
a heavy cover of *brush*. They may be seen feeding a few feet
from cover in early morning and early evening. The ears and
tail are relatively *small* for a rabbit.
   **Similar species:** — Desert Cottontail; grayish, larger, ears
longer. Blacktail Jackrabbit; larger, open areas.

**MARSH RABBIT.** *Sylvilagus palustris.*         pp. 140, 146
   **Recognition:** — Head and body, 14–16 in.; ear, 2½–3 in.; wt.,
2½–3½ lb. This *dark brown*, coarse-haired, *small-footed* rabbit
prefers *wet* situations with dense vegetation. They readily take
to water. The feet are *reddish brown* above, darker below. The
tail is small and inconspicuous, dingy white below.
   **Similar species:** — Eastern Cottontail; hind feet whitish above,
large rusty nape patch, conspicuous white tail.

**SWAMP RABBIT.** *Sylvilagus aquaticus.*         pp. 140, 146
   **Recognition:** — Head and body, 14–17 in.; ear, 3½–4 in.; wt.,
3½–6 lb. This rich *brownish-gray* rabbit prefers *wet* areas along

streams and sloughs. The hair is coarse for a rabbit. The hind feet are *rusty above*, and the nape patch is *small* and indistinct.
**Similar species:** — Eastern Cottontail; rusty nape patch distinct, hind feet whitish.

**PIGMY RABBIT.** *Sylvilagus idahoensis.* pp. **140**, 143
   **Recognition:** — Head and body, 8½–11 in.; ear, 2¼–2½ in.; wt., ½–1 lb. In the *dense sagebrush* of the lower areas, these small *slate-gray* rabbits with a *pinkish tinge* make runways. They are difficult to see in the dense cover. They are the *smallest* of the rabbits and may be distinguished from all others on size alone.
   **Similar species:** — Cottontails; larger, conspicuous white tails

# Even-toed Hoofed Mammals: Artiodactyla

## Peccaries: Tayassuidæ

**PECCARY.** *Pecari angulatus.* pp. **132**, 154
   **Recognition:** — Head and body, 36 in.; height, 20–24 in.; wt., 40–50 lb. This *pig-like* mammal, grizzled black and grayish, lighter over the front of the shoulder, has but *three toes* on each hind foot. It prefers oak-covered hills.
   **Similar species:** — Domestic Pigs; four toes on each hind foot

## Domestic Pigs: Suidæ

**EUROPEAN WILD BOAR.** *Sus scrofa.*
   In *Georgia, North Carolina, Tennessee, Texas, New Hampshire,* and on some of the islands off southern California (*Santa Cruz*) are feral pigs or European wild boars that have been liberated. Nowhere do these overlap the range of the Peccary, which is a native wild animal.

## Deer: Cervidæ

THIS family includes *hoofed* mammals that have *antlers* which are *shed each year.* It includes our Deer, Elk, Moose, and Caribou.

**ELK.** *Cervus canadensis.* pp. **141**, 154
   **Recognition:** — Height, 4½–5 ft.; wt., females, 500–600 lb., males, 700–900 lb. This large "deer" prefers semi-open forests.

# BATS, SHREWS, AND MOLES

### (All Natural Size)

Plate 26                                                   153

## MICE, VOLES, AND RATS

(All Natural Size)

1. **PIGMY MOUSE** (*Baiomys*)                    pp. *102*, 101

2. **WESTERN HARVEST MOUSE** (*Reithrodon-
   tomys*)                                        pp. *100*, 101

3. **HOUSE MOUSE** (*Mus*)                        pp. *137*, 136

4. **MEADOW JUMPING MOUSE** (*Zapus*)             pp. *139*, 138

5. **WOODLAND JUMPING MOUSE** (*Napæozapus*) pp. *139*, 138

6. **NORTHERN GRASSHOPPER MOUSE** (*Ony-
   chomys*)                                       pp. *99*, 96

7. **DEER MOUSE** (*Peromyscus*)                  pp. *103*, 106

8. **HISPID COTTON RAT** (*Sigmodon*)             pp. *110*, 111

9. **WHITETHROAT WOODRAT** (*Neotoma*)            pp. *112*, 113

10. **RICE RAT** (*Oryzomys*)                     pp. *110*, 111

11. **BOREAL REDBACK VOLE** (*Clethrionomys*)     pp. *122*, 123

12. **PINE VOLE** (*Pitymys*)                     pp. *135*, 134

13. **MEADOW VOLE** (*Microtus*)                  pp. *126*, 123

14. **SAGEBRUSH VOLE** (*Lagurus*)                pp. *135*, 134

15. **SOUTHERN BOG LEMMING** (*Synaptomys*) pp. *115*, 116

16. **MOUNTAIN PHENACOMYS** (*Phenacomys*)        pp. *119*, 118

17. **HUDSON BAY COLLARED LEMMING** (*Di-
    crostonyx*)                                   pp. *117*, 118

18. **MUSKRAT** (*Ondatra*)                       pp. *135*, 134

19. **FLORIDA WATER RAT** (*Neofiber*)            pp. *135*, 134

20. **NORWAY RAT** (*Rattus*)                     pp. *137*, 136

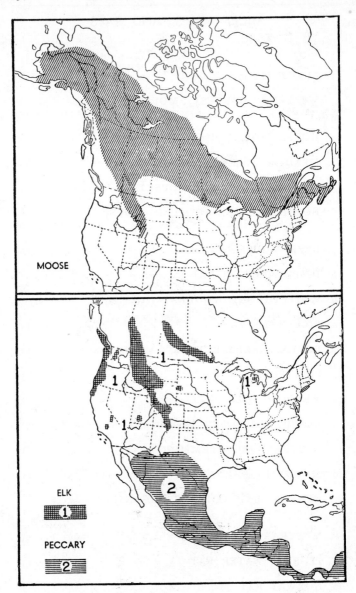

MOOSE

ELK

1

PECCARY

2

In the West they spend the summers in the mountains and the winters in the valleys. The large, *pale-yellowish* rump patch, small *white* tail, general *reddish brown* body (chestnut brown neck with a mane in males), and *huge spreading antlers* on males in late summer and autumn will serve to distinguish the elk.

**Similar species:** — Moose; brown rump. Mule Deer; black on tail. Whitetail Deer; no rump patch. Caribou, whitish neck.

**MULE DEER.** *Odocoileus hemionus.* pp. **148**, 158
**Recognition:** — Height, 3–3½ ft.; wt., 125–200 lb. The Mule Deer is found in the forests and brushy areas within its range. It is *reddish* in summer, *blue-gray* in winter. Some have a whitish rump patch; the tail is either *black-tipped or black on top*. The ears are *large* and the antlers, on males, branch *equally*, not prongs from a main beam.

**Similar species:** — Whitetail Deer; tail white on tip, antlers with main beam and prongs from it. Elk; no black on tail, larger. Woodland Caribou; no black on tail, side of neck whitish. Moose; dark brown, larger.

**Remarks:** — The Blacktail Deer of the Pacific Slope, formerly regarded as a distinct species (*Odocoileus columbianus*) is now regarded as a subspecies of the Mule Deer.

**WHITETAIL DEER.** *Odocoileus virginianus.* pp. **148**, 158
**Recognition:** — Height, 3–3½ ft.; wt., 50–275 lb. A large *white flag* wagging back and forth and disappearing into the woods indicates a Whitetail Deer on the move. They are *reddish* in summer, *blue-gray* in winter. The antlers, on males, consist of a *main beam with prongs* issuing from it. A loud, *whistling snort* from the woods, in morning or evening, means that a deer has scented you.

**Similar species:** — Mule Deer; black tip on tail, prongs of antlers not from a main beam. Elk; larger, yellowish rump patch. Woodland Caribou; whitish rump patch and neck. Moose; no white.

**Remarks:** — The Key Deer, a "toy" race of the Whitetail, weighing in the neighborhood of 50 pounds or less, is now so rare in the Florida Keys that conservationists are very concerned about its future.

**MOOSE.** *Alces americana.* pp. **141**, 154
**Recognition:** — Height, 5–6½ ft.; wt., 700–1300 lb. This large, dark brown animal prefers dense forests bordering shallow lakes. By its *large size, overhanging snout*, and pendant *"bell"* on throat, as well as its ungainly appearance, it may be distinguished from all other mammals. Males have massive, *palmate, flat antlers* with small prongs projecting from the borders. Often seen *in or near water*.

# POCKET MICE, KANGAROO RATS, POCKET GOPHERS, CHIPMUNKS, AND SQUIRRELS

## (All Natural Size)

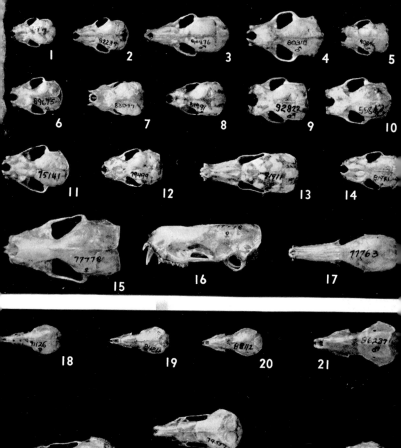

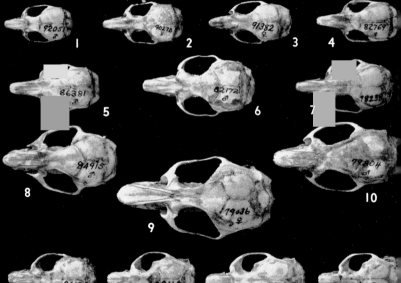

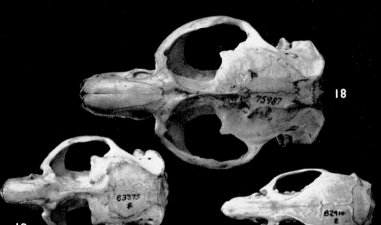

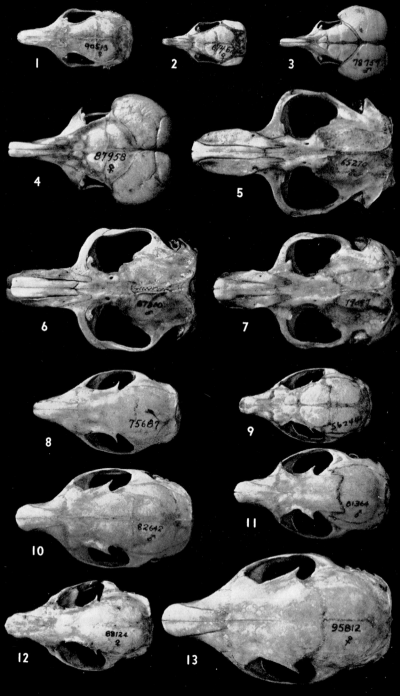

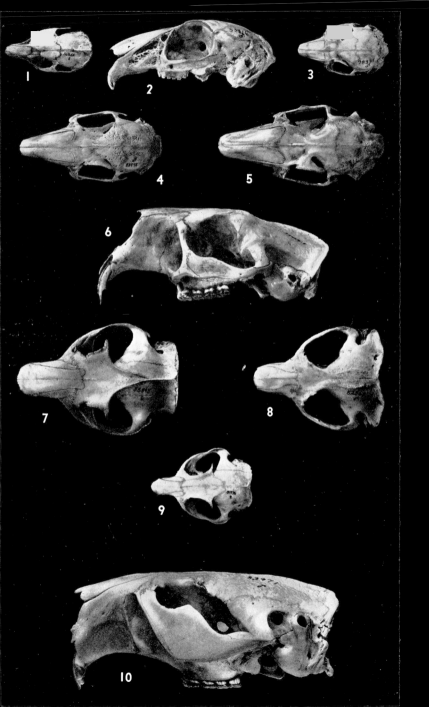

Plate 28                                             157

# RABBITS, HARES, AND MISCELLANEOUS RODENTS

### (All One-half Natural Size)

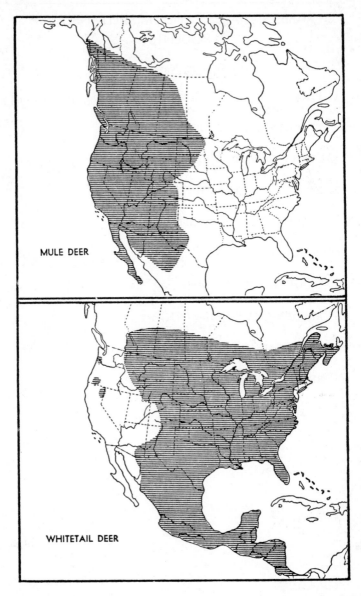

MULE DEER

WHITETAIL DEER

Similar species: — Elk; pale yellow rump patch. Deer; smaller, white on some part of body. Caribou; whitish on rump and neck.

**WOODLAND CARIBOU.** *Rangifer caribou.* pp. **141**, 160
   **Recognition:** — Height, 3½–4 ft.; wt., 150–400 lb. The Woodland Caribou is a heavy-set "deer" with *large feet* and *rounded*, not pointed, hoofs. Both sexes have *semi-palmated antlers* with one prominent brow tine down over the nose. They are brownish with *whitish on neck* and *rump* and *white above each hoof*. Prefer *muskegs*.
   Similar species: — Moose; dark brown, no white, hoofs pointed. Elk; neck chestnut brown. Mule Deer; black-tipped tail. Whitetail Deer; side of neck and rump not whitish.

**BARREN GROUND CARIBOU.** *Rangifer arcticus.* pp. **141**, 160
   **Recognition:** — Height, 3½ ft.; wt., 150–375 lb. Similar, in general, to the Woodland Caribou except slightly paler (in far north *nearly white*); antlers (on both sexes) more slender. After the southward migration in autumn the two occur together, in winter, in Manitoba and Saskatchewan, but in summer, after the northward migration, their ranges are usually separate.
   Similar species: — Moose; dark brown. Mule Deer, black on tail. Sheep and Goat; unbranched horns.

**GREENLAND CARIBOU.** *Rangifer tarandus.* p. 160
   **Recognition:** — Height, 3½ ft.; wt., 150–300 lb. Found chiefly along coast of *Greenland*.
   Similar species: — Muskox; unbranched horns, hair of body reaches nearly to ground.
   **Remarks:** — The Reindeer of Siberia has been introduced in parts of Alaska.

# Pronghorn: Antilocapridæ

THERE is but one species in this family. It is a purely North American mammal. They have true horns, a bone core covered with a horny sheath, but are peculiar in that the sheath is shed each year. *Both sexes have horns.*

**PRONGHORN.** *Antilocapra americana.* pp. **148**, 162
   **Recognition:** — Height, 3 ft.; wt., 100–125 pounds. An animal of the *open prairies* and *sagebrush flats*, this pale, *tan* antelope may be distinguished by its *large white rump patch*, white lower sides, two broad *white bands across the throat*, and slightly curved horns, each with a single *prong projecting forward*. Usually seen in groups.
   Similar species: — Bighorn Sheep; massive coiled horns, no

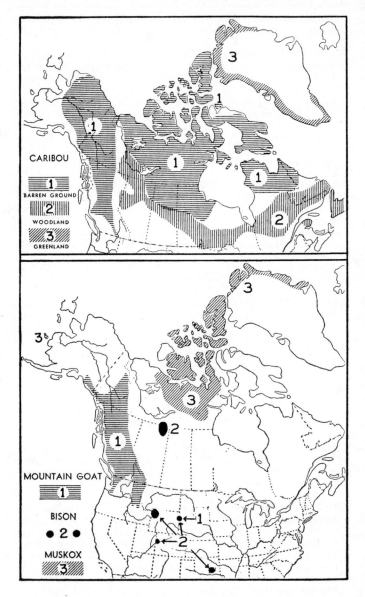

white bands across throat.  Mule Deer; black on tail.  Whitetail
Deer; no white rump patch.

# Bison, Goats, Sheep, Oxen: Bovidæ

THIS is the family to which our Domestic Cattle, Sheep, and Goats
belong.  Members have *true horns* which are *never shed* and which
are *not branched*.  Horns are present on *both sexes*.

**BISON.**  *Bison bison.*                                pp. **149**, 160
 **Recognition:** — Height, 5–6 ft.; wt., 800–2000 lb.  This large,
 dark brown beast with *massive head*, a *high hump on* its *shoulders*,
 and *long shaggy hair on shoulders and front legs*, is typically a
 *grassland* animal.  Both sexes have horns.
 **Similar species:** — Domestic Cattle; not dark brown, usually no
 large hump on shoulders.

**MUSKOX.**  *Ovibos moschatus.*                          pp. **141**, 160
 **Recognition:** — Height, 3–5 ft.  In the *far north*, this brownish ox
 may be recognized by its long fur that *hangs skirt-like nearly to
 its feet*.  The broad flat horns are *plastered close to the skull* with
 the curved tips pointing forward.  Both sexes have horns.  When
 approached Muskoxen form a defensive circle.
 **Similar species:** — Barren Ground Caribou; hair not concealing
 most of legs, antlers, not horns.

**BIGHORN SHEEP.**  *Ovis canadensis.*                    pp. **149**, 162
 **Recognition:** — Height, 3–3½ ft.; wt., 125–275 lb.  This brown
 to grayish-brown sheep has a *creamy white rump* and *massive
 horns* (smaller in females) that spiral back, out, and then forward
 to complete an arc.  At home in the *rugged mountainous country*,
 it is usually seen in bands of six or more.
 **Similar species:** — Mountain Goat; white.  Deer; with branched
 antlers or none.
 **Remarks:** — The Bighorn Sheep of the Southwestern desert
 mountains, a pale race, has been the subject of recent atten-
 tion by conservationists.

**WHITE SHEEP.**  *Ovis dalli.*                           pp. **149**, 162
 **Recognition:** — Height, 3–3¼ ft.; wt., 125–200 lb.  This
 stocky, *white or whitish* sheep (nearly black in the south of its
 range) is found in the *inaccessible mountain areas* of the Northwest.  Both sexes have horns, massive in the males, smaller in
 females.  Usually seen in bands of six or more.  Included here is
 the "Stone Sheep," a blackish color phase, and the "Fannin
 Sheep," an intermediate phase.

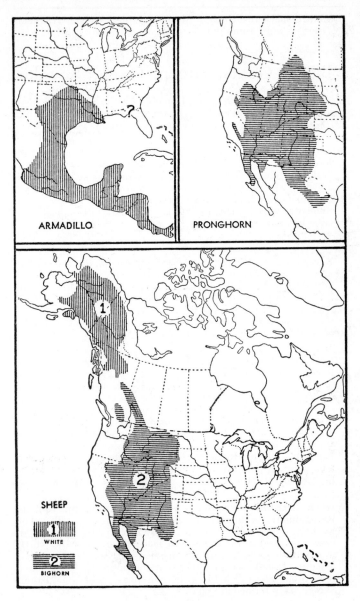

ARMADILLO

PRONGHORN

SHEEP

1
WHITE

2
BIGHORN

**Similar species:** — Mountain Goat; long fur, a beard, small, slender, black horns that curve slightly backward.

**MOUNTAIN GOAT.** *Oreamnos americanus.*          pp. **149**, 160
  **Recognition:** — Height, 3–3½ ft.; wt., 125–300 lb. On the *rocky crags near snow line*, this *white* goat with long fur and short, *smooth, black horns* that curve slightly backwards may be seen at a distance by the adventurer.
  **Similar species:** — White Sheep; horns massive, yellowish, and spiral-shaped.

# Sloths, Armadillos: Xenarthra
# Armadillos: Dasypodidæ

THIS is chiefly a tropical family. They have *degenerate teeth,* and the body is covered with a *protective "armor" of horny material.* Small, scattered hairs grow from between the plates.

**ARMADILLO.** *Dasypus novemcinctus.*          pp. **132**, 162
  **Recognition:** — Head and body, 15–17 in.; tail, 14–16 in. This peculiar *"armored"* mammal is about the size of a house cat. The body, tail, and top of head are *covered with horny material.* They roll into a ball for protection. It is the only mammal here included that has a protective cover of armor plate. It prefers low brushy areas, and is extending its range northward. By introduction, it is now common in parts of Florida.

# Dugongs and Manatees: Sirenia
# Manatees: Trichechidæ

**MANATEE.** *Trichechus manatus.*          p. **171**
  **Recognition:** — Length, 7–13 ft. In the *shallow waters* along the coast, including *lagoons* and *river mouths*, lives this sluggish aquatic mammal with *broad head, thick lips,* front flippers, and a broad, horizontally flattened and rounded tail. There are no hind legs (flippers). The muzzle is adorned with stiff bristles. The Manatee eats aquatic vegetation.
  **Range:** — From Beaufort, North Carolina, south to the Florida Keys, and along the coast of the Gulf of Mexico.
  **Similar species:** — Whales and Porpoises; usually in deep water some distance from shore, tails not rounded.

## WEASEL AND RACCOON FAMILIES

(All One-half Natural Size)

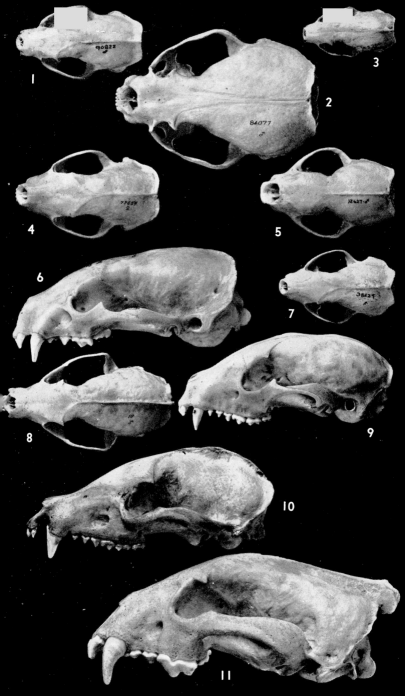

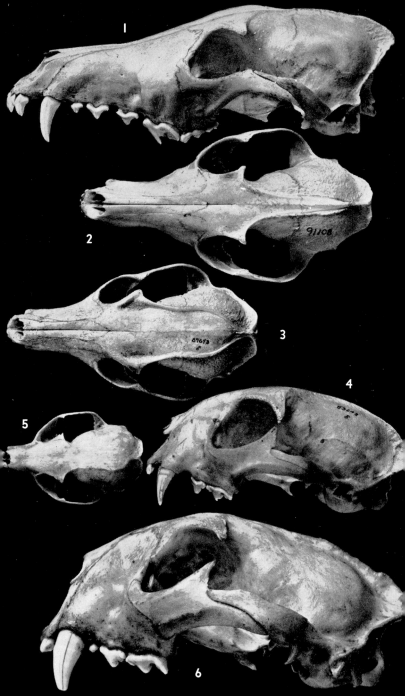

Plate 30                                    165

# DOGS AND CATS

(All One-half Natural Size)

# Whales and Porpoises: Cetacea

THESE are strictly *marine* mammals as far as North America is concerned. They are *fish-like* in general appearance except that the *tail fluke is horizontal*, not vertical. Also, they breathe air and must come to the surface periodically. Just before they break water, they expell air, and the vapor one sees as they "blow" is the water carried up by the force of the expelled air and the condensation of moisture in that air. The large whales usually are not seen at close range, unless washed up on a beach, and are difficult for the novice to identify. Porpoises and dolphins play off the bows of boats and may be seen at close range, making identification easier.

# Baleen Whales: Balænidæ

WHALES *without teeth*, but with *strips of whalebone*, baleen, hanging from the roof of the mouth.

**ATLANTIC RIGHT WHALE.** *Eubalæna glacialis.*
　　**Recognition:** — Length, 35–55 ft. This large, *blackish* whale, sometimes pale on the belly, has *no dorsal* (back) *fin*, and the skin on the throat is *smooth*. It is a whalebone whale, has no teeth, but has long strips of *black whalebone* hanging from the roof of the mouth. The spout, 10–15 ft. high, comes out *in two columns* which diverge to form a V.
　　**Range:** — Chiefly in the North Atlantic, south as far as South Carolina.

**PACIFIC RIGHT WHALE.** *Eubalæna sieboldi.*　　　　　　p. **171**
　　**Recognition:** — Length, 60–70 ft. This large whalebone whale is similar to the Atlantic Right Whale, but larger. *No dorsal fin; throat smooth;* spout *in two divergent columns,* V-shaped, 15 ft. high.
　　**Range:** — California north to the Aleutian Islands.

**BOWHEAD WHALE.** *Balæna mysticetus.*　　　　　　　　p. **171**
　　**Recognition:** — Length, 50–65 ft. The Bowhead is found only in the *polar* and *subpolar* seas, usually near the *edge of the ice*. It has an extremely large head, *more than one-third of length of animal,* and *no dorsal fin.* It is dark, grayish brown. When loafing, a part of its back may project above the water.
　　**Range:** — Circumpolar; polar and subpolar seas.

# Gray Whales: Rhachianectidæ

THIS family has *baleen, not teeth*, in the mouth.

**GRAY WHALE.** *Rhachianectes glaucus.*     p. **171**
  **Recognition:** — Length, 35–45 ft. This medium-sized, *blotched grayish-black* whale is often seen, especially in migration, fairly close inshore. It is rather slender and its spouts are *quick and low* (about 10 ft. high). It has *two to four longitudinal folds* on the throat and the baleen is a little over a foot in length. There is a slight hump, but *no fin*, on the back.
  **Range:** — Pacific Coast.

# Finback Whales: Balænopteridæ

BALEEN whales without teeth.

**FINBACK WHALE.** *Balænoptera physalus.*     p. **171**
  **Recognition:** — Length, 60–70 ft. This large, *flat-headed* whale, with *many longitudinal furrows* on the throat, has a *small dorsal fin* a short distance in front of the tail. The back is *gray* and the belly is *white*. The baleen is streaked *purple and white*. The columnar spout, 15–20 ft. high, is accompanied by a loud *whistling sound*. It rises as a narrow column then expands into an ellipse. Sometimes, these whales come close to ships.
  **Range:** — Atlantic and Pacific Coasts.

**RORQUAL.** *Balænoptera borealis.*     p. **171**
  **Recognition:** — Length, 50 ft. Similar to the Finback, but smaller, and with a relatively larger dorsal fin. The baleen is *black*. This is a rare whale.
  **Range:** — Atlantic and Pacific.

**PIKED WHALE.** *Balænoptera acutorostrata.*     p. **171**
  **Recognition:** — Length, 20–30 ft. This small rare finback with *whitish baleen* prefers coastal waters. The dorsal fin is *far back* and has a *curved tip*. A broad *white band* crosses the upper side of the flipper. The throat is *furrowed*.
  **Range:** — Atlantic and Pacific.

**BLUE WHALE.** *Sibbaldus musculus.*     p. **171**
  **Recognition:** — Length up to 100 ft.; wt., up to 150 tons. This is the *largest animal* that is known to man, past or present. It is

## MISCELLANEOUS

(Numbers 1–4, One-half Natural Size)

1. **ARMADILLO**  (side view) (*Dasypus*)          pp. *163*, 162

2. **ARMADILLO** (top view)                        pp. *163*, 162

3. **VIRGINIA  OPOSSUM** (top view) (*Didelphis*)     pp. *1*, *2*

4. **VIRGINIA  OPOSSUM** (side view)               pp. *1*, *2*

(Numbers 5–7, One-fourth Natural Size)

5. **PECCARY**  (*Pecari*)                         pp. *151*, 154

6. **BLACK  BEAR**  (*Ursus americanus*)          pp. *32*, 33

7. **BIG  BROWN  BEAR**  (*Ursus middendorffi*)   pp. *34*, 33

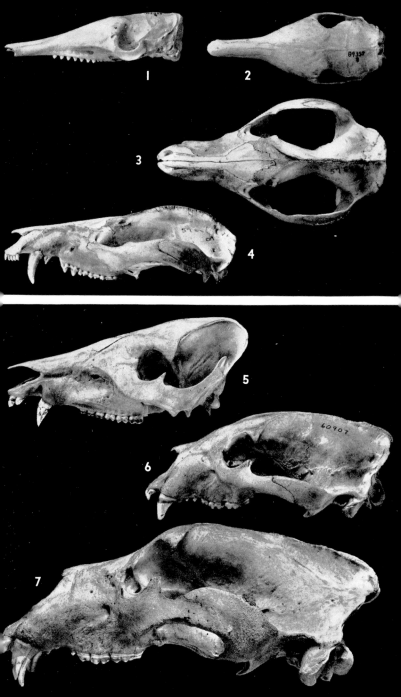

Plate 32                                    169

# HOOFED MAMMALS

### (All One-sixth Natural Size)

1. **MOOSE** (antlers shed) (*Alces*)                    pp. *155,* 154

2. **BARREN GROUND CARIBOU** (antlers removed) (*Rangifer*)                    pp. *159,* 160

3. **WHITETAIL DEER** (antlers shed) (*Odocoileus*) pp. *155,* 158

4. **ELK** (female, no antlers) (*Cervus*)                    pp. *151,* 154

5. **PRONGHORN** (horn sheaths removed) (*Antilocapra*)                    pp. *159,* 162

6. **WHITE SHEEP** (horn sheaths removed) (*Ovis*) pp. *161,* 162

7. **BISON** (horn sheaths removed) (*Bison*)                    pp. *161,* 160

slaty to *bluish gray* above, *yellowish or whitish* on the belly. The throat has many longitudinal *furrows*, and the small dorsal fin is far back on the body. The baleen is *bluish black*. The spout is *vertical* and may be 20 ft. high.

**Range:** — Atlantic and Pacific Coasts, commonest near pack ice.

**HUMPBACK WHALE.** *Megaptera novæangliæ.*    p. 171
   **Recognition:** — Length, 40–50 ft. This is a relatively short, thick-bodied whale with *long pectoral fins* (equal to distance from eye to end of snout) and a small dorsal fin well back on the body. It is black except for the *white, furrowed throat and breast.* The flippers have *fleshy knobs* along their front borders and the fluke is *irregular* in outline on its posterior border. The spout is an *expanding column* about 20 ft. high.
   **Range:** — Pacific and Atlantic Coasts.

# Sperm Whales: Physeteridæ

MEMBERS of this family have *teeth*, not baleen.

**SPERM WHALE.** *Physeter catodon.*    p. 173
   **Recognition:** — Length, 40–60 ft. This *square-snouted, large-headed* whale has a relatively small, *narrow lower jaw.* There is *no dorsal fin.* It is bluish gray above, paler below. The spout is prolonged and *directed forward* at a distinct angle.
   **Range:** — Pacific and Atlantic, between Arctic and Antarctic circles.

**PIGMY SPERM WHALE.** *Kogia breviceps.*    p. 173
   **Recognition:** — Length, 9–13 ft. This is one of the *smallest* of the whales. It has a *broad protruding snout* and a *narrow lower jaw* set with many teeth. It is black above, grayish white below. It is seldom seen.
   **Range:** — Warm waters of both coasts, north to Nova Scotia.

# Dolphins and Porpoises: Delphinidæ

MEMBERS of this family have *teeth.*

**SPOTTED DOLPHIN.** *Stenella plagiodon.*    p. 173
   **Recognition:** — Length, 5–7 ft. This small grayish-black dolphin has numerous small *white spots* on its back. The belly is pale gray. The rather *long snout* is separated from the forehead by a distinct *transverse groove.* It has a dorsal fin.
   **Range:** — Atlantic Coast, from North Carolina to Texas.

**LONGBEAK DOLPHIN.** *Steno rostratus.*
   **Recognition:** — Length, 7–8 ft. An inhabitant of *temperate*

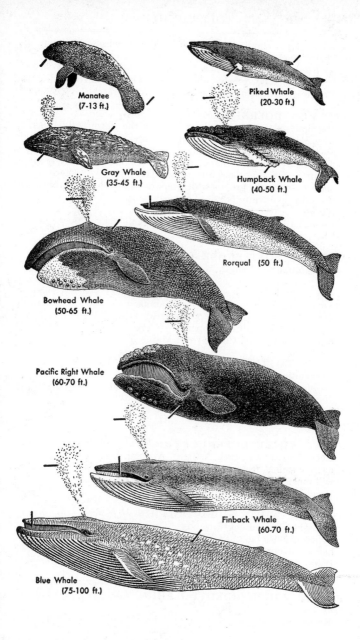

Manatee
(7-13 ft.)

Piked Whale
(20-30 ft.)

Gray Whale
(35-45 ft.)

Humpback Whale
(40-50 ft.)

Rorqual (50 ft.)

Bowhead Whale
(50-65 ft.)

Pacific Right Whale
(60-70 ft.)

Finback Whale
(60-70 ft.)

Blue Whale
(75-100 ft.)

waters, this small dolphin, black above, white (including the beak) below, is rare along the North American coasts. There is *no transverse groove* between beak and forehead. The slender beak is *compressed* from side to side. This is a rare species.
**Range:** — Atlantic and Pacific, temperate waters.

**COMMON DOLPHIN.** *Delphinus delphis.*                     p. **173**
  **Recognition:** — Length, 6½–8½ ft. In the warm and temperate waters, usually some distance from shore, one is likely to see this average-sized dolphin playing in front of a ship. The back and flippers are *black*, the flanks are *yellowish*, and the belly is *white*. Around each eye is a white ring. The *white eye-rings* are connected, across the groove which separates the beak from the forehead, by two white lines. The beak is about 6 in. long.
  **Range:** — Atlantic and Pacific.
  **Remarks:** — The Pacific Dolphin is thought by some to be distinct, *Delphinus bairdi.*

**ATLANTIC BOTTLENOSE DOLPHIN.** *Tursiops truncatus.*
  **Recognition:** — Length, 9–12 ft. This is the *commonest* dolphin along the Atlantic Coast. It may be recognized by its *large* size and general *grayish* coloration, slightly paler beneath than on back. The relatively *short beak* (about 3 in. long) is separated from the forehead by a *transverse groove.* The lower jaw is slightly *longer* than the upper.
  **Range:** — Atlantic Coast, from Maine to Texas.

**PACIFIC BOTTLENOSE DOLPHIN.** *Tursiops gilli.*      p. **173**
  **Recognition:** — Length, 10–12 ft. A rather large dolphin, grayish-black above, white beneath, except for dark area from vent to fluke, and with *white on the upper lip*, may be seen off the west coast.
  **Range:** — Pacific Coast.

**RIGHT WHALE DOLPHIN.** *Lissodelphis borealis.*        p. **173**
  **Recognition:** — Length, 5–8 ft. A small, black dolphin with a narrow *white belly strip* from breast to tail, and with *no dorsal fin*, will most certainly be of this species.
  **Range:** — Pacific Coast.

**ATLANTIC WHITE–SIDED DOLPHIN.** *Lagenorhynchus acutus.*
  **Recognition:** — Length, 7–9 ft. This dolphin may be recognized by its blackish back, white belly, and a *pale area* along either side below the dorsal fin. There are *yellowish streaks* along the sides. It has a *prominent dorsal fin* and a rather *short, blunt nose.*
  **Range:** — Atlantic Coast, south to Cape Cod.

**PACIFIC WHITE–SIDED DOLPHIN.** *Lagenorhynchus obliquidens.*                                                           p. **173**
  **Recognition:** — Length, 7–9 ft. This average-sized dolphin has

Spotted Dolphin
(5-7 ft.)

Common Dolphin
(6½-8½ ft.)

Right Whale Dolphin
(5-8 ft.)

Pacific White-sided Dolphin
(7-9 ft.)

Pacific Bottlenose Dolphin
(10-12 ft.)

Whitebeak Dolphin
(7-10 ft.)

Pigmy Sperm Whale
(9-13 ft.)

Grampus
(9-13 ft.)

Atlantic
Killer Whale
(15-30 ft.)

Sperm Whale
(40-60 ft.)

a greenish-black back, a *pale stripe along each side*, and a white belly. Its nose is blunt.

**Range:** — Pacific Coast, south to California.

**WHITEBEAK DOLPHIN.** *Lagenorhynchus albirostris.* p. **173**
  **Recognition:** — Length, 7–10 ft. In the North Atlantic one is likely to encounter this medium-sized, blackish dolphin with a *pale stripe* along each side, a whitish belly, and a *white beak*, about 2 in. long.
  **Range:** — Extreme North Atlantic, south to Labrador.

**ATLANTIC KILLER WHALE.** *Grampus orca.* p. **173**
  **Recognition:** — Length, 15–30 ft. If seen at sea, the first indication of a killer whale would probably be the *large, exposed dorsal fin* cutting the surface of the water. If it exposes a jet-black body with *white extending up on the side* posteriorly, it is this species. It also has a clear white spot behind each eye and a white belly. The nose is blunt and the jaws are set with many teeth.
  **Range:** — Atlantic Coast.

**PACIFIC KILLER WHALE.** *Grampus rectipinna.*
  **Recognition:** — Length, 20–30 ft. Characters as given for the Atlantic Killer Whale.
  **Range:** — Pacific Coast.

**GRAMPUS.** *Gramphidelphis griseus.* p. **173**
  **Recognition:** — Length, 9–13 ft. The Grampus is rather *blunt-nosed* with a dark gray or blackish body marked with numerous *irregular streaks.* The head is tinged with *yellow*, the belly is grayish white and the *slender flippers* are mottled grayish.
  **Range:** — Atlantic and Pacific.

**FALSE KILLER.** *Pseudorca crassidens.* p. **175**
  **Recognition:** — Length, 13–18 ft. This small, black, *slender* whale has a relatively small, *recurved dorsal fin* just in front of the middle of the body. The snout is blunt and rounded, and the head is flattened.
  **Range:** — Atlantic and Pacific.

**COMMON BLACKFISH.** *Globicephala ventricosa.* p. **175**
  **Recognition:** — Length, 14–28 ft. *Uniformly black*, the Blackfish has a rather large, recurved dorsal fin that is well forward of the middle of the body. The flippers are about *one-fifth* the length of the body. The forehead is *high* and *bulges forward.* They normally travel in large schools. Schools are occasionally stranded on the beach.
  **Range:** — Atlantic.

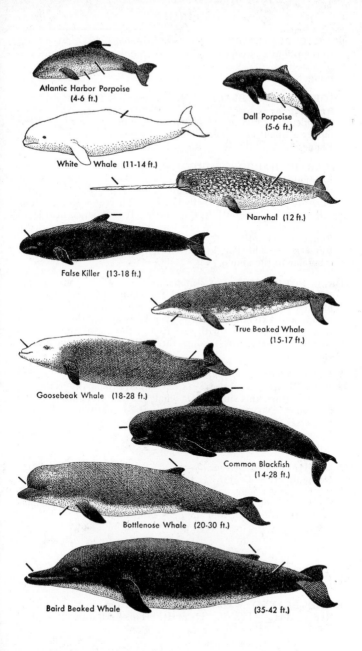

Atlantic Harbor Porpoise
(4-6 ft.)

Dall Porpoise
(5-6 ft.)

White Whale (11-14 ft.)

Narwhal (12 ft.)

False Killer (13-18 ft.)

True Beaked Whale
(15-17 ft.)

Goosebeak Whale (18-28 ft.)

Common Blackfish
(14-28 ft.)

Bottlenose Whale (20-30 ft.)

Baird Beaked Whale          (35-42 ft.)

**PACIFIC BLACKFISH.** *Globicephala scammoni.*
    **Recognition:** — Length, 14–16 ft.  Similar to the Common Blackfish.
    **Range:** — Pacific.

**SHORT-FINNED BLACKFISH.** *Globicephala brachyptera.*
    **Recognition:** — Length, 15–20 ft.; flipper, 2½–3 ft.  This species is difficult to distinguish from the Common Blackfish.  The flipper is about *one-sixth* as long as the body.
    **Range:** — Atlantic Coast, north to New Jersey.

**ATLANTIC HARBOR PORPOISE.** *Phocœna phocœna.*  p. **175**
    **Recognition:** — Length, 4–6 ft.  The Harbor Porpoise is a *small*, thick-bodied animal with a blunt snout.  The back is *black*, the sides are *pinkish*, and the belly is *white*.  There is a *dark line* from the corner of the mouth to the flipper.  It is common near shore and in harbors.
    **Range:** — Atlantic.
    **Remarks:** — The Pacific Harbor Porpoise, *Phocœna vomerina*, is similar to the above.

**DALL PORPOISE.** *Phocœnoides dalli.*                           p. **175**
    **Recognition:** — Length, 5–6 ft.  The Dall Porpoise is strikingly marked.  It is *black* except for a *large white area* across the vent region and extending slightly over halfway up the sides; the front edge about even with the front of the dorsal fin.
    **Range:** — Pacific Coast, south rarely to Santa Barbara Islands, California.

**WHITE WHALE.** *Delphinapterus leucas.*                         p. **175**
    **Recognition:** — Length, 11–14 ft.  Found principally in the cold *Arctic* waters, this small *white* whale may be recognized by size and color.  No other cetaceans have these characters.  There is no dorsal fin.
    **Range:** — Atlantic and Pacific, chiefly in cold waters, rarely south as far as New Jersey.

**NARWHAL.** *Monodon monoceros.*                                 p. **175**
    **Recognition:** — Length, 12 ft.  The Narwhal is peculiar in that the male has a *long, spirally twisted tusk projecting forward* from the blunt snout.  This tusk may reach a length of 9 ft.  The back is mottled gray and the belly is white.
    **Range:** — Arctic Seas.

# Beaked Whales: Ziphiidæ

MEMBERS of this family have *teeth*, sometimes small, but *no baleen*.

**BAIRD BEAKED WHALE.** *Berardius bairdi.*               p. **175**
    **Recognition:** — Length, 35–42 ft.  This is a rare and little-

known whale. It is black with a *whitish area on the lower belly*. The snout is formed into a definite beak; the dorsal fin is small and set far back on the body.

**Range:** — Pacific Coast, south to California.

**SOWERBY WHALE.** *Mesoplodon bidens.*
    **Recognition:** — Length, 16 ft. A rare and little-known species, this beaked whale has a dorsal fin well back on the body. It is *dark gray* above, paler on the sides and belly.
    **Range:** — North Atlantic, south to Massachusetts.
    **Remarks:** — Two other similar species, *Mesoplodon densirostris* (length, 12 ft.) and *M. europæus* (length, 22 ft.) are also rarely encountered in the North Atlantic.

**TRUE BEAKED WHALE.** *Mesoplodon mirus.*      p. **175**
    **Recognition:** — Length, 15–17 ft. A small whale, slaty-black on top, paler on belly, and with *two anteriorly-converging grooves on the throat*. The dorsal fin is well back on the body.
    **Range:** — Southeast coast of United States.

**PACIFIC BEAKED WHALE.** *Mesoplodon stejnegeri.*
    **Recognition:** — Length, 17 ft. This is a rare, blackish whale with gray on the belly. Its snout is elongated into a beak and the dorsal fin is small.
    **Range:** — Pacific Coast, south to Oregon.

**GOOSEBEAK WHALE.** *Ziphius cavirostris.*      p. **175**
    **Recognition:** — Length, 18–28 ft. This small whale is variable in color, gray to black on back with occasional white on head and back. The sides are brownish or spotted and the belly is usually whitish. Grooves on the throat converge toward the front. The body is thick, and there is a distinct *keel from the dorsal fin to the tail*. *No notch between flukes*. Usually travel in schools of 30 or more.
    **Range:** — Atlantic and Pacific.

**BOTTLENOSE WHALE.** *Hyperoodon ampullatus.*      p. **175**
    **Recognition:** — Length, 20–30 ft. This small whale of the northern waters is black to light brown or yellowish with *whitish about the head* and a whitish belly. The small dorsal fin is well back on the body. The forehead of the male *rises abruptly* from the short beak, and old males may be recognized by a *whitish patch on the forehead* and a *white dorsal fin*.
    **Range:** — Arctic and Atlantic.

# Dental Formulæ

THE FOLLOWING list of dental formulæ for the land mammals may aid in identifying skulls that are picked up in the field. The symbols I, C, P, and M refer to incisors, canines, premolars, and molars,

respectively. The formula $I \frac{5-5}{4-4}$, $C \frac{1-1}{1-1}$, $P \frac{3-3}{3-3}$, $M \frac{4-4}{4-4} = \frac{26}{24} = 50$

means that there are 5 incisors on each side in the upper jaw and 4 on each side in the lower jaw. Similarly, with the canines, premolars, and molars. Further, that there are 26 teeth, in all, in the upper and 24 in the lower jaw, or a total of 50 teeth. There is only one North American land mammal with this formula, the Opossum (*Didelphis*). Identification from the Opossum skull can, therefore, be positive by counting the teeth. Suppose you have a skull with a total of 36 teeth. It could be either of two moles, a bat, or a River Otter. If it has 20 teeth above and 16 below it is an Eastern Mole (*Scalopus*); if it has 16 above and 20 below it is a Big-eared Bat (*Corynorhinus*), the map (p. 28) will tell you the species; if it has 18 above and 18 below, it is either a Shrew-mole (*Neürotrichus*) or a River Otter (*Lutra*). If found anywhere but in the northwestern United States it would be an Otter, but if found within the range of the Shrew-mole, you will note that it has 4 incisors above and 2 below, whereas the River Otter has 6 above and 6 below. You can also refer to the photographs of skulls (pp. 152, 164) which should indicate that it is either a mole or a flesh-eater. For many of the rodents, with 16, 20, or 22 teeth, one cannot come so close to the species as in the above examples. The pictures, again, might help some, but for positive identification they should be sent to a specialist. Scientific names of the genera are given after the dental formulæ. Reference to the proper place in the text may be gained through the index. (p. 189).

| | Incisors | Canines | Pre-Molars | Molars | U and L | Total | Identifies Land Mammals Below |
|---|---|---|---|---|---|---|---|
| U | 5-5 | 1-1 | 3-3 | 4-4 | 26 | = 50 | Didelphis |
| L | 4-4 | 1-1 | 3-3 | 4-4 | 24 | | |
| U | 3-3 | 1-1 | 4-4 | 3-3 | 22 | = 44 | Parascalops, Scapanus, Condylura |
| L | 3-3 | 1-1 | 4-4 | 3-3 | 22 | | |
| U | 3-3 | 1-1 | 4-4 | 2-2 | 20 | = 42 | Ursus, Thalarctos, Vulpes, Urocyon, Canis, Alopex |
| L | 3-3 | 1-1 | 4-4 | 3-3 | 22 | | |
| U | 3-3 | 1-1 | 4-4 | 2-2 | 20 | = 40 | Procyon, Nasua, Bassariscus |
| L | 3-3 | 1-1 | 4-4 | 2-2 | 20 | | |
| U | 2-2 | 1-1 | 3-3 | 3-3 | 18 | = 38 | Myotis, Pecari |
| L | 3-3 | 1-1 | 3-3 | 3-3 | 20 | | |
| U | 3-3 | 1-1 | 4-4 | 1-1 | 18 | = 38 | Martes, Gulo |
| L | 3-3 | 1-1 | 4-4 | 2-2 | 20 | | |
| U | 3-3 | 1-1 | 3-3 | 3-3 | 20 | = 36 | Scalopus |
| L | 2-2 | 0-0 | 3-3 | 3-3 | 16 | | |
| U | 2-2 | 1-1 | 3-3 | 3-3 | 18 | = 36 | Neürotrichus |
| L | 1-1 | 1-1 | 4-4 | 3-3 | 18 | | |
| U | 2-2 | 1-1 | 2-2 | 3-3 | 16 | = 36 | Corynorhinus |
| L | 3-3 | 1-1 | 3-3 | 3-3 | 20 | | |
| U | 3-3 | 1-1 | 4-4 | 1-1 | 18 | = 36 | Lutra |
| L | 3-3 | 1-1 | 3-3 | 2-2 | 18 | | |
| U | 2-2 | 1-1 | 2-2 | 3-3 | 16 | = 34 | Mormoops, Macrotus |
| L | 2-2 | 1-1 | 3-3 | 3-3 | 18 | | |

## DENTAL FORMULÆ (continued)

| | Incisors | Canines | Pre-Molars | Molars | U and L | Total | Identifies Land Mammals Below |
|---|---|---|---|---|---|---|---|
| U | 2-2 | 1-1 | 2-2 | 3-3 | 16 | | |
| L | 3-3 | 1-1 | 2-2 | 3-3 | 18 | = 34 | Pipistrellus, Euderma |
| U | 3-3 | 1-1 | 3-3 | 1-1 | 16 | | |
| L | 3-3 | 1-1 | 3-3 | 2-2 | 18 | = 34 | Mustela, Spilogale, Mephitis, Taxidea |
| U | 0-0 | 1-1 | 3-3 | 3-3 | 14 | | |
| L | 3-3 | 1-1 | 3-3 | 3-3 | 20 | = 34 | Cervus, Rangifer |
| U | 3-3 | 1-1 | 3-3 | 3-3 | 20 | | |
| L | 1-1 | 1-1 | 1-1 | 3-3 | 12 | = 32 | Sorex, Microsorex, Blarina |
| U | 2-2 | 1-1 | 1-1 | 3-3 | 14 | | |
| L | 3-3 | 1-1 | 2-2 | 3-3 | 18 | = 32 | Eptesicus |
| U | 1-1 | 1-1 | 2-2 | 3-3 | 14 | | |
| L | 3-3 | 1-1 | 2-2 | 3-3 | 18 | = 32 | Lasiurus, Tadarida mexicana, Tadarida cynocephala |
| U | 3-3 | 1-1 | 3-3 | 1-1 | 16 | | |
| L | 3-3 | 1-1 | 3-3 | 2-2 | 16 | = 32 | Enhydra |
| U | 3-3 | 1-1 | 2-2 | 1-1 | 14 | | |
| L | 3-3 | 1-1 | 3-3 | 2-2 | 18 | = 32 | Conepatus |
| U | 0-0 | 0-0 | 3-3 | 3-3 | 12 | | |
| L | 3-3 | 1-1 | 3-3 | 3-3 | 20 | = 32 | Odocoileus, Alces, Rangifer, Antilocapra, Bison, Ovibos, Ovis, Oreamnos |
| U | 0-0 | 0-0 | { 8-8 | | 16 | | |
| L | 0-0 | 0-0 | { 8-8 | | 16 | = 32 | Dasypus |
| U | 3-3 | 1-1 | 2-2 | 3-3 | 18 | | |
| L | 1-1 | 1-1 | 1-1 | 3-3 | 12 | = 30 | Cryptotis |

DENTAL FORMULÆ (continued)

|   | Incisors | Canines | Pre-Molars | Molars | U and L | Total | Identifies Land Mammals Below |
|---|----------|---------|------------|--------|---------|-------|-------------------------------|
| U | 2-2 | 1-1 | 2-2 | 3-3 | 16 |  |  |
| L | 0-0 | 1-1 | 3-3 | 3-3 | 14 | = 30 | Chœronycteris |
| U | 2-2 | 1-1 | 2-2 | 2-2 | 14 |  |  |
| L | 2-2 | 1-1 | 3-3 | 2-2 | 16 | = 30 | Leptonycteris |
| U | 1-1 | 1-1 | 1-1 | 3-3 | 12 |  |  |
| L | 3-3 | 1-1 | 2-2 | 3-3 | 18 | = 30 | Nycticeius, Dasypterus |
| U | 1-1 | 1-1 | 2-2 | 3-3 | 14 |  |  |
| L | 2-2 | 1-1 | 2-2 | 3-3 | 16 | = 30 | Tadarida macrotis, Tadarida femorosacca, Eumops |
| U | 3-3 | 1-1 | 3-3 | 1-1 | 16 |  |  |
| L | 3-3 | 1-1 | 2-2 | 1-1 | 14 | = 30 | Felis |
| U | 3-3 | 1-1 | 1-1 | 3-3 | 16 |  |  |
| L | 1-1 | 1-1 | 1-1 | 3-3 | 12 | = 28 | Notiosorex |
| U | 1-1 | 1-1 | 1-1 | 3-3 | 12 |  |  |
| L | 2-2 | 1-1 | 2-2 | 3-3 | 16 | = 28 | Antrozous |
| U | 3-3 | 1-1 | 2-2 | 1-1 | 14 |  |  |
| L | 3-3 | 1-1 | 2-2 | 1-1 | 14 | = 28 | Lynx |
| U | 2-2 | 0-0 | 3-3 | 3-3 | 16 |  |  |
| L | 1-1 | 0-0 | 2-2 | 3-3 | 12 | = 28 | Lepus, Sylvilagus |
| U | 0-0 | 0-0 | { 7-7 | } | 14 |  |  |
| L | 0-0 | 0-0 | { 7-7 | } | 14 | = 28 | Dasypus |
| U | 2-2 | 0-0 | 2-2 | 3-3 | 14 |  |  |
| L | 1-1 | 0-0 | 2-2 | 3-3 | 12 | = 26 | Ochotona |

DENTAL FORMULÆ (*continued*)

| | Incisors | Canines | Pre-Molars | Molars | U and L | Total | Identifies Land Mammals Below |
|---|---|---|---|---|---|---|---|
| U | 1-1 | 0-0 | 2-2 | 3-3 | 12 | | Marmota, Citellus, Cynomys, Eutamias, Tamiasciurus, Glaucomys, |
| L | 1-1 | 0-0 | 1-1 | 3-3 | 10 | = 22 | Sciurus carolinensis, Sciurus griseus, Sciurus aberti, Aplodontia |
| U | 1-1 | 0-0 | 1-1 | 3-3 | 10 | | Tamias, Tamiasciurus, Sciurus niger, Sciurus apache, Sciurus ari- |
| L | 1-1 | 0-0 | 1-1 | 3-3 | 10 | = 20 | zonensis, Thomomys, Geomys, Cratogeomys, Liomys, Perognathus, |
| | | | | | | | Dipodomys, Microdipodops, Castor, Erethizon |
| U | 1-1 | 0-0 | 1-1 | 3-3 | 10 | | Zapus |
| L | 1-1 | 0-0 | 0-0 | 3-3 | 8 | = 18 | |
| U | 1-1 | 0-0 | 0-0 | 3-3 | 8 | | Reithrodontomys, Onychomys, Baiomys, Peromyscus, Oryzomys, |
| L | 1-1 | 0-0 | 0-0 | 3-3 | 8 | = 16 | Sigmodon, Neotoma, Synaptomys, Lemmus, Dicrostonyx, Phena- |
| | | | | | | | comys, Clethrionomys, Microtus, Lagurus, Pitymys, Neofiber, Onda- |
| | | | | | | | tra, Rattus, Mus, Napaeozapus |

# References

For the student whose interest carries him beyond the limits of this book, we have included a short list of references. This list is far from complete. If there is a fairly recent work covering a state or province it will be the only one listed for that area. The bibliography contained therein will guide the interested person to other references. Old publications, which often are not available except in larger universities and colleges, have purposely been omitted.

The *Journal of Mammalogy*, a quarterly published by The American Society of Mammalogists, is devoted entirely to articles on mammals, chiefly of North America. The serious student will want access to this Journal as well as to the *North American Fauna* series, published by the U.S. Department of the Interior (formerly the Department of Agriculture). In addition to the above, there is a *Catalogue of Canadian Recent Mammals* by Rudolph M. Anderson (Bulletin National Museum of Canada, No. 102, Biological series, No. 31, pp. vi + 238. 1947) and a *List of North American Recent Mammals* by Gerrit S. Miller, Jr. (U.S. National Museum Bulletin, No. 128, pp. xvi + 673. 1924). The latter two are checklists and will not help in identification beyond giving the names of the species and subspecies and their approximate ranges. Miller's Checklist is quite out of date. It is expected that a revised edition will be published in the near future. References for the states and provinces follow.

*Alabama*
> Howell, A. H.  A biological survey of Alabama.  North Amer. Fauna, 45; 1–88.  1921.

*Alaska*
> Dufresne, Frank.  Alaska's animals and fishes.  New York, A. S. Barnes and Co., xviii + 297, illustr.  1946.

*Alberta*
> Rand, A. L.  Mammals of the eastern Rockies and western plains of Canada.  Dept. Mines and Resources, Bull. Nat. Mus. Canada, 108; viii + 237, illustr.  1948.
> Soper, J. D.  Mammals of Wood Buffalo Park, northern Alberta and District of Mackenzie.  Jour. Mamm. 23:119–45, illustr.  1942.
> Soper, J. D.  Mammal notes from the Grande Prairie — Peace River region, Alberta.  Jour. Mamm. 29:49–64, illustr.  1948.

*Arizona*
> Burt, W. H.  Additional notes on the mammals of southern Arizona.  Jour. Mamm. 14:114–22.  1933.
> Cahalane, V. H.  Mammals of the Chiricahua mountains,

Cochise county, Arizona. Jour. Mamm. 20:418–40, illustr.
1939.

Doutt, J. K.   A systematic study of a collection of mammals
from southern Arizona.   Ann. Carnegie Mus. 23:241–74,
illustr.   1934.

Hatfield, D. M.   Mammals from south-central Arizona.   Bull.
Chicago Acad. Sci. 6 (8):143–57, 8 figs.   1942.

*Arkansas*

Black, J. D.   Mammals of northwestern Arkansas.   Jour.
Mamm. 17:29–35.   1936.

Black, J. D.   Notes on Arkansas mammals.   Jour. Mamm.
21:187–91.   1940.

*British Columbia*

Carl, G. Clifford, and George A. Hardy.   Flora and fauna of
the Paradise Mine area, British Columbia.   Rept. Prov. Mus.
Nat. Hist. and Anthrop. for 1944, Victoria, C 18–C 38, pl. 1.
1945.

Cowan, I. McT.   The vertebrate fauna of the Peace river district of British Columbia.   Occ. Papers British Columbia
Prov. Mus., Victoria, 1:1–102, illustr.   1939.

Cowan, I. McT., and J. A. Munro.   Birds and mammals of
Revelstoke National Park.   Canadian Alpine Jour.  29 (1):100
–21.   1945.

Hall, E. R.   Remarks on the affinities of the mammalian fauna
of Vancouver Island, British Columbia, with descriptions of
new subspecies.   Univ. Calif. Publ. Zoöl. 38:415–23.   1932.

Hall, E. R.   Mammals collected by T. T. and E. B. McCabe
in the Bowron Lake region of British Columbia.   Univ. Calif.
Publ. Zool. 40:363–86, illustr.   1934.

Munro, J. A.   Observations of birds and mammals in central
British Columbia.   Occ. Papers British Columbia Prov. Mus.
6; 165.   1947.

Munro, J. A., and I. McT. Cowan.   Preliminary report on the
birds and mammals of Kootenay National Park, British Columbia.   Canad. Field-Nat., Sutton West, 58 (2):34–51.   1944.

Racey, K., and I. McT. Cowan.   Mammals of the Alta Lake
region of southwestern British Columbia.   Report Prov., Mus.
Nat. Hist. for 1935, Victoria, H 15–H 29, illustr.   1936.

Swarth, H. S.   Mammals of the Atlin region, northwestern
British Columbia, Jour. Mamm. 17:398–405.   1936.

*California*

Grinnell, J., J. S. Dixon, and J. M. Linsdale.   Fur-bearing
mammals of California, their natural history, systematic
status, and relations to man.   Univ. Calif. Press (2 vols.).
i–xii + 777, illustr.   1937.

Ingles, L. G.   Mammals of California.   Stanford Univ. Press.
xx + 258, illustr.   1948.

*Colorado*

Warren, E. R.   The mammals of Colorado, their habits and

distribution. Univ. Oklahoma Press. xvii + 330, illustr. 1943.

*Connecticut*

Goodwin, G. G. The mammals of Connecticut. State of Conn. Geol. and Nat. Hist. Surv. Bull. 53: 1–221, illustr. 1935.

*Florida*

Sherman, H. B. A list of the recent land mammals of Florida. Proc. Fla. Acad. Sci. 1:102–28. 1936.

*Georgia*

Harper, Francis. The mammals of the Okefenokee Swamp region of Georgia. Proc. Boston Soc. Nat. Hist. 38 (7):191–396, illustr. 1927.

*Idaho*

Davis, W. B. The recent mammals of Idaho. Caldwell, Idaho, The Caxton Printers, Ltd. 400 pp., illustr. 1939.

*Illinois*

Necker, W. L., and D. M. Hatfield. Mammals of Illinois. Bull. Chicago Acad. Sci. 6 (3):17–60, illustr. 1941.

*Indiana*

Lyon, M. W., Jr. Mammals of Indiana. Amer. Mid. Nat. 17:1–384, illustr. 1936.

*Iowa*

Scott, T. G. Mammals of Iowa. Iowa State College, Jour. Sci. 12 (1):43–97. 1937.

*Kansas*

Black, J. D. Mammals of Kansas. 13th Bien. Rept. Kan. State Board Agric. 116–217, illustr. 1938.

*Keewatin District*

Sutton, G. M., and W. J. Hamilton, Jr. The mammals of Southampton Island. Mem. Carnegie Mus. 12, pt. 2, sec. 1:9–111, illustr. 1932.

*Kentucky*

Bailey, V. Cave life in Kentucky. Mainly in the mammoth cave region. Amer. Mid. Nat. 14 (5):385–635, illustr. 1933.
Welter, W. A., and D. E. Sollberger. Notes on the mammals of Rowan and adjacent counties in eastern Kentucky. Jour. Mamm. 20:77–81. 1939.

*Labrador*

Hantzsch, B. Contributions to the knowledge of extreme northeastern Labrador (translated by M. B. A. Anderson). Canad. Field Nat. 46, 1:7–12; 2:34–36. 1932.
Jackson, C. F. Notes on the mammals of southern Labrador. Jour. Mamm. 19:429–34. 1938.
Strong, W. D. Notes on mammals of the Labrador interior. Jour. Mamm., 11:1–10. 1930.
Weaver, R. L. Notes on a collection of mammals from the southern coast of the Labrador peninsula. Jour. Mamm. 21:417–22. 1940.

*Louisiana*

Lowery, G. H., Jr.  Checklist of the mammals of Louisiana and adjacent waters.  Occ. Papers Mus. Zool., Louisiana State Univ., Baton Rouge, 13; 213–57, illustr.  1943.

*Mackenzie District*

Harper, F.  Mammals of the Athabaska and Great Slave Lakes region.  Jour. Mamm. 13:19–36, illustr.  1932.

*Maine*

Manville, R. H.  Notes on the mammals of Mount Desert Island, Maine.  Jour. Mamm. 23:391–98.  1942.

*Manitoba*

Breckenridge, W. J.  Mammals collected in northern Manitoba.  Jour. Mamm. 17:61–62.  1936.

Green, H. U.  Mammals of the Riding Mountain National Park, Manitoba.  Canad. Field-Nat. 46 (7):149–52.  1932.

*Maryland*

Goldman, E. A., and H. H. T. Jackson.  Natural history of Plummers Island, Maryland.  IX, Mammals, Proc. Biol. Soc. 52:131–34.  1939.

*Massachusetts*

Warfel, H. E.  Notes on some mammals of western Massachusetts.  Jour. Mamm. 18:82–85.  1937.

*Michigan*

Burt, William H.  The mammals of Michigan.  Univ. Mich. Press. 288 + xv, illustr.  Sept. 1948 (revised ed.).

*Minnesota*

Swanson, Gustav, Thaddeus Surber, and Thomas S. Roberts. The mammals of Minnesota.  Minnesota Dept. Conserv. Tech. Bull., No. 2, 108 pp., illustr.  1945.

*Mississippi*

Cook, F. A.  Game animals of Mississippi.  Surv. Bull. Miss. State Game and Fish Commission, Jackson, v + 42 (mimeographed).  1943.

*Missouri*

Bennitt, R., and W. O. Nagle.  A survey of the resident game and fur-bearers of Missouri.  Univ. Mo. Studies 12 (2):1–215. 1937.

Schwarz, F.  Mammals of Missouri.  Bull. St. Louis. Nat. Hist. Mus. Assoc. 1:38–44.  1920.

*Nevada*

Hall, E. Raymond.  Mammals of Nevada.  Univ. Calif. Press.  xi + 710, illustr.  1946.

*New Brunswick*

Morris, R. F.  The land mammals of New Brunswick.  Jour. Mamm. 29:165–76.  1948.

*Newfoundland*

Bangs, Outram.  The land mammals of Newfoundland. Bull. Mus. Comp. Zool., Harvard College. 54:507–16.  1913.

*New Mexico*
    Bailey, V.   Mammals of New Mexico.   North Amer. Fauna
    53:1–412, illustr.   1931.
*North Dakota*
    Bailey, V.   A biological survey of North Dakota.   I. Physiog-
    raphy and life zones.   II. The mammals.   North Amer.
    Fauna 49:1–226, illustr.   1927.
*Nova Scotia*
    Smith, R. W.   The land mammals of Nova Scotia.   Notre
    Dame, Amer. Mid. Nat. 24:213–41.   1940.
*Ohio*
    Bole, B. P., Jr., and P. N. Moulthrop.   The Ohio recent mam-
    mal collection in the Cleveland Museum of Natural History.
    Sci. Publs. Cleveland Mus. Nat. Hist. 5 (6):83–181.   1942.
*Oklahoma*
    Blair, W. F.   Faunal relationships and geographic distribution
    of mammals in Oklahoma.   Amer. Mid. Nat. 22 (1):85–133,
    illustr.   1939.
*Ontario*
    Cross, E. C., and J. R. Dymond.   The mammals of Ontario.
    Roy. Ont. Mus. Zool. Handbook 1:1–56, illustr.   1929.
*Oregon*
    Bailey, V.   The mammals and life zones of Oregon.   North
    Amer. Fauna 55:1–416, illustr.   1936.
*Pennsylvania*
    Grimm, W. C., and H. A. Roberts.   Mammal survey of south-
    western Pennsylvania.   Penna. Game Comm., Harrisburg, 99
    pp.   1950.
    Richmond, N. D., and H. R. Rosland.   Mammal survey of
    northwestern Pennsylvania.   Penna. Game Comm. and U.S.
    Fish and Wildlife Service, 67 pp.   1949.
*Quebec*
    Goodwin, G. G.   Mammals of the Cascapedia Valley, Quebec.
    Jour. Mamm. 10:239–46.   1929.
*Saskatchewan*
    Banfield, F. A.   Notes on Saskatchewan mammals.   Canadian
    Field-Nat., Ottawa, 55 (8):117–23, illustr.   1941.
*South Carolina*
    Penney, J. T.   Distribution and bibliography of the mammals
    of South Carolina.   Jour. Mamm. 31:81–89.   1950.
*South Dakota*
    Over, William H., and Edward P. Churchill.   Mammals of
    South Dakota.   Mus. and Dept. Zool., Univ. South Dakota,
    Vermillion, 1–56 (mimeographed).   1941.
*Tennessee*
    Kellogg, R.   Annotated list of Tennessee mammals.   Proc.
    U.S. Natl. Mus. 86 (3051):245–303.   1939.

*Texas*
  Taylor, W. P., and W. B. Davis.  The mammals of Texas.
  Game, Fish, and Oyster Comm., Austin., Bull. 27:1–79, illustr.
  1947.
*Utah*
  Hall, E. R., and D. H. Johnson.  Mammals from Millard
  County, Utah.  Proc. Utah Acad. Sci. Arts & Letters 15:121–
  122.  1938.
  Long, W. S.  Notes on the life histories of some Utah mam-
  mals.  Jour. Mamm. 21:170–80.  1940.
  Presnall, C. C.  Mammals of Zion-Bryce and Cedar Breaks.
  Zion-Bryce Mus. Bull. 2:1–20, illustr.  1938.
  Presnall, C. C., and E. R. Hall.  Ranges and relationships of
  certain mammals in southwestern Utah.  Utah Acad. Sci. Arts
  & Letters 13:211–13.  1936.
*Vermont*
  Osgood, F. L., Jr.  The mammals of Vermont.  Jour. Mamm.
  19:435–41.  1938.
*Virginia*
  Handley, C. O., Jr., and C. P. Patton.  Wild mammals of
  Virginia.  Comm. Game and Inland Fisheries, Richmond,
  vi + 220, illustr.  1947.
*Washington*
  Dalquest, W. W.  Mammals of Washington.  Univ. Kan.
  Publ., Mus. Nat. Hist., 2:1–444, illustr.  1948.
*West Virginia*
  Kellogg, R.  Annotated list of West Virginia mammals.  Proc.
  U.S. Nat. Mus. 84 (3022):443–79.  1937.
  Wilson, L. W., and J. E. Friedel.  A list of mammals collected
  in West Virginia.  Proc. West Virginia Acad. Sci. for 1941,
  Philippi, vol. 15 (West Virginia Univ. Bull. ser. 42) 8–11; 85–
  92.  1942.
*Wyoming*
  Bailey, Vernon.  Animal life of Yellowstone Park.  Sierra
  Club Bull. 12 (4):333–45, illustr.  1927.

# Index

THE READER will find it most practical to go directly to the illustrations and the maps for identification. In most cases it will not be necessary to refer to the text.

Page numbers in *italics* refer to the distribution maps, those in **bold face** type refer to the illustrations. These are placed only after the common English names of the species. They are not used after the scientific names.

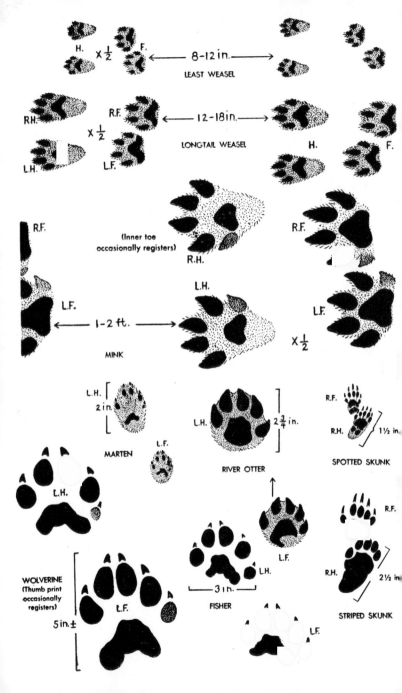

H. X ½ F. ← 8-12 in. → **LEAST WEASEL**

R.H. R.F. ← 12-18 in. → **LONGTAIL WEASEL** H. F.
L.H. X ½ L.F.

R.F. (Inner toe occasionally registers) R.F.
R.H.
L.F. L.H.
← 1-2 ft. → **MINK** X ½ L.F.

L.H. 2 in. L.H. 2¾ in. R.F.
**MARTEN** L.F. L.H. R.H.
**RIVER OTTER** 1½ in.
**SPOTTED SKUNK**

L.H.
L.F. R.F.

**WOLVERINE** (Thumb print occasionally registers) L.H. L.F. R.H. 2½ in.
5 in. ± L.F. ← 3 in. → **FISHER** **STRIPED SKUNK**
L.F.